George Washington:
Soldier and Man

George Washington, from a painting by John Trumbull in City Hall. New York City (*Courtesy of Hellmich Bros.*)

NORTH CALLAHAN

George Washington
Soldier and Man

WILLIAM MORROW & COMPANY, INC., NEW YORK 1972

Illustration credits: Prints Division, The New York Public
Library, Astor, Lenox and Tilden Foundations

21450

Copyright © 1972 by North Callahan

Printed in the United States of America.
Library of Congress Catalog Card Number 74–170230

To John C. Pemberton III

CONTENTS

Frontispiece: George Washington

Introduction   xi

Map   xvi

Illustrations between pages 182 and 183

    I *A Charmed Life*   1

   II *Washington Assumes Command*   16

  III *The Boston Dilemma*   34

  IV *New York: A Crisis*   42

   V *Triumph in New Jersey*   65

  VI *Portentous Withdrawal*   85

 VII *Rest and Resurgence*   114

VIII *A Difficult Time in New Jersey*   142

  IX *Variety in the Northeast*   162

   X *Hardship and Betrayal*   183

XI	On Land, Sea and in the Offing	208
XII	The Reckoning at Yorktown	222
XIII	Aftermath	255
XIV	Appraisal	273
	Bibliographical Note	281
	Index	285
	About the Author	295

INTRODUCTION

WITH ALL DUE REGARD to the great number of books that have been written on George Washington, there is still no adequate single volume about him as a soldier and man. This, then, is the purpose of this book: to show him as the fighting man and human being who led others to the victories that resulted in the creation of the United States of America—which he was then unanimously elected to head.

Much of this new approach is the result of years spent in studying the voluminous papers of Henry Knox and Daniel Morgan, two of Washington's best generals and friends. From this research, I have written two published biographies. These men were close to their chief, and their letters, along with other documents, reveal new facets of the commander of the army as well as of the man himself. Extensive research in the George Washington papers as well as in many original documents relating to the American Tories, along with new interpretations lately given by eminent scholars in this early period of American history, has, I believe, enhanced my knowledge and viewpoint.

As the late biographer Douglas Southall Freeman said, "Few emulate what they cannot hope to duplicate. Youth, conscious of its failings, is suspicious of other youth supposed to have none. Where complete virtue does not create skepticism, it arouses resentment . . . Americans will be relieved and shocked to know that Washington was sometimes violent, emotional, resentful—a human being and not a monument in frozen flesh."

It seems therefore fitting in this day of confusion of values that the life of Washington be held up again as an example to be emulated. He had a reason to lead a revolution, for he and his associates had a constructive plan with which to follow it. Unlike Robespierre—or his modern counterparts for that matter—Washington sought not destruction but a wholesome, material improvement of the status quo. Reluctant to fight, once in the conflict he was resolutely determined to acquit himself well.

To the scholar with an eye for footnotes, it is suggested that most of the important research on the life of Washington has already been done and amply annotated in both the monumental work of Douglas Freeman and the more recent volumes of James Thomas Flexner, among others. However, any quote or other historical detail included in this book is authenticated. It would appear that the usual visible scholarly apparatus is not necessary in a comparatively concise account, especially when such academic spadework, already accomplished, is easily available elsewhere in standard works.

Attention may here appropriately be called to the main repositories of the papers of George Washington, namely in the Manuscript Division of the Library of Congress and the impressive collection now being compiled at the University of Virginia. Other documents relating to him can be found in many places, from Harvard University to the Huntington Library in California. A number are now in convenient printed form.

The Henry Knox papers, from which much of this account is drawn, are in the Massachusetts Historical Society in Boston and have fairly recently been made available on microfilm. Documents concerning Daniel Morgan, another rewarding source, are not so plentiful; they are located mainly in the New York Public Library. The Nathanael Greene papers in the Library of Congress and in the Rhode Island Historical Society are also among the numerous primary sources from which this account is taken.

The story of George Washington is endless. Its main fabric has been woven, but there is still room for a new pattern, and hopefully a fuller impression of this man who often walked alone.

N.C.

Of all men in history, not one so answers our expectations as Washington. Into whatever part of his life the historian puts his probe, the result is always satisfactory.

EDWARD CHANNING

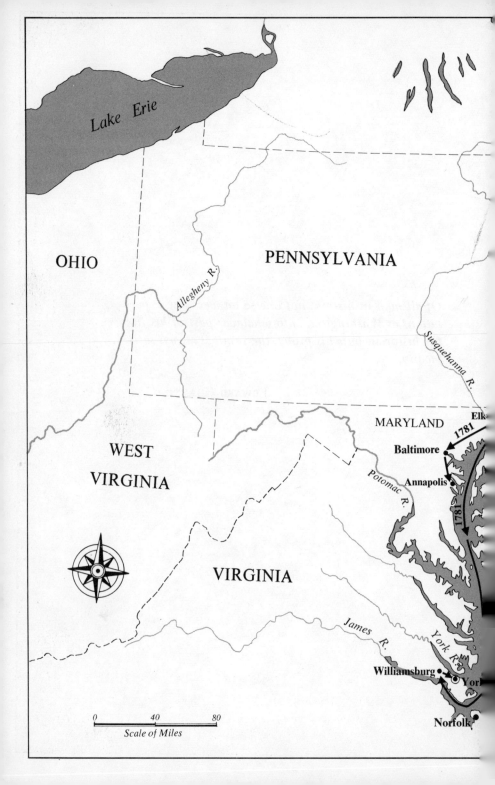

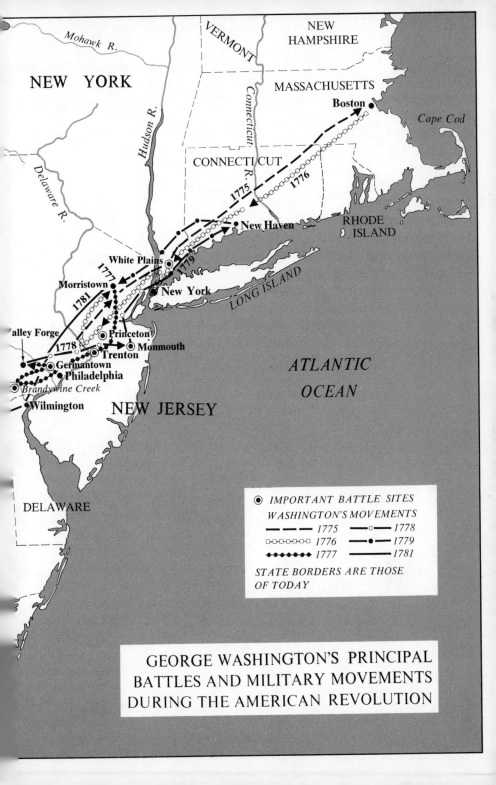

GEORGE WASHINGTON'S PRINCIPAL
BATTLES AND MILITARY MOVEMENTS
DURING THE AMERICAN REVOLUTION

George Washington:
Soldier and Man

I A CHARMED LIFE

A REMARKABLE THING about the life of George Washington is that, instead of being a battlefield casualty, he lived out an eventful span of almost three-score-years-and-ten. He certainly challenged death on more than one occasion, even admitting at one time that he liked to hear "the bullets whistle." So often did he experience this "liking" that he won the admiration of his comrades and foes alike. They felt he was absolutely fearless.

This quality of bravery probably inspired a later disciple of Washington, Theodore Roosevelt, to declare, "He is not fit to live who is afraid to die." But the man who perhaps came the closest to ending the career of Washington was Lieutenant Colonel Patrick Ferguson, a colorful Scottish officer in the British army. Aroused by the "boasted skill of the American marksmen" in the early stages of the Revolution, Ferguson invented the first breech-loading rifle used in the British forces.

During the seesaw Battle of Brandywine Creek near Philadelphia in the summer of 1777, Ferguson was stationed with his riflemen in a thick wood. "We had not lain long," he later recalled, "when a rebel officer marked by a hussar dress, passed toward our army, within a hundred yards of my right flank, not perceiving us." [Ferguson's new rifle was deadly accurate at two hundred yards.] "He was followed by another dressed in dark green and blue, mounted on a bay horse, with a remarkably high cocked hat. I ordered three good shots to steal near to and fire at them; but the idea disgusting me, I recalled the order. The hussar, in returning, made a circuit, but the other officer passed within a hundred yards of us, upon which I advanced from the woods toward him. Upon my calling, he stopped; but after looking at me, he proceeded. I could have lodged half a dozen balls in or about him but it was not pleasant to fire at the back of an unoffending individual who was acquitting himself very coolly of his duty—so I let him alone.

"The day after, rebel officers who were wounded told us that General Washington was all the morning with the light troops, and only attended by a French officer in hussar dress, he himself dressed and mounted in every point as above described. I am not sorry that I did not know at the time who it was."

Three years later, Colonel Ferguson was not to find his American opponents so gallant. Commanding the Tories at the Battle of King's Mountain in the Carolinas, Ferguson was fatally riddled with bullets as he rode among his troops. He left the account of having Washington in his rifle sights in a letter now preserved in Edinburgh. Not far to the southward in the northern English county of Yorkshire whose mountains dwindle off as they stretch toward London, the ancestors of George Washington had sired a progeny which was to extend into the New World and lessen to a considerable degree the extent of the British Empire.

On the sundial in the herb garden of Washington's birthplace at Bridges Creek, near Fredericksburg, Virginia, there is an inscription that reads: "Here a matchless flower came to birth—Time paused and blessed the spot."

Although time did not stand still, it marked here what

was probably the most propitious moment in American history. George Washington was born on February 11 (old style), February 22 (new style), in 1732, the same year that Lord North, British prime minister during the American Revolution, was born. George's father, Augustine Washington, had gone to school in England, had been a sailor and later had fallen heir to a large Virginia estate. The future general and President could claim "Cavalier" ancestry on both sides. His great-grandfather John Washington had come to America from England in 1657 and settled at Bridges Creek. George's mother was much younger than her husband and below him in social status; her ancestors had also left England at the time of the uprising of the Puritans.

Young Washington grew up on a plantation, one thousand acres of which stretched for a mile along the Potomac River in Westmoreland County. Although not as pretentious as the elegant estates of Shirley and Westover on the James River, the plantation had a comfortably substantial house, a one-and-a-half-story brick dwelling with dormer windows and large outside chimneys. In 1735 Augustine moved to a larger plantation, still near Fredericksburg but with ten times the number of acres. Though he was a strong and vigorous man, Augustine Washington died suddenly in 1743 from what was called gout of the stomach.

George was eleven when his father passed away and was left under the guardianship of another son, Lawrence Washington, offspring of Augustine's first marriage. Lawrence Washington inherited much of the parental estate, and George lived most of the time with Lawrence at the estate known as Mount Vernon. Until 1747 George attended school irregularly, studying Latin, moral precepts and mathematics. But best of all he loved the outdoors, where he became skillful at raising tobacco and livestock and practicing the elements of surveying. He also developed a handsome and legible handwriting, though his spelling was then and always far from perfect. Never an intellectual like Thomas Jefferson and John Adams, Washington nevertheless at an early age gained basic concepts of life that were even more valuable. Apparently he made some study of the works of Alexander Pope and Joseph Addison, as shown by the style of his personal letter writing.

An important step in the early life of Washington began when he turned to surveying as a full-time job, working for Thomas, Lord Fairfax, a mature bachelor who had come to America in 1746 to preside over a huge estate in Northern Virginia. Washington lived with a cousin at Belvoir, which adjoined Mount Vernon. Fairfax, trying to protect his lands, on which Pennsylvania squatters were beginning to settle, sent a surveying party to the Shenandoah Valley in 1748, among which was the sixteen-year-old George Washington. During this challenging enterprise, the young man kept a diary, in which he described the hardships of the wilderness, such as sleeping under a thin blanket thickened by lice and fleas. He saw Indians carrying scalps and encountered some Pennsylvania-German settlers who impressed him as being quite ignorant and unable to express themselves in understandable language.

Upon his return, Washington, with the help of Lord Fairfax, obtained the position of public surveyor for Fairfax County. He was kept busy for almost two years, his surveying trips taking him far into the western wilderness where he learned to cope with the exigencies of nature and the hostility of the Indians. There is no doubt that these experiences shaped and strengthened his character and taught him how to endure a strenuous life. This, of course, was to stand him in good stead in the trials to come.

Going beyond the picturesque Appalachian horizon, Washington came more and more into contact with the far-stretching western lands. They represented a great opportunity not only for national expansion but for personal gain, a double fascination that remained with him as long as he lived. For he was to become not only a soldier who would lead men through the wild fastnesses but also a major speculator in western holdings. This last interest was to becloud his reputation in the minds of some, but it did help to spur the winning of the West. Not only did he work in the wilderness, but after Lord Fairfax moved into the Shenandoah Valley and constructed a huge log structure called Greenway Court after his English estate, Washington was often entertained there. He seemed especially to enjoy the large Fairfax library, which included many of the English novels of the day.

In 1752, at the age of twenty, George Washington lost one of the important influences of his life. His half-brother Lawrence died at Mount Vernon of tuberculosis, and George was made the executor of his will and the residuary heir of his estate.

Then Sarah Washington, daughter of Lawrence and the direct inheritor of the estate, died within two months leaving no descendants, so George became manager of the large plantation. He entered upon his new duties, however, in a somewhat weakened condition. Not long before, he had accompanied Lawrence on his voyage to Barbados for his health. This was George's only sea journey, and he was to remember it, for on Barbados he contracted smallpox, a then uncontrolled disease, which left his face permanently pockmarked. In fact this was the only occasion upon which Washington ever left the United States, although later he was often invited to do so.

For the next several years he was busy with his duties and the social life at Mount Vernon. Washington liked to ride to hounds, to dance and to attend occasional theatrical performances. He was slightly over six feet tall and strongly built, an impressive if not handsome man. Although he enjoyed the company of ladies, he usually felt awkward among them, perhaps because of his height, his size and especially his big hands and feet. Lafayette later remarked that Washington had the largest hands he had ever seen.

Washington was unusually fond of horseback riding, and well he might have been, since it was a natural pursuit in which he greatly excelled. He was said to be truly a majestic figure when clad in uniform and astride his white charger. His imposing physical characteristics doubtless gave him tremendous confidence in himself, which was added to by his increasing number of admirers. He had previously compiled a book on conduct in which he stressed that everything that one does in company should be with respect to those present; that one should never frighten a friend; in the presence of others, a person should not hum to himself or drum with fingers or feet; pity should be shown to an offender and when reprimanding another it should be done in private and with mildness; and one should never act like a peacock.

Washington and his mother did not get along very well. She never forgot that her name had been Mary Ball, and she was said to have been an awesome person who kept her children quiet just by her presence. Stern, argumentative and with a high temper, she made no bones about her personality or its effect on others. Washington's letters to his mother usually began with the salutation "Honored Madam," and he did not write many. She hardly ever visited him at Mount Vernon, and he seemed to be glad of it, apparently fearing she would be too unconventional and uninhibited there. She later became an embarrassment to him, for in her old age she unjustifiably complained of being neglected and of not having enough money. She lived until 1789 and was able to enjoy the pride of her son's inauguration as the first President of the United States.

The office of adjutant of the local military district, one of four in Virginia, was left vacant in 1752 and George coveted this position. Accordingly, he obtained it, with an annual salary of one hundred pounds and duties that were not too demanding. Though the salary was not great, the military region was a large one, extending in southern Virginia from the James River to the North Carolina boundary. This brought young Washington active experience in a new country, command of men and the title of major.

His military duties, however, took up only part of the time of the youthful Virginian, and his energy and personality soon thrust him prominently into community affairs as well. Whether from choice or conformity Washington became first an active member and then a vestryman of the Episcopal Church. With the same verve and orderliness he had shown in his military duties, he took over the affairs of his plantation. Displaying a natural leadership, he soon became recognized as a systematic and wise manager of his property. By 1757 he had more than four thousand acres to supervise, using both white and slave labor.

For anyone interested in a military career, this was a propitious time. In 1753, Governor Robert Dinwiddie of Virginia decided to warn the French against encroaching on British land in the Ohio Valley. He sent word to make this clear, but the messenger failed to reach the proper French authorities. Dinwiddie then determined to send Washington. The major started for the French post with an interpreter, a guide, servants and traders. They left Cumberland, Maryland, in the middle of a cold November and reached what is now Waterford, Pennsylvania, without incident. There the French commander of Fort Le Boeuf, fortified with plenty of wine, received Washington courteously but told him "it was their absolute design to take possession of the Ohio, and, by God, they would do it."

The French commander gave Washington a letter of reply to Governor Dinwiddie amounting to a polite refusal to comply with English orders. Washington was disgusted but dutifully received the message. On his return home he encountered bad weather and went by canoe as far as possible. But when it was necessary to travel by land, Washington and his guide, Christopher Gist, found that the going was hazardous. At one remote spot the party met some French and Indians. This was wilderness country, known as Devil's Backbone in the forest, which a British soldier had described as a desolate country full of bold Indians, bears and rattlesnakes. So Washington and Gist were understandably alarmed when one of the Indians fired at them from a distance of fifteen paces. Fortunately he missed.

In this dim and neutral zone between the British and the French, the Indians fought not so much for either side as for themselves. Washington did not yet understand this situation. Another time, while crossing the Allegheny River on an improvised raft, Washington fell into the icy river; luckily he saved himself by catching hold of one of the raft logs. He had to spend the night in water-soaked clothes on an island. Gist was not so fortunate. His fingers and some of his toes were frozen.

Despite such hardships, Washington and his guide arrived at Williamsburg on January 16, 1754. Governor Dinwiddie was impressed with the physical endurance and strength of will the young Virginian had shown. The governor asked Washington for a report, to be put in the hands of his legislature the next day. Washington worked through the night writing this account and then apologized for not having time to put it in proper form or to correct the wording. Even so, it was good enough to be published both in Virginia and in England, and a few copies of *The Journal of Major George Washington* exist today. This journal warned of the forthcoming conflict between the British and French. Governor Dinwiddie was sufficiently impressed with the report to send it to London in order to convince his superiors that help was needed in America. The Assembly of Virginia thought enough of the report to vote Washington an honorarium of fifty pounds.

Although other colonies were asked to share the burden of preparations, Virginia was to carry the brunt of it and voted Dinwiddie ten thousand pounds and the authority to raise six companies of soldiers. Within five days after his return from his arduous journey, Washington was called upon to enlist and train these volunteers; he was promoted to lieutenant colonel. He regarded these troops mainly as idle men without home or clothing. Washington, second in command to Colonel Joshua Fry, set out immediately for the Ohio territory with raw troops who had no uniforms, little training or discipline, few supplies and lacked spirit for the occasion. At least he was somewhat at home by now in the wilderness; his superior, Colonel Fry—born in England and educated at Oxford—died without ever reaching his men. So Washington was left in full charge, beset not only with the foregoing difficulties but with a lack of wagons and horses as well as ammunition and drill sergeants.

Before Washington reached the French, he was met at Will's Creek by a messenger who informed him that the fort at the forks of the Ohio, at the present site of Pittsburgh, had been renamed Fort Duquesne and was already in French hands. Although more men from Virginia reached him as well as some from South Carolina, Washington was still faced with misfortune. Even so, he went forward at the rate of about four miles a day with his small and untrained forces. He arrived at a place called Great Meadows, within forty miles of the French position, where he erected a sort of amateurish fort, appropriately named Necessity. He then made a surprise attack upon an advance party of thirty Frenchmen and killed a third of them, including the leader, Coulon de Jumonville, taking the rest prisoners. On the body of Jumonville was found a letter addressed to the commander of the English troops on the territory of the King of France, ordering the Americans to depart. This Washington ignored as being presumptuous.

He now continued to advance, but not for long. The whole French force of some seven hundred men including Indians, under the command of Jumonville's brother, swept down upon him. Washington, with his three hundred and fifty soldiers, quickly fell back into Fort Necessity, but it did not live up to its name. Badly situated in an indefensible hollow and handicapped by a nearby hill from which the attackers could look down into the fort, the bastion was foredoomed. The French and Indians, attacking skillfully from behind trees with plenty of ammunition and overwhelming numbers, were aided by a heavy rainfall. The fort was compelled to surrender within nine hours. The enemy surged into the watery creek bottom from three forested sides, and Washington had no chance. Even so, his stand was far from glorious. Too much rum had made some of his men drunk, and now there were thirty dead, seventy wounded and more had deserted.

So the future commander-in-chief of the American armies in the Revolution ended his first major military effort in ignominious disaster. The French, elated by the victory, insisted that Washington sign a vague document of surrender. He did so by the light of a flickering candle in a rainstorm. The terms allowed his motley band of colonial soldiers to march back to Virginia with the honors of war, little as they were. But Washington had to promise that Virginia would not build another fort on the Ohio for a year and was forced to sign a paper taking responsibility for the "assassination" of Jumonville. Washington said later that he did not understand exactly what he was signing, because it was partly written in French. Although the military action was not a big one, it has been described by some historians as the starting point of the French and Indian War. It did bring out the courage, bravery and tough character of

George Washington. "I have heard the bullets whistle," he wrote to his brother, "and believe me, there is something charming in the sound."

But even Washington's strong personal qualities could not change the fact that this short campaign of 1754 was ineptly managed both from Williamsburg and London as well as where it was carried out. The unfavorable consequences brought criticism of Washington from British officials to the effect that he was brash, hasty, too ambitious, inexperienced and unmilitary. From the situation he did learn some lessons of how Indians fought and how warfare in the wilderness should not be conducted. Back at headquarters relations grew cool between Washington and Governor Dinwiddie, resulting in Washington's resignation from the service in October, 1754.

The young provincial colonel, however, was not allowed to enjoy Mount Vernon for very long. The following February, General Edward Braddock and his British army arrived in Virginia as part of a campaign to defeat the French. Braddock was a brusque but energetic veteran of forty-five years of military service, well-trained in European warfare but contemptuous of the colonial soldiers. He offered Washington the courtesy rank of colonel and invited him to join the forthcoming expedition as his aide-de-camp. Although Washington had recently resigned a commission, he accepted the offer. As he told a friend, "My inclinations are strongly bent to arms." Braddock apparently was fair enough to allow his aide to express himself frankly, for in their conferences, when the general criticized the colonials for failing to deliver supplies, Washington warmly defended them. He suggested that Braddock divide his army and leave half of it to come later with wagons and supply trains, moving the rest forward quickly against Fort Duquesne before it could be reinforced. As was later shown, this would have been a wise decision.

On June 16, half the twenty-two hundred men Braddock had assembled pushed forward against Duquesne, but it was not until the seventh of July that they were near the fort. It was a colorful procession of British and Virginians entering the forest with bands playing, banners waving, the officers in resplendent and shiny uniforms, wagons, cannons, horses and cattle passing in long and noisy array across the rippling shallows of Turtle Creek. It was an inviting spectacle for the enemy, quietly lying in wait behind the protective trees and rocks. Washington himself had wanted to lead the advance guard with his Virginians but unfortunately became ill from dysentery and could take little active part. He did manage to join the troops on July 8 riding in a covered wagon. By this time, the French had advanced a force of some nine hundred men, two-thirds of whom were Indians. Braddock was not completely taken by surprise as some accounts indicate, but once he had crossed the Monongahela River, he found his column was in so narrow a passageway that it could not properly maneuver. So the struggling red- and blue-coated force was soon surrounded by Indians, who poured a withering fire into it from behind their forested concealment.

Braddock gave a command to charge, and his troops valiantly tried to carry out the attack, but to no avail. Through the confusion and smoke the war whoop sounded and the scalping knife flashed. The British regulars broke and ran like sheep pursued by dogs. Washington's Virginians, in his own words, "behaved like men and died like soldiers." Braddock fought superbly. Washington, despite his dysentery, showed great energy, coolness and poise, even though he had to use a pillow instead of a saddle. He seemed everywhere at once, following Braddock bravely, trying to rally the men to push forward, especially his Virginians. Colonel Washington exposed his own person as recklessly as did the brave Braddock, who finally was fatally wounded when his fifth horse was shot from under him. Washington himself had two horses shot and his clothing pierced by four bullets, although he was not hurt. This seemingly miraculous ability to lead his men in the face of danger and emerge always unscathed remained with him throughout his military career. The Virginian was at Braddock's side when he died, heard him mutter praise for the colonial troops and in his last breath say of the French and Indians, "You shall better know how to deal with them another time."

Braddock was buried in the middle of the trail over which his forces retreated, and no marker was placed above the grave so that the corpse would not be scalped or mutilated. The wagons then moved across the burial place, obliterating any trace of it.

In August of 1755, when only twenty-three years of age, Washington was made commander-in-chief of all Virginia forces. But these forces were no match for the Indians, who now ran wild through the countryside, spreading panic and devastation. Washington's untrained militia ranged in number between three hundred and nine hundred men. A Maryland captain with a royal commission refused to obey Colonel Washington, so the latter rode northward and placed the matter before their British commander in America, Colonel William Shirley of Massachusetts. The *Boston Gazette* announced the news of Washington's arrival and stated he had "deservedly a high reputation for military skill and valor, though success has not always attended his undertakings." Washington won his point, but this achievement seemed not to amount to so much when he learned that even before he arrived in Boston, Governor Shirley had appointed Governor Horatio Sharpe of Maryland to command the troops to be used in an expedition against Fort Duquesne.

Washington felt like resigning his commission again but did stay on for more than a year, struggling with the difficulties of defending the frontier. He became a stern commander, insisting that a cowardly deserter be put to death in the presence of newly drafted men. For swearing, his men received twenty-five lashes; drunkenness was rewarded with fifty. In November of 1757 Washington again became so ill, of the same "bloody flux," that his doctor ordered him home. But he returned to duty five months later in time to command the advance guard of troops under General John Forbes who, taking a lesson from the late catastrophe of Braddock, carried out a successful campaign against Fort Duquesne, captured it and renamed it Fort Pitt. With this triumph behind him, Colonel George Washington resigned his commission the latter part of 1758.

In the early days of the next year, he was married to Martha Dandridge, the widow of Daniel Parke Custis, a plump and pleasant woman his age, who had two children and one of the largest fortunes in Virginia. However, she was never to bear a child for Washington. The man who was to be called "the Father of His Country" never had a child of his own. From this time until the American Revolution, Washington devoted himself to his duties as a rich Virginia planter. He was industrious, prompt and a good manager, caring for his hundreds of slaves, rotating his crops and breeding horses and cattle. For each year he kept an exact account of his expenses and income. His house was often full of guests and friends, its elegant interior and magnificent view of the Potomac the scene of a gay social life. Washington was an active member of the Virginia House of Burgesses and was present when Patrick Henry intoned his resolution against the Stamp Act in May of 1765. But there was comparatively little at this time to indicate the greatness that George Washington was eventually to achieve.

The master of Mount Vernon resumed his active interest in western lands, but his eyes were soon turned in the opposite direction by the Boston Tea Party of December, 1773, which added to his fears of British tyranny and of economic monopoly. John Adams reported in his diary on August 31, 1774, that "Colonel Washington made the most eloquent speech at the Virginia Convention that was ever made. Said he, 'I will raise one thousand men, subsist them at my own expense, and march myself at their head for the relief of Boston.' "

A week later, Washington was a delegate to the First Continental Congress. When it met in Philadelphia on September 5, 1774, he was the only one present in a military uniform. The forty-two-year-old soldier-civilian could hardly have worn such dress incidentally; it actually drew attention to him when military affairs were discussed, and doubtless contributed to his selection soon afterward as commander-in-chief of the Continental forces in the forthcoming War of Independence.

II WASHINGTON ASSUMES COMMAND

THE MAN SELECTED as commander-in-chief of the Continental army was impressive in more ways than one. Washington stood a head taller than most of those around him. He had large bones and classical features, his complexion appeared weathered and at times pallid. His eyes were grayish-blue, his hair brown. Standing, walking or astride his horse, he was majestic.

Nor did his appearance belie his substance. Already his military experience was more widespread and renowned than that of any other man in the colonies. He was also probably the richest in material assets. He was an aristocrat who had chosen to turn away from aristocracy and cast his lot with struggling merchants, planters and artisans. His influence, although not always immediate, was effective.

The fact that Washington was a southerner was not the only reason that the astute John Adams nominated him as commander-in-chief. Adams, among others, realized that to give New England too much dominance in the forthcoming campaigns would be to run a risk of fastening a rigid sectionalism on the rest of the new nation. Virginia must be won over, and Washington was its outstanding citizen; he would furnish just the symbol necessary for a great enterprise.

Washington protested with sincerity that his abilities were not equal to the task, but his humility only further convinced the delegates of his moderation and soundness of judgment. There would be a strong and safe man at the helm who had already won their respect. He had been rather quiet in the Congress, but with his firm chin and pleasing countenance he had made more impression than had others more verbose. His sincerity was unquestioned, and when he talked, in a voice more agreeable than strong, he looked his listener full in the face. Adams thought him modest, virtuous, amiable, generous and brave.

Washington's commission, which designated him "General and Commander In Chief of the United Colonies," was dated June 19, 1775. He received it on the twentieth and started for Boston on the twenty-first. Congress voted him a salary of five hundred dollars a month and expenses, but he graciously declined it. He did, however, agree to keep an account of his expenses, and this he did meticulously, noting in his ledgers the cost of everything from a buckle for his shoes to a magnificent horse. By the end of the war, Washington's expense account, despite his commendable intentions, had amounted to what would be considered a substantial salary. But it was in inflated Continental money; despite later comments to the contrary, his accounts were not padded.

In his orders of June 20, Washington found a clause that stated that he was to prosecute the conflict with the advice of his council of war. Some historians have questioned the value of this order, which was to influence the course of the war, believing that Washington took these instructions too literally. Before making major decisions he would ordinarily ask the advice of his generals, and the length of these deliberations won him the name among some critics of "the Fabian general," because of his sometimes cautious delays and avoidance of battles. A few thought the course of the military campaign was too often dictated by a majority vote of his generals rather than by his own judgment. This, however, is doubtful. He was of a deliberating nature, and with the meager resources at his command, he wanted to be as certain as possible of the outcome before he committed his forces against the well-trained professionals of the British army. He felt himself more an instrument of the Congress than an independent military leader and indeed at times was driven to distraction by petty congressional directives. It must be remembered also that owing to his natural modesty he never seemed to have great confidence in his own ability as a soldier.

Washington left Philadelphia in a cavalcade that included some of his future officers and a number of delegates to Congress and was accompanied by members of the local militia with flags flying and music playing. From the safety of a spectator's seat, stocky little John Adams watched with envy the big men who passed in uniform. He noted that he was a poor creature, worn out by scribbling, who must watch others wear the laurels he had dreamed of earning. He had hoped to be a soldier, but this was never to be. He would fight his battles in the chambers of governments.

Arriving in New York, Washington and his entourage found the city divided between rebels and Tories. Embarrassingly, the colony's royal English governor, William Tryon, was being welcomed almost at the same time. Washington arrived first—characteristically—and was greeted by members of the Provincial Congress, ministers of the churches and Patriot and Tory leaders. One observer noted that the very people who met the rebel generals in the morning, five hours later joined in acclaiming the returning royal governor.

While in New York, Washington sent Major General Philip Schuyler to take command of all the troops in the colony and to occupy positions on Lake George and Lake

Champlain. Schuyler, wealthy aristocrat and future father-in-law of Alexander Hamilton, was to have an unsuccessful career as a general. His participation was to vary with both the political and military tides. Though an able man, he was never to realize fully the prominent part he had hoped to play in the conflict. At the time of his meeting with Washington, however, his orders were to keep an eye on Governor Tryon to make sure that he did not interfere with the Patriot cause.

Washington and the rest of the party continued on to Cambridge, Massachusetts, arriving July 2, 1775. Here he immediately took command of the newly formed army. Although there is an appealing legend that he did this in a ceremony under an elm tree on Cambridge Common, this appears to have no basis in fact.

The discerning and highly expressive Abigail Adams wrote to her husband John in mid-July that "I was struck with General Washington. You had prepared me to entertain a favorable opinion of him but I thought the half was not told me. Dignity, with ease and complacency, the gentleman and soldier, look agreeably blended in him. Modesty marks every line and feature of his face."

A few days later Surgeon James Thacher recorded in his *Journal*, "I have been much gratified this day with a view of General Washington. His Excellency was on horseback, in company with several military gentlemen. It was not difficult to distinguish him from all others; his personal appearance is truly noble and majestic, being tall and well-proportioned. His dress is a blue coat with buff-colored facings, a rich epaulette on each shoulder, buff under dress, and an elegant small sword; a black cockade in his hat."

The new general found that most of his men had not yet seen military service. On the whole they seemed brave and intelligent but had little knowledge of what was necessary for military success, such as cleanliness of dress and lodging, proper exercise and strict temperance. Despite this he was optimistic.

In general orders of August 22, 1775, Washington said, "The General does not mean to discourage the practice of bathing whilst the weather is warm enough to continue it, but he expressly forbids any persons doing it near the bridge in Cambridge, where it has been observed and complained of that many men, lost to all sense of decency and common modesty, are running naked upon the bridge, whilst passengers and even ladies of the first fashion in the neighborhood, are passing over it, as if they meant to glory in their shame." Washington's attitude is indicated in a letter he wrote to Schuyler in late 1776. "There is not a difficulty," Washington said, "that you very justly complain of, that I am not every day experiencing; but we must bear up against them, and make the best of mankind as they are, since we cannot have them as we wish."

There was one phase of the new army, however, that disturbed Washington. That was the New England "leveling spirit"; every man was thought to be as good as any other. Many of the officers had been elected by their units, and to Washington, this was military heresy. There should be proper distinction between officers and privates; every officer should be a gentleman. Otherwise officers could not maintain the necessary dignity and position over their men and could not give orders and expect them to be instantly obeyed. To him, the idea that familiarity breeds contempt was truer in the military system than anywhere else. When Washington found that one of his officers who had been a former barber was seen shaving a man and that another had carried a large piece of beef to his tent he was horrified.

One reason for such lack of distinction was that there were few uniforms in the American army, making it difficult to tell an officer from a private. Washington let it be known that to identify himself he would wear a light-blue ribbon across his breast between his coat and waistcoat. This item he duly entered in his expense account to the tune of three shillings and four-pence. (As has been noted, Washington had a uniform for dress occasions.) Major generals were to wear purple ribbons, brigadier generals pink ones and aides-de-camp green. Field officers wore red or pink cockades in their hats, captains yellow or buff and subalterns green. Sergeants appeared with knots of red cloth on the right shoulder, corporals with green.

Proper uniforms for the men were one of Washington's first objectives. He believed they would unite the army and accordingly proposed to Congress the procurement of ten thousand hunting shirts. Apparently the colorful garb of the riflemen of Captain Daniel Morgan of Virginia appealed to Washington. He asked that the shirts be long and loose, made of tow cloth and belted at the waist with double shoulder capes, worn outside the breeches. Congress approved the request; but though Washington had a search made in several colonies, he had to abandon the coveted project because tow cloth was so scarce. So his army continued to have a motley appearance.

Lack of uniforms was not the only difficulty facing him. He sorely needed information but had little opportunity to acquire it. He did not even know the population of the colonies, the strength of their militia or what military supplies they had on hand. It has been estimated that in 1775 there were no more than twenty gunsmiths in all the colonies, and some of these were Tories.

In his first general order Washington asked the adjutant of each regiment for a complete inventory of men and supplies. The answers did not all come in until a week had passed, and then they showed a total of 16,770 men enrolled, 1,598 of whom were on the sick list, 1,429 absent for other reasons. This left 13,743 present and on duty. The army was immediately reorganized into six brigades of six regiments each and three divisions of two brigades each. General Artemas Ward was placed in charge of one division, which constituted the right wing of the army posted at Roxbury. A fat, elderly man, active in his church, he had previously commanded the troops around Boston. General Charles Lee, eccentric, acid-tongued and unpredictable, was in charge of another division at Prospect Hill. He had been a professional soldier and had served under Braddock. The Americans were impressed by his comparatively long military experience. In charge of the third division, stationed at Cambridge, was Major General Israel Putnam, an odd and colorful officer, courageous and energetic, with a roughness that made him popular with the troops. He was the only one of the four major generals unanimously chosen by Congress. Interestingly enough, not one of the four ever became outstanding or even served out the entire war. Men such as Henry Knox and Nathanael Greene were to emerge from the lower ranks and outshine them.

Although Washington did not at first understand the New England troops, he had been in warm agreement with the revolutionary leaders of that region. British Captain Robert Mackenzie of Boston, who had served with Washington in the French and Indian War, wrote Washington in September, 1775, denouncing Massachusetts for its trend toward independence. Washington replied defending the state, pointing out that it had been imposed upon by Britain and stating that regarding the New England people, "none of them will ever submit to the loss of those valuable rights and privileges which are essential to the happiness of every free state, and without which life, liberty and property are rendered totally insecure." John and Samuel Adams, as well as the militant Elbridge Gerry, also supported Washington in most of his military activities.

General Lee, typically outspoken, noted that the military situation was just the reverse of what he had expected. Having been assured that there were plenty of engineers in the service, he claimed to find not one. Nor could he discover a single gunner, though he had been promised an expert corps of artillery. The latter difficulty, however, was soon remedied.

One of the first and most pressing problems to face Washington was that of feeding his army. Here they were in and around Boston after having been summoned unexpectedly two months before. Rushing from their homes, the men had not expected to stay long and had brought along only bits of food, which had long since been consumed. Massachusetts had provided well for feeding its men, but the more distant colonies faced greater difficulty. Governor Jonathan Trumbull of Connecticut tried hard to supply his forces. Rhode Island had a royal governor, who of course did not cooperate. New Hampshire eventually contributed its share of rations.

Washington had been authorized by Congress to feed his men at the expense of the new government and he appointed Joseph Trumbull of Connecticut as commissary general. Trumbull succeeded nobly under trying circumstances. The daily ration consisted of fresh beef, pork or fish along with beans, peas, rice, milk and bread. Spruce beer was the daily drink, and when it was not available, molasses was used.

Washington was heartened when Captain Daniel Morgan and two companies of expert riflemen from his native colony came into camp. Morgan was a soldier after Washington's own heart. A man of magnificent physique and courage —he had been a teamster in the southern wilderness—Morgan was to become as near a folk hero as the Revolutionary War produced. Huge, unpolished but undaunted, he was probably the best field officer of the Continental army. His men, like the other riflemen, were alike in many respects, a large proportion of them being Scotch-Irish, tall and accustomed to the outdoors. They wore round wool hats, hunting shirts, breeches, stockings and leather shoes or moccasins. Lettered on the front of their shirts was the motto "Liberty or Death." Morgan and his men had ridden six hundred miles in twenty-one days on their trek from Virginia.

Rifle companies from Maryland and Pennsylvania also arrived. The rifle was to figure more importantly in Washington's overall strategy than has been generally realized. It would play a weighty role in the fighting at Quebec, Saratoga, the Cowpens and King's Mountain. Unlike the musket, which was the customary infantry weapon, this long and slender gun had spiral grooves inside its barrel, that made the bullet rotate in its flight and thereby increased its accuracy. Though rifles had been used in Europe for many years, the Kentucky rifle, first produced by German and Swiss gunsmiths in Pennsylvania, was a more slender weapon. Its barrel was about five feet long and carried a ball weighing around half an ounce. In the hands of an expert it was deadly. Musket fire at point-blank range was effective from only about fifty to one hundred yards, whereas Morgan's riflemen could pick off men as far as two hundred and fifty yards away.

The rifle, however, was not without its problems. With its small bore and grooves it fouled up more often than the musket; the barrel frequently had to be cleaned. But more important, it took longer to reload than did the musket. A small disk of greased linen or buckskin was placed on the muzzle. The ball was then laid upon it and rammed down the barrel. A musket could be loaded in about half the time, and in close-quarter fighting, delay could be disastrous. (This difficulty was remedied at the Battle of Oriskany. Two riflemen were placed together behind trees, one firing at the Indians and British while the other was reloading.)

The riflemen were an individualistic lot, and this proved troublesome to Washington. Accustomed to acting on their own in the woods, they soon grew tired of the tedium of camp. They would amuse themselves by sniping at long distance at the British sentries or anyone else who exposed themselves along the enemy lines. Their potshots were so accurate that the redcoats became extremely careful not to be seen.

This firing, however, was not particularly effective and was regarded by Washington mainly as a waste of ammunition. He ordered it stopped, thereby angering the frontiersmen. Some were confined for being unruly, but companions soon freed them from the guardhouse; Washington had to strengthen the guard to prevent a mutiny.

Maintaining discipline was one of the new commander's greatest difficulties. Militia officers were elected for their popularity, not their military ability. Washington valued the personal regard of the men for their officers, but he realized from experience that respect and immediate obedience were much more important, particularly during combat. Some officers placed their pay in a common fund, enlisted men sharing equally with them. Others knowingly drew more pay and provisions than the number of men in their charge warranted, thus defrauding the government.

The same rebel spirit that had caused the common people to take up arms against the British made them reluctant to obey their own officers. Officers and men were often equal in birth and fortune. In many of the regiments they had been neighbors and friends before the war. Washington learned that "men cannot bear to be commanded by others that are their superiors in nothing but in having had the good fortune to get a superior commission." Some Massachusetts men complained that Washington expelled some of their officers in order to replace them with his own Virginians. This charge had little validity but did cause him worry.

Washington had written to Martha on June 18, 1775: "My Dearest: I am now set down to write you on a subject which fills me with inexpressible concern, and this concern is greatly aggravated and increased when I reflect upon the uneasiness I know it will cause you. It has been determined in Congress that the whole army raised for the defense of the American cause shall be put under my care, and that it is necessary for me to proceed to Boston immediately to take upon me the command of it. You may believe me, my dear Patsy, when I assure you in the most solemn manner that, so far from seeking this appointment, I have used every endeavor in my power to avoid it [but he alone did appear in uniform at the meeting of Congress when he was selected], not only from my unwillingness to part with you and the family, but from a consciousness of its being a trust too great for my capacity, and that I should enjoy more real happiness in one month with you at home than I have the most distant prospect of finding abroad, if my star were to be seven times seven years. But as it has been a kind of destiny that has thrown me upon this service, I shall hope that my undertaking it is designed to answer some good purpose."

Washington believed in the time-honored adage, "To command, one must first learn to obey." Throughout his long career whenever he had to choose between being respected or being loved, he chose the former.

Some felt he was cold and hard, but all believed him fair. In disciplining the men, persuasion was tried, then admonition given. If these did not work, the court-martial and the lash often followed. The average sentence was thirty-nine strokes laid on the bare back by a cat-o'-nine-tails, a leather thong interspersed with metal pellets. Washington even recommended to Congress that a maximum of five hundred strokes be allowed, but this request was refused. Flogging may seem cruel today, but Washington believed it an effective measure that prevented more drastic punishment.

Washington had read that three things kept soldiers active: natural bravery, hope of reward and fear of punishment. He recommended to his officers that they read Humphrey Bland's *Treatise on Military Discipline*.

In order to keep the men out of trouble, he tried to keep

them occupied. Improvised latrines were covered up and new ones dug each week. Trash was burned immediately. Company streets were swept early each morning. Camp kitchens were inspected daily so that food would be clean and properly served. Any sentry caught lagging in guard duty was heavily punished. Furloughs could not be applied for unless there were good reasons. Strict orders were issued that prostitutes be immediately run out of camp; drunken soldiers received a flogging.

The situation regarding military service of Negroes was mixed. In general blacks appeared anxious to serve, but in July of 1775, the Massachusetts Provincial Congress decided against enlisting them. On December 30, however, General Washington authorized his recruiting officers to admit free Negroes to the service and recommended to the Continental Congress that this be made a continuing rule. Congress approved but with the provision that only free Negroes who served in the army at Cambridge could reenlist. A considerable number of Negroes did serve in the army, especially in the northern campaign. Southern plantation owners generally did not favor using black troops. They feared that eventually the Negroes would become armed and turn against their owners.

In midsummer Washington protested to the British general Thomas Gage, commander in Boston, about the indiscriminate treatment of captured American officers. Gage replied that the men he took prisoners were not officers at all but civilians whom he could have treated as criminals.

The young army was growing, however, and this furnished still another headache for Washington. Supplies were short. In early August he had less than ten thousand pounds of gunpowder, an estimated nine cartridges per man. Then he asked Congress for more, but by September he only had twelve or fifteen rounds per man, compared with the British allotment—usually sixty cartridges for each redcoat!

In September Washington recommended to his council of war an attack on the city of Boston, but his plan was frowned upon. It did not seem promising enough and, too, his officers still hoped for a change in the attitude of the British.

As if this were not discouraging enough, Washington began to be puzzled by the personality of the New Englanders, many of whom seemed to him to be indifferent to the cause. Many of the men planned to return home. This made Washington furious. The Connecticut troops especially aroused his wrath when they refused to reenlist after they were given a bounty. He requested that they stay at least until December 10, when they could be replaced by other militia from Massachusetts and New Hampshire. They replied by leaving on December 1. Washington, utterly chagrined and disgusted, compared them with mercenaries basely deserting the cause of their country. As they departed they received boos, hisses, stones and insults from the other soldiers. By December 1 only about thirty-five hundred men had reenlisted, and many of these only because furloughs had been granted them.

Besides the shortage of powder, money was hard to obtain. Washington, almost at the end of his endurance, exclaimed to his secretary Joseph Reed, "Those who are employed to sign the Continental bills are not able nor inclined to do it as fast as they are wanted. They will prove the destruction of the army if they are not more attentive and diligent. Such a dearth of public spirit and want of virtue, such stock-jobbing and fertility in all the low arts to obtain advantages of one kind or another, in this great change of military arrangement, I never saw before, and pray God I may never be witness to again. . . . Could I have foreseen what I have, and am likely to experience, no consideration upon earth should have induced me to accept this command."

The wonder was that under the circumstances Washington could keep together any army at all. He wrote to Congress on September 21, 1775, complaining that he was pained and distressed "to see the winter fast approaching upon a naked army, the time of their service within a few weeks of expiring." He reminded the lawmakers that his paymaster had "not a single dollar in hand" and that the commissary general had strained his credit to the utmost, with the quartermaster general in an equally dire situation. Washington feared his troops would mutiny. "I am of the opinion," he stated, "that if the evil is not immediately remedied and more punctually observed in the future, the army must absolutely break up."

Washington was a wealthy man, and it was not easy for him to understand the hardships and sacrifices the enlisted man underwent upon leaving his home and occupation. Perhaps this was fortunate; had he understood he might have been too sympathetic and not as steadfast in his purpose. At Mount Vernon, the work of the plantation went on under the supervision of his cousin Lund (though he did not always do a good job). But a soldier who had left a small farm uncultivated did not have a field hand to take his place. A tiny shop left unattended except by a wife or by children loomed large in the mind of a lonely soldier. To the enlisted man drawing low and often irregular army pay, therefore, a bounty usually appeared not only desirable but justified.

One criticism of the new army was that it was not active enough, and Washington now found a refreshing auxiliary enterprise that promised brighter horizons. For a long time Americans had wanted to make Canada a fourteenth colony and thus present a united continental front to the British. The British, it was also feared, might come down the Saint Lawrence to the Hudson River and thereby split the colo-

nies. Rumor had it that the English were even now negoti-
ating with the Iroquois Indians in an effort to persuade
them to attack the American fort on Lake Champlain.
Washington prodded General Schuyler into action. Schuyler,
with the northern army, planned to launch an expedition
from Fort Ticonderoga into Canada.

To create a diversion, Washington sent a force of a thousand men into Canada from Boston. They were placed under
the command of bold and dashing Benedict Arnold, then
a colonel. With him went Daniel Morgan's company, those
restless riflemen, who were now to be given a chance to
utilize their great energy. They were to proceed up the
coast to the Kennebec River in Maine, along its forested
banks to the Dead River portages and down the Chaudière
to the Saint Lawrence River opposite the city of Quebec.

Schuyler's force was to approach Quebec from the west.
He and Arnold by a pincers movement were to overcome
the city, now held by British General Sir Guy Carleton. It
was a good plan, and its prospects pleased Washington. But
no one could have foreseen the practical difficulties and
unexpected contingencies. Washington saw in the courageous Arnold just the type of man needed for the formidable
push through uncharted wilderness. But though daring,
Arnold was unpredictable.

Reports of the expedition to Quebec are not wanting. So
many journals or diaries were kept that it has proven one of
the most recorded as well as one of the most interesting
enterprises in our history. On a bright summer day on Cambridge Common the soldiers were given a hero's send-off by
cheering crowds. Many of these men in their drab tunics
would never see their homeland again. There was a great
celebration, and by the time the ships carrying Arnold's
troops reached their destination on the coast of Maine the
pilots of the vessels had become so intoxicated they could
not see shore.

The little fleet reached Gardiner, Maine, on September 22. Arnold inspected some two hundred boats that had been prepared and found them poorly constructed. But the force moved on anyway, guided by Indians who said they knew the forest trail. The Virginia riflemen at first set a fast pace as the advance unit, but even Daniel Morgan found the going rough. The bateaux soon were broken in the stony streams; the men were forced to wade through icy waters when they could not make their way along the shrub-covered banks. Many became ill. Winter set in early that year, and food was scarce. Soldiers ate cartridge boxes, shoes and soap, and even devoured a favorite dog that had accompanied them. Starving, many fell to the ground and had to be abandoned. The records of this terrible journey are not often clear as to the activities of Arnold. But they do emphasize the leadership of Morgan, with his great stamina and spirit.

By the time they reached the Chaudière they resembled gaunt, walking skeletons. It appeared that they would never reach their objective. Just when it seemed that they would all die of starvation, a herd of cattle appeared around a bend in the river. Morgan and his men fell upon them and devoured the flesh raw.

Finally the decimated American force stood on the banks of the Saint Lawrence and looked across at the high, beetling cliffs of Quebec, hoping for victory. But it was not to be. The mid-November wind blew so strongly that the small force was delayed in crossing the river. The British, meanwhile, had intercepted a message from Arnold to American General Richard Montgomery, learned of the expedition and prepared themselves for the onslaught. Arnold and Morgan finally got their men across at night by canoes, climbed the Plains of Abraham and challenged the British under Colonel Allan Maclean of the Royal Highland Emigrants. But the redcoats were not to be drawn out prematurely, so the Americans had to fall back and await the arrival of Montgomery from Fort Ticonderoga.

This officer was also having difficulty, for among his men there was "an unhappy homesickness." Many of them claimed they were too feeble for military duty. They set out southward and "instantly acquired health" as soon as they were well on their way home. Leaving garrisons at Saint Johns in Montreal, Montgomery sailed down the river with three hundred men to join Arnold's force. Now the combined troops laid siege to Quebec. But the hard winter had grown worse, the snow as high as the second story of the houses. Food ran short, and smallpox broke out among the Americans. While the British were being reinforced by more soldiers and some sailors, the Americans on December 31 would face the enlistment expirations of a considerable number of their men. So Montgomery and Arnold conferred and decided on a two-pronged attack.

As the snow began to fall, the assault began late Saturday afternoon, December 30. Arnold led his column up toward the Palace Gate, while Montgomery and his men slipped along ice-filled Wolfe's Cove. Rockets signaled the attack at five o'clock, but the siege was not a surprise. A drunken sailor on the British side pulled the lanyard of a cannon for his last shot before he ran, the ball killing General Montgomery instantly. Arnold was carried off the field with a bullet through his leg. Lieutenant Aaron Burr tried to rally some of the men, but without success. Daniel Morgan assumed command of Arnold's contingent and bravely led the way forward. Though he suffered a bruised knee and received powder burns on his face, he did not pause until asked to do so by his fellow officers.

Meanwhile General Carleton had secured firm control over his defenses, and the Americans began to be surrounded. They fired as best they could, but many of their flintlocks were damp from the snow. Grapeshot and musket fire greeted them at every turn in the winding streets. Morgan, refusing to face defeat, led numerous charges. Finally surrounded, his back against a wall, he slashed with his huge sword and cried that he would never surrender. After being beseeched both by his own men and by the enemy, Morgan, weeping with anger, handed his big sword to a nearby priest, saying, "Not a scoundrel of these cowards shall take it out of my hand." Thus Canada was permanently lost to the United States.

To Washington the loss of this battle was a bitter blow. The colonies were disappointed in him, although he was not directly responsible for the failure of the Canadian expedition. He also had at this time the painful duty of court-martialing Lieutenant Colonel Roger Enos. Enos had commanded the rear party of Arnold's expedition. When the going had become rough, he had sent his supplies forward, withdrawn his men and returned to Cambridge. His excuse that he felt he had fulfilled his mission was not accepted by the indignant Washington.

Many Americans, especially those who had little or no knowledge of the exigencies of war, were growing restive, because no spectacular victory had been achieved. In the ill-fated Canadian expedition, much money had been spent; around five thousand casualties had been suffered from death, illness, desertion and capture. The fact that some good leadership—that of Morgan and Arnold—had evolved from the attempt did not change the sad fact that the struggle to obtain a fourteenth colony had ended in abysmal failure. Not only had Canada not been taken, but now Carleton's army was growing. It was feared that he would soon strike at the Americans in the south. Washington must now seek a new and, if possible, more victorious path.

III THE BOSTON DILEMMA

ALTHOUGH THE EXPEDITION to capture Canada had failed, Washington now had a challenging new plan. He would like to take the dramatic step of attacking the British in Boston. His council of war, however, as well as his own prudence held him back.

In late September he had written a long letter to Congress vividly setting forth the condition of his troops and calling attention to their needs. The young army would fall apart, he wrote, unless there were new enlistments. Washington wrote well, as the many volumes of his missives, both personal and official, testify. He had an open, florid but convincing style that revealed a rare and effective talent for expression. Often his writings have a literary quality; in no small measure they show a key to his success.

For example, the letter he wrote to Congress in September resulted in the appointment of a committee comprising Benjamin Franklin, Thomas Lynch and Benjamin Harrison. Its purpose was to consult with Washington and with New England representatives about the most effectual method of continuing and supporting a Continental army. The committeemen journeyed to Cambridge and conferred with Washington for five days. From this fruitful meeting came congressional resolutions calling for an army of 30,732 officers and men divided into 26 regiments of 728 men each, exclusive of riflemen and artillery. Their pay and rations were determined, and brown was designated as the color of their uniforms, each colony to be indicated by a distinctive facing.

Washington now sought some means of increasing his supplies. He improvised a kind of navy, modeled on those fitted out by some of the colonies for protection. The besieged British in Boston received their supplies by water, mostly from England and the West Indies. Six armed American schooners, known as "Washington's Navy," soon were preying on British vessels and capturing ammunition and clothing that were of significant help.

The Continental army around Boston now contained about seventeen thousand men. The siege of the city was apparently effective except that there was no immediate prospect for victory. Washington had read in European military manuals that sieges were won by the use of artillery. He had virtually none.

In seeking a solution to this problem, Washington made one of his happiest discoveries. He found Henry Knox. A fat and genial Bostonian, Knox was to become in many ways his right-hand man. He had had some experience with artillery in the local Massachusetts militia. Though married to a socially prominent Tory, he was nonetheless an ardent patriot and had converted her to his beliefs. Young Knox had been present at the Boston Massacre and had tried to prevent it.

He owned a bookstore and avidly read European volumes on military tactics and strategy, especially on the use of artillery. Soon after Washington had reached Cambridge, Knox joined him. He brought with him his willing wife, who carried her husband's militia sword sewn inside the lining of her petticoat as they escaped through British lines.

Knox and Washington liked each other immediately.

Here was one New Englander Washington understood. He asked Knox if he would go to distant Fort Ticonderoga to bring back fifty-five pieces of heavy artillery that had been captured from the British. Knox responded with an enthusiastic affirmative. Had he known what lay in store for him, he surely would have been less eager.

Characteristically, Knox lost no time in starting. Wishing to see the city, he made his way to New York on horseback. He found it impressive but materialistic; the people, he thought, were quite profane, and mostly Tories. Knox then went to Albany and Ticonderoga.

At Fort George he spent the night in a one-room cabin beside the road with a captured British officer, young Lieutenant John André. The two found they had much in common. They were about the same age, and both were interested in literature and military matters. Here the similarity was to end. Knox was to become head of American artillery and later the first Secretary of War. André was to attain infamy as a spy—General Henry Knox, five years later, would sit on the general court-martial that tried and sentenced André to be hanged.

Meanwhile at Boston, the winter wore on. The men's clothing, designed for summer, was too scant to keep them warm. Blankets and fuel were also lacking. Soldiers were forced to eat their provisions raw, because there was not enough wood with which to cook; they had already burned the surrounding rail fences and trees for a mile around the camp.

But with all these woes, the civilian soldiers suffered most from homesickness. Longing for their families, shops and farms, they grew increasingly weary of camp life. They had agreed to serve for a certain length of time. When their enlistments expired, they expected to go home.

John Adams understood their state of mind better than Washington. He wrote to Congress, "It is not in the pages of history perhaps to furnish a case like ours. To maintain a post within musket shot of the enemy for six months together, without powder, and at the same time to disband one army and recruit another within that distance of twenty-odd British regiments is more than probably ever was attempted."

So disgusted was Washington with this attitude of the troops that he wrote Joseph Reed, "I have often thought how much happier I should have been if instead of accepting a command under such circumstances, I had taken my musket on my shoulder and entered the ranks, or, if I could have justified the measure to posterity and my own conscience, had retired to the back country and lived in a wigwam."

But Washington did not show his unhappiness to the rank and file. On January 1, 1776, the very day after many enlistments had expired, he ordered a new flag hoisted high on a pole at the American headquarters on Prospect Hill in Somerville, Massachusetts, "in compliment to the United Colonies." The flag had thirteen alternate red and white horizontal stripes, its canton was the Union Jack of Great Britain. In the orders that proclaimed the new flag, it was also noted that "This day giving commencement to the new army which, in every point of view is Continental, the general flatters himself that a laudable spirit of emulation will now take place and pervade the whole." As a matter of fact, he now had a paper strength of only 8,212 men with 5,582 present and fit for duty. Even so Washington was determined to attack as soon as he had sufficient artillery.

The British in Boston, under General Sir William Howe, were not much better off. Although their defenses were well prepared, only eleven thousand men manned them. These were beset with scurvy and smallpox. Someone characterized their situation as "really rotten." About the only food the redcoats had was salt meat, dried peas and, on occasion,

fish. They had found to their misfortune that much of the
food sent from England spoiled during the long voyage or
was captured by the new Revolutionary navy. The cold
New England winter caused such a shortage of firewood
that churches, houses and wharves were broken up and used
for fuel. The British, as a matter of fact, would have abandoned Boston sooner had they possessed enough ships to
evacuate both the soldiers and the Tories. Washington and
Howe realized one another's weakness, but each knew he
could not successfully mount a battle for control of the city.

In the meantime cheering words reached Washington's
ears. Knox was on his way with the heavy artillery. He had
arrived at Ticonderoga in early December and had selected
fifty-five cannon, long guns, short pieces and heavy mortars,
ranging in weight from one hundred pounds to fifty-five
hundred pounds each. How to transport such a massive
cargo over snow and ice through an uncharted country for
some three hundred miles? Using rollers, skids and sledges,
Knox managed to assemble his strange caravan. The teams
of horses and oxen were driven by both soldiers and civilians. Knox managed to get the procession underway by
December 9. Strong sleds helped to move the artillery over
frozen Lake George. Here six tons of it broke through the
ice and sank, but fortunately most was recovered. General
Schuyler contributed horses and slaves, helping to continue
the tortuous journey eastward from Albany. Through the
Berkshires they went, over an Indian trail that later was to
be used by British General John Burgoyne on his withdrawal from Saratoga. The cannon were pulled up each hill
and then slid down on the opposite side. At Westfield, Massachusetts, a curious crowd gathered to examine and fondle
the guns. They brought out cider and whiskey, which was
welcomed by the cold and tired teamsters. Knox obligingly
fired his biggest gun, nicknamed "The Old Sow" because of
its shape and size.

By the time they reached Springfield, the ground was beginning to thaw under the melting snow. This made the going more difficult. The weather soon became cold again, the ground froze and Knox moved on to Framingham. It was now January 25. John Adams came out to see the sight, which he doubtless reported to Washington. Knox reported immediately to Washington's headquarters where the gratified commander-in-chief received him with his "noble train of artillery." Knox was forthwith commissioned a colonel and placed in charge of the army's big guns.

Washington had been increasingly anxious to have the guns, without which any military action was stymied. On February 16 he called a council of war and proposed an assault on the British across the frozen harbor of Back Bay. This was an impulsive idea of Washington's, with which the council did not agree because of its riskiness. The expedition over the ice would have been hazardous. Then, too, the British had more men inside Boston than Washington realized at the time. The alternate plan agreed upon was to seize and fortify Dorchester Heights, the adjoining hills southeast of Boston. Mounting the captured guns on Dorchester Heights would not only bring the city of Boston within range but also jeopardize shipping in the harbor. Supplies vital to the besieged garrison would be cut off; British defenses at Castle William and on Boston Neck at the south of the city would be endangered also.

Fortifications must be set up quickly, Washington realized, or the maneuver would fail to surprise the British. Colonel Rufus Putnam suggested that prefabricated forts be constructed of bundles of logs, baskets of earth and bales of hay. These would be fronted by a frieze of sharpened stakes supported by barrels of earth. Should the breastworks be attacked, some barrels could be rolled down the steep hillside. This plan was enthusiastically accepted, the materials were prepared and the heavy guns were assembled at Roxbury.

Under the command of Israel Putnam, the brigades of

Nathanael Greene and John Sullivan opposed any possible British attack across Boston Neck. Under cover of night on March 2, Knox's artillery on the Cambridge side of the lines opened fire to attract the attention of the British. This was repeated the following night. On March 4, Washington opened a thunderous bombardment, using up his scarce ammunition, but with good purpose. A party of twelve hundred soldiers supported by eight hundred more, with three hundred sixty loaded oxcarts bringing up the rear, left Roxbury for Dorchester Heights. There the revolutionaries worked feverishly through the night to complete the rough but elaborate fortifications.

When General Howe awoke the next morning, late as was his custom, he faced an astonishing sight. On Dorchester Heights there had appeared as if by magic two formidable redoubts looking down upon him. To add to his discomfiture, British Admiral Molyneux Shuldham announced that he could not keep his ships in the harbor because of this new threat. Howe must either leave or drive the Americans out of their new stronghold. Howe's first impulse was to blast them out with his cannon, but he found to his chagrin that the guns could not be elevated enough to catch the new redoubts in their sights. Although he had previously decided to evacuate Boston, William Howe was not one to run away without a fight. He ordered some two thousand men to go by boat to the Dorchester Peninsula, and attack the Americans with bayonets.

Often in the history of warfare the elements play a part. This night over Boston a fierce storm broke. It continued throughout the next day, drenching the boats and breaking on the shore. Howe called off his attack to wait out the storm, but by then it was too late. The Dorchester Heights fortifications had been completed. The Ticonderoga cannon, ironically of British make, were now in American hands and frowning down upon Boston. So Howe ordered the evacuation to proceed. Watching from the heights, Washington must have had a great feeling of exultation at having thus attained his objective without fighting.

He could have bombarded some of the outgoing vessels, but he was glad to see them leave and carried on only occasional cannonading as a reminder. Howe had promised if he were not attacked he would not burn Boston, and Washington had this in mind. He also wanted to spare the thousand fleeing Tories who left with the British. Anyone would have felt compassion at the plight of these exiles who were leaving their homes and possessions forever with no certain haven in view. The ships were so crowded it was difficult for them to sail out of the harbor. In one cabin of an already heavily laden ship, for example, were thirty-six men, women, and children.

British army stores, cavalry and artillery horses had been abandoned in Boston. By Saint Patrick's Day, March 17, the last British soldier had gone, and the fleet was anchored five miles out, making Washington wonder if some trick was being played. Howe was bound for New York, but first he sailed to Halifax, Nova Scotia, where he landed his cargo of unfortunate Tories.

On March 20, Washington and his Continentals took complete possession of Boston.

IV NEW YORK: A CRISIS

NEW YORK NOW HELD a fascination for Washington. From a military standpoint it was to occupy much of his thought throughout the war. His success at Boston had given him confidence. Though still far from a seasoned commander, he had learned valuable lessons.

Washington rightly reasoned that following the British evacuation of Boston on March 17, 1776, the redcoats would attack New York. So the very next day he sent most of his army in that direction. It consisted of three companies of Virginia riflemen, a rifle regiment from Pennsylvania, three brigades under Generals William Heath, John Sullivan and Nathanael Greene and Henry Knox's artillery. Israel Putnam was in charge of this force, while five regiments stayed in Boston under the lethargic General Artemas Ward.

Washington had mellowed as a commander, but he was still having discipline problems with his troops. On February 27, 1776, he had issued orders that "all officers, non-commissioned officers and soldiers are positively forbidden playing at cards and other games of chance. At this time of public distress, men may find enough to do in the service of their God and their country, without abandoning themselves to vice and immorality. As the season is now fast approaching when every man is expected to be drawn into the field of action, it is highly important that he should prepare his mind as well as everything necessary for it."

Another order, one of the first off-limits commands in our history was issued by Washington in the spring of 1776. It stated eloquently that "The gin shops and other houses where liquors have been heretofore retailed within or near the lines are strictly forbidden to sell any for the future to any soldier in the army, and the inhabitants of said houses near the lines are immediately to move out of them; they are to be appropriated to the use of the troops.

"If any soldier of the army shall be found disguised with liquor, as has been too much the practice heretofore, the general is determined to have him punished with the utmost severity, as no soldier in such situation can be either fit for defense or attack. The general orders that no sutler in the army shall sell to any soldier more than one half pint of spirit per day."

Though he was strong-willed and had little sense of humor, Washington had acquired tolerance for his soldiers. His experience had shown him that given the proper circumstances and a dose of inspiration, good soldiers would fight no matter what their origin.

On April 3, 1776, the Corporation of Overseers of Harvard College voted Washington the degree of Doctor of Laws, the second time in one hundred and forty years that the institution had conferred this honor. It stated in part: "There is the greatest propriety in conferring such honor on . . . the accomplished general who . . . without hesitation left all the pleasures of his delightful seat in Virginia, and the affairs of his own estate . . . without accepting any reward that he might deliver New England from the unjust and cruel arms of Britain."

General Washington himself arrived in New York City on April 13, just as the leaves on the shade trees of Brooklyn

Heights were beginning to emerge. He set about at once arranging for the defense of the city, which he was positive would soon be needed. He was convinced of the value of holding New York against the British; and this objective was to cost him time and men unnecessarily.

The eccentric Charles Lee had first been sent to Connecticut to recruit volunteers. Lee had then gone on to New York to prepare its defenses and disarm the Tories. He advised Washington—who at this time regarded his opinions highly—to make the city a battleground. Lee, however, had time only to plan certain broad defensive measures and organize a New York, New Jersey and Connecticut militia before he was ordered by Congress to take command in the South. New York's defense was left in the hands of Brigadier General William Alexander, better known as Lord Stirling. Born in New York, his noble title was recognized by his ancestral Scotland but not by the English Parliament. Stirling was able and brave but too fond of the bottle. Washington wrote to him about New York: "It is the place that we must use every endeavor to keep from them. For should they get that town, and the command of the North River, they can stop the intercourse between the northern and southern colonies, upon which depends the safety of America."

New York was then about a square mile in size on the southern end of Manhattan. Lee's plan had been to place fortifications all around the lower part of the island and on Brooklyn Heights so that the Continental guns could dominate the city. Washington generally agreed with these plans, although he varied them to some extent. Colonel Knox insisted on placing the artillery, but most of it was to see little use here. Ships' hulks were sunk in the East and North rivers, and plans were made for constructing a huge chain, two thousand feet long, to be stretched across the North River some miles to the north.

By May, Washington's force in New York had grown to

about ten thousand. Now he placed lookouts on the heights of Staten Island in New York Harbor to watch for the enemy. On the east bank of the North River in Upper Manhattan, a bastion was constructed and appropriately named Fort Washington. It was protected by a steep promontory of land, rocks and woods. On the New Jersey bank a similar fortification was built and called Fort Lee. On paper the defensive position looked promising.

In the meantime, New York's Tories had become increasingly aware of the tall, conspicuous Virginian directing his army in their midst. Gouverneur Morris and a secret committee of the New York Provincial Congress informed Washington that an intrigue was going on right under his nose. Royal Governor William Tryon had set up headquarters on the British warship *Duchess of Gordon* in the harbor. With the Tory mayor, David Matthews, Tryon was recruiting local men to serve in the British army. These soldiers would join in a British attack on the city. It was rumored that this "Tory plot" also included a plan to assassinate Washington and his leading generals.

In intelligence activities, Washington often acted with dispatch; this was no exception. On June 22 Mayor Matthews was arrested in Flatbush and charged with allegiance to a foreign authority. Also implicated were a number of Americans, including Thomas Hickey, a member of Washington's personal bodyguard. Technically Matthews could not be charged with treason, but the military rules governing Hickey were more clear. He was court-martialed. Matthews was never convicted in connection with the assassination plot. He was, however, kept in jail as an example for any other Tory who might be similarly tempted.

One member of his guard, a drummer named William Greene, confessed all he knew and begged the mercy of the court. Gilbert Forbes, another, also gave testimony about his fellow conspirators; these two got off fairly easily.

Sergeant Hickey alone was stubborn. He had obviously

lied and did not show remorse. A gallows was erected near
the Bowery, and Hickey was taken there after he was court-
martialed. He contemptuously refused the service of a chaplain, maintaining his rebellious attitude almost to the end.
As the noose and blindfold were placed on him he burst
into tears. Then he wiped them away and calmly faced his
executioner. He was the first soldier in Washington's army
to be hanged.

In general orders, Washington stated that he hoped the
case would be a warning to every soldier. He counseled that
the best way to avoid such crimes and their consequences
was to stay away from temptation and to avoid especially
lewd women—Hickey had confessed they had first led him
astray. The Hickey plot, which Washington did nothing to
play down, darkened the cause of the Tories throughout
the colonies.

On July 9, 1776, the Declaration of Independence was
read to the assembled army in New York at 6 P.M. Washington remarked, "The general hopes that this important
event will serve as a fresh incentive to every officer and
soldier to act with fidelity and courage, knowing that now
the peace and safety of his country depend, under God,
solely on the success of our arms, and that he is now in the
service of a state possessed of sufficient power to reward his
merit, and advance him to the highest honors of a free
country."

The lookouts on the Staten Island heights had not long
to wait. Scores of ships soon appeared in the harbor loaded
with the largest expeditionary force England had ever sent.
In a few days, one hundred and thirty warships and transports unloaded almost ten thousand men. These were followed by one hundred and ninety-three other vessels carrying
additional soldiers.

Within the British camp on Staten Island there were now twenty-seven regiments of the line; four grenadier, four light infantry and two guards battalions; three artillery brigades; one regiment of light dragoons and eight thousand Hessians. In command were Generals William Howe, Henry Clinton, Lord Percy, Lord Cornwallis and Leopold von Heister, all veteran officers.

Supporting this powerful army were ten British ships of the line, twenty frigates boasting twelve hundred guns and numerous transports. They were manned by over ten thousand sailors. (All this had cost the British government almost a million pounds.)

One description went as follows: "Onlookers gazed with awe on a pageant such as America had never seen before—five hundred dark hulls, forests of masts, a network of spas and ropes and a gay display of flying pennants. There were ships of the line with frowning sides, three-tiers of guns and high forecastles; there were graceful frigates, alert and speedy, tenders and galleys to land the thousands of men from the unwieldy transports."

To oppose this ominous array, Washington had by now less than twenty thousand inexperienced and undisciplined recruits quickly drawn from shop and farm, with meager arms led by amateur officers. But he believed in their fighting hearts and in their desire to support the recently announced Declaration of Independence. He had issued orders that his men keep their firearms ready at all times, even at night. He was disturbed by the women and children running about noisily and unpredictably; they might have a demoralizing effect upon his inexperienced men.

The Howe brothers, General William and Lord Richard, did not relish the idea of fighting the Americans. They remembered that these colonists had had a statue of their brother erected in Westminster Abbey after he had died in the fighting for Ticonderoga during the French and Indian War. Too, the Howes were Whigs, and a Tory government sat in London. But though they were opposed to the government of Lord North, they were loyal to their sovereign. The Patriots, demonstrating other feelings, at about the time of their arrival pulled down a leaden statue of George III on Bowling Green in New York City.

Admiral Richard Howe at this time sent a flag of truce to the American forces requesting a conference with "Mr. Washington." Adjutant General Joseph Reed replied that he knew of no such person. The messenger then produced a letter addressed to "George Washington, Esquire." Reed stated that he could not receive a letter addressed in such a manner. The redcoat returned disappointed to Admiral Howe. Washington told Congress that more than mere protocol was involved. The commander-in-chief felt it his duty to his country to insist on proper respect for his position. He also felt that the British would try again.

They did. This time it was William Howe who sent a flag to ask if his adjutant general could have an interview with "General Washington." But when Lieutenant Colonel James Patterson, the adjutant, arrived, he carried a letter again addressed to "George Washington, Esq., etc. etc." This was promptly refused, whereupon Patterson disclosed its contents. It contained only an inquiry about a British officer who had been captured at Montreal and had complained about his treatment. To this, Washington replied that Ethan Allen and other revolutionaries had been treated as badly by the British. Patterson said that such matters were beyond the jurisdiction of General Howe. He added that it was the hope of his superiors that a reconciliation was still possible. The Howe brothers, he said, had been designated peace commissioners by the King. Washington found this unconvincing; he felt that innocent men needed no pardons. He pointed out that it was really Congress with whom the commissioners should negotiate. At this point Patterson gave up his effort, thanked Washington for his offer of lunch, and left.

The British now abandoned their efforts at peace and began preparing for war. Perhaps Washington felt some relief. He must also have sensed the great danger. He told his men they could withstand the assault; he pointed out that in their courage and action they might well be responsible for the fate of unborn millions. Had he been sufficiently familiar with European warfare, he would have known he did not stand a chance against the Howes' juggernaut.

At eight on the morning of August 22, an advance British force of four thousand—infantry, dragoons, grenadiers and Hessian Jaegers—set sail under Clinton and Cornwallis and landed on Long Island. Beneath the covering guns of the warship *Rainbow* they landed and drew up in smart formation. Soon five thousand more disembarked and took up positions nearby, and by noon as many more. Washington, biding his time, felt he should not try to oppose these landings. He doubtless could not have, because of the protecting guns of the fleet.

He had positioned Colonel Edward Hand and some two hundred Pennsylvanians at an outpost on Denyse Point near where the redcoats had landed. All this small detachment could do was watch the enemy eat some of the luscious apples on the surrounding trees and then march inland, burning the standing grain and killing as many cattle as possible. Hand's group was then captured. Cornwallis quickly occupied the village of Flatbush. For the next three days, all the rebels could do was pepper the British with grapeshot and snipe at them in an effort to disconcert them.

Washington was aware of these landings, but he was informed that they amounted to only eight or nine thousand men. Thus it was somewhat understandable that he kept three-quarters of his army on the New York side. His intel-ligence, however, should have told him that the main Brit-ish attack would come on Long Island. General Greene, meanwhile, had become sick with a fever and had to be replaced by General Sullivan. Washington visited the Long Island headquarters and not being sure of Sullivan's ability, placed Putnam, the senior major general, in overall com-mand on Brooklyn Heights, with Sullivan second. More reinforcements were now sent to Long Island, bringing Putnam's forces to around ten thousand. After having spent several hours in this area, Washington rightly reasoned that the British would attack soon.

In his Manhattan headquarters, George Washington was asleep in the early morning hours of August 27, 1776. At 1 A.M. he was awakened by the sound of firing on Long Island. By the time dawn had arrived he could make out the shape of British ships headed toward the battle. Imme-diately, Washington ordered a small boat and made for the scene of action.

When he arrived he was told that Jamaica Pass, a strategic point leading inward, had been held by the Americans. But this information was false. Colonel Samuel Miles had been assigned responsibility for the pass by Sullivan. (Both later denied such responsibility.)

Washington did not see any need to intervene in the orders his officers had given. However, he was apparently apprehensive. He told some of his men: "If I see any man turn his back today, I will shoot him through. I have two pistols loaded. But I will not ask any man to go further than I do. I will fight as long as I have a leg or an arm. . . . Quit yourselves like men, like soldiers, for all that is worth living for is at stake."

Soon heavy firing broke out. General Stirling's men sta-tioned on the Gowanus Road had seen English troops advancing in the dark and let loose a volley at them. It was learned that General James Grant's division was moving slowly but strongly against the rebels. Putnam ordered Stirling to meet the British threat with his reserve brigade. Here for the first time an American unit met a British force in an open field in formal position. As day dawned, British infantry and artillery tried to break Stirling's formation, but his Maryland and Delaware Continentals stood firm. For hours, English cannon fire continued, but they had been stopped, for the time being at least, by Stirling's stand.

Colonel Miles, meanwhile, had for some reason begun to realize that holding Jamaica Pass was important. He marched eastward with his five hundred men, following the trails along tree-filled Brooklyn Heights. Suddenly he found himself in the midst of the main British army. Clinton had been led to the site by three Tory farmers. Both British and Americans were surprised at confronting each other at the pass. After exchanging some musket shots, Miles and his men were overrun and captured. A few managed to escape through the woods and hurried back to Putnam's headquarters, where they reported the advance of the British through Jamaica Pass. Whether Washington was there at this time is not clear. But action was taken to meet the threat.

Sullivan tried hard to hurl his force at the invaders, but found to his dismay that he was caught between the British and Hessians. The last Washington heard of Sullivan was that he was seen with a smoking pistol in each hand just before he and several hundred of his troops were forced to surrender. In addition to this catastrophe, Washington heard that numbers of his men had been bayoneted by Hessians even after they had given up. The Germans displayed a professionalism unknown to the raw Americans. For a while Stirling stood his ground. Then, finding himself surrounded, he surrendered to the Hessians.

It was a disastrous defeat. The defenders had lost about

fifteen hundred men, the English three hundred. The redcoats now pressed against the remaining American fortifications in Brooklyn, expecting orders to carry the last ramparts. But these orders did not come—for which Washington was thankful. Howe and Clinton had had enough experience in assaulting rebel lines at Bunker Hill and Charleston. They did not wish to risk great loss. Howe decided to use a siege approach, a tactic with which Washington never became fully familiar.

Washington doubtless expected a British assault. Were it to be successful, the result could be decisive for the colonies. His army would be pushed back to the East River and destroyed. He must hold his line, he reasoned. He still had some seven thousand troops who had not taken part in the battle; these, he felt, had a reasonable opportunity of holding the onslaught. Sending his wounded back across the river, he asked to have reinforcements moved to Brooklyn from Manhattan. Then he rode along his lines to inspect his defenses and strengthen the morale of his men. Reinforcements did arrive on the morning of August 28, and now the American strength in Brooklyn was nearly twelve thousand. He breathed more easily.

There was still great danger ahead. Three-fifths of Washington's troops were now in Brooklyn, the rest in Manhattan. If they decided to do so, the British could move up the East River or the Hudson to cut off the rebel forces. Washington has been blamed for not using a cavalry patrol to ferret out the positions and intentions of the enemy, but he had no real cavalry. Nor had he asked for any (strangely enough, as he himself was a superb horseman). Had he availed himself of the five hundred so-called "light dragoons" who had ridden 'over from Connecticut—actually farmers mounted on rough country horses and armed with fowling pieces—more of his intelligence reports might have been true. As it was, Washington did not use the mounted troopers.

There was some skirmishing throughout the next day, and he encouraged his men to keep up their fire, not only to make a show of resistance but to maintain morale. The British had begun to dig parallel and approach trenches in the manner of European siegecraft. He could see that their sea power and numbers were too much for him. How to withdraw without letting the British know and thereby risking a possibly annihilating attack was his problem. He kept his decision a secret, even from his most trusted aides, until late in the afternoon of the twenty-ninth.

"Nine thousand disheartened soldiers, the last hope of their country, were penned up," commented the English historian, George Trevelyan, "with the sea behind them and a triumphant enemy in front, shelterless and famished on a square mile of open ground." Had Howe realized it, he could have stormed this position, captured Washington and his staff and ended the war right there.

When Washington called his generals together on the twenty-ninth, he had for once already made up his mind. Instead of asking for a council of war, he told them of his plan for retreat. Their troops must believe reinforcements were arriving soon to replace them. Actually, all supplies and artillery were to be prepared for early evacuation.

At twilight the boats began to arrive across the East River. Headed by the Marblehead Mariners under Colonel John Glover, scores of slender vessels edged the Brooklyn shore to take the fleeing units aboard. Carefully prepared and supervised, the project went well. As the evening wore on, unfavorable wind and tides from the northeast threatened to drive them aground. By midnight, however, this danger had subsided. Rain began to fall; though it added to their discomfort it also served to muffle the sounds of the moving troops. The operation was proceeding smoothly, when suddenly a cannon went off by accident. The roar frightened the Americans into thinking the enemy had heard it, but apparently they had not.

At about 2 A.M., General Thomas Mifflin was told by a Washington aide that the boats were ready for his unit. The command seemed premature to Mifflin, but he finally ordered his troops to the shore. There he found an indignant Washington wondering why Mifflin had come so soon. When the latter remonstrated that he had received orders to do so, Washington assured him that it was a mistake. Mifflin then obediently and skillfully led his men back to their trenches. Within two hours, he had authentic orders to embark, which he did quickly and silently.

Dawn was now breaking, and a Tory woman warned the British that the Americans were up to something. Redcoats began reconnoitering to see what was going on. Some peered over the American breastworks and became suspicious. Perhaps they would have succeeded in blocking the retreat had not nature intervened. A thick fog settled over the boats, screening all activity. The evacuation proceeded. Washington himself was in one of the last boats to leave. As he wrote to Congress, he had hardly been off his horse and had never closed his eyes once in the forty-eight hours before the retreat. All during the long and anxious night, he rode his gray horse through the lines of his men, cheering and calming them and personally supervising every detail of the operation.

Ironically, Washington's success was his retreat; Howe's, his attack. Though honored for his feat, Washington had won no battle, gained no victory. He has been praised by historians as masterful; he performed a seemingly impossible feat. But he had neglected to defend Jamaica Pass and thus allowed Howe to encircle his army and drive it backward. Howe, on the other hand, did not use his opportunity to attack the American lines. If not for Washington's retreat, Long Island might have been the last battle of the American Revolution. As it was, it became only another serious setback. Gloom spread over the colonies, and Washington was first to admit it. He wrote Congress that the defeat had dispirited his soldiers.

As is every leader who loses a cause, Washington was blamed by many for the American failure. In turn, he complained of a lack of confidence in his men, writing to Congress: "With the deepest concern, I am obliged to confess my want of confidence in the generality of the troops. . . . Till of late, I had no doubt in my own mind of defending this place, nor should I have yet if the men would do their duty."

Most of his generals did not know the terrain of the battleground. Added to this difficulty, the raw militia could not and would not stand up against the seasoned British regulars in the open field. Intelligence of the size and location of the enemy forces was faulty.

Nevertheless, some of the sharpest criticism has been aimed at Washington himself. He was somewhat familiar with the territory; he should have altered the disposition of his troops. He sent no cavalry to reconnoiter. At times, Washington did not even seem aware of how bad a situation his army was in.

The criticism of Washington was not directed toward his character but his ability. Some officers pined for the presence of General Charles Lee. The paymaster was two months behind, and this of course did not help morale. The rebels were exhausted and wet. Their supplies were in great disorder. As his men deserted by companies and even regiments, Washington wished he had never heard of the war, much less assumed its leadership.

Colonel John Haslet of Delaware wrote to Caesar Rodney on September 4, 1776, in reference to Washington: "The general I revere; his character for disinterestedness, patience and fortitude will be had in everlasting remembrances, but the vast burden appears much too much his own. Beardless youth and inexperience regimented are too much about him. The original scheme for the disposition of the army appears to have been on too narrow a scale, and everything almost sacrificed, or endangered for the preservation of New York and its environs, all which deserve from every honest American damnation. We have alarm upon alarm. Orders now issue, and the next moment reversed. Would to heaven General [Charles] Lee were here, is the language of officers and men."

Washington knew that something must be done. In early September he reorganized the army into three divisions, placed to meet Howe's anticipated movements. Washington had special concern for northern Manhattan. It was suggested that New York City be burned to prevent its use by the British as winter quarters, for he could see already that he would be unable to hold it much longer. To this idea, General Greene gave enthusiastic approval. He wrote Washington: "The city and island of New York are no objects for us. . . . the country is struck with panic; any capital loss at this time may ruin the cause. . . . A general and speedy retreat is absolutely necessary. . . . I would burn the city and suburbs. . . . It will deprive the enemy of an opportunity of barracking their whole army together. . . . Anyhow, two-thirds of the city of New York and the suburbs belong to the Tories, so why worry about its loss by burning?" But Congress rejected the idea.

A council of war decided unanimously to evacuate the city as soon as the military supplies could be removed. Wagons, horses and boats were commandeered even as British warships began to move up the East River. Washington, sensing the direction of Howe's move, changed his headquarters to Harlem Heights and had his men start digging entrenchments across Upper Manhattan.

To the president of Congress on September 8, 1776, Washington wrote: "History, our own experience, the advice of our ablest friends in Europe, the fears of the enemy, and even the declaration of Congress demonstrate, that on our side the war should be defensive."

Sunday, September 15, 1776, was a bright day under a clear, blue sky enhanced by a smart breeze. Five British frigates lined up along the center of the East River and anchored. By 10 A.M., eighty-four flatboats filled with red-coats shoved off from the Long Island shore. Soon the ships opened fire on the American entrenchments on the New York shore. Some seventy large guns belched shot and shell into breastworks that were little more than ditches with dirt piled up at waterside. The bombardment lasted for two hours, then stopped. The troop-laden boats came on then, looking, as one observer said, like "a clover field in full bloom." As they neared the Manhattan shore at Kip's Bay—about where Thirty-fourth Street is now—the light infantry headed ashore and entered the island with little opposition.

Apparently no one had thought to inform Washington of what was taking place. As soon as he heard the firing, he rode at full gallop from Harlem. Where Lexington Avenue now crosses Forty-second Street, he met his men in confused retreat. Indignantly, he tried to stop them, ordering them to take to the walls or the cornfields. But the sight of British grenadiers and Hessian Jaegers broke the nerve of the defending militia. Washington and Putnam now tried to rally the men behind the walls, but to little avail.

Washington completely lost his temper. "He dashed his hat upon the ground in a transport of rage" and cried out, "Are these the men with whom I am to defend America?" In violent desperation, the distraught commander-in-chief snapped a pistol at them and with his riding crop hit the fleeing officers and soldiers in his frantic efforts to get them to stop.

By now he was alone. A line of British and Hessians bore down upon him with bayonets fixed. Overcome by despair, the general simply sat on his horse, paying no attention to the onrushing danger. Then two anxious aides rushed to his side, grabbed the bridle of his horse and led him from the field. Musket balls rained from the redcoats, but the

British cheered the bravery of the American leader. Perhaps they chose not to kill him. Nathanael Greene felt that Washington preferred death to such ignominy.

After he had regained his composure, Washington tried to salvage as much as he could from the disaster. His chief concern now was to prevent his troops in Lower Manhattan from being cut off by a British move across the island. Putnam was dispatched to the south to lead the force there up to Harlem and out of danger. Washington ordered the heavy artillery and other supplies abandoned. Then he deliberately followed his panicky men as they fled to the north. As for Putnam, dense but capable, he reached Lower Manhattan and sent the troops scurrying up the island. It was a very hot day and dust impeded their march. Putnam rode up and down encouraging them, though he knew little of the roads. Captain Aaron Burr, his aide, helped him. Among those who reached safety was heavy Henry Knox, whom Washington had thought lost. When Knox showed up at Harlem Heights, he was embraced by his commander.

Again Washington tried to reorganize his army, now numbering around fifteen thousand. He left about a third of them to hold Kingsbridge for fear the British would turn through the Bronx. The rest were assigned to three lines of trenches between what is now 130th and 150th streets. He was not sure that even with these fortifications, his soldiers would stand up to the enemy. The flight from Kip's Bay had further shaken his confidence.

The place to which the patriots retreated was on the slender neck of land between the Harlem and Hudson rivers in Upper Manhattan. Soon after daylight on September 16, a Connecticut battalion under Lieutenant Colonel Thomas Knowlton crossed to reconnoiter the small wooded valley where West 125th Street is now. Working westward through underbrush and boulders, the rebels approached the spot where Grant's Tomb now stands and were met by two battalions of redcoats. Knowlton retired just as Washington and his adjutant, Lieutenant Colonel Joseph Reed were arriving. Other English troops appeared on the side of the valley and jeered at the retreating Americans. The redcoats, according to Reed, "in the most insulting manner sounded their bugle horns as is usual in a fox chase. I never felt such a sensation before. It seemed to crown our disgrace."

A fox hunter himself, Washington apparently felt the insult deeply, recognizing the notes as the signal of a fox gone to earth. After questioning Reed, he learned that the enemy were only some three hundred in number. The insult was just too much after Kip's Bay. The general decided to teach the British a lesson. He ordered Knowlton and some additional troops to go back across what is now Morningside Heights and come up behind the enemy. Simultaneously, other American infantrymen were to fire and feign an advance from the front. This plan worked. The redcoats fell for the ruse, ran down the hill toward the advancing rebels and started firing. Washington, however, was dismayed to hear premature firing from the flank on which Knowlton had advanced. This alerted the British, and they fell back instead of walking into the trap. Knowlton and his major, Andrew Leitch, were fatally wounded. Washington, sobered and saddened, kept his composure; he sent some Maryland and New England troops to reinforce the assault. As a result, the English were forced to retreat.

By this time the skirmish was developing into a major battle and nearly five thousand men were engaged on each side. Washington noted through his glass that even more British were coming to join their comrades. His men were acting better than they had during yesterday's disgraceful rout. The British now moved back into a field of buckwheat, having been put to flight by some well-aimed rebel artillery fire. They were soon reinforced by more light infantry and the famous Scottish Black Watch. Then, at about 2 P.M., the redcoats and the Scotsmen both retreated. Into an orchard, down a slope and up a hill they went, Americans pursuing. For the discouraged Washington, it was a grand sight. In order not to run the risk of a reverse, he withdrew his troops.

In six hours, the British had lost 70 dead and 200 wounded; the Americans 30 dead and 90 wounded (although reports of the casualties were conflicting). Though small in scope, the Battle of Harlem Heights was not minor in its effect: the Americans had viewed the crimson backs of the British as they fled, and it was a heartening spectacle. It showed the British commanders that their opponents could fight with bravery and resolution. Some revolutionaries who had run like scared rabbits at Kip's Bay helped to drive the English back more than a mile before they withdrew in good order. The engagement had a lasting effect on the Americans throughout the rest of the fighting in New York.

Despite this temporary "victory," Washington still had his administrative problems. Desertion and plundering by his men were chief among them, and he carelessly blamed the militia and inferior officers. "It is not in the power of words," he wrote home, "to describe the task I have to perform. Fifty thousand pounds would not induce me again to undergo what I have done. . . . Such is my situation that if I were to wish the bitterest curse to an enemy on this side of the grave, I should put him in my stead with my feelings."

Testy John Adams sent a letter to his friend Henry Knox on September 29, 1776, from the Congress in Philadelphia. "Pray tell me, Colonel Knox," he wrote, "does every man to the Southward of Hudsons River, behave like a hero, and every man to the Northward of it, like a poltroon or not? The rumors, reports and letters which come here upon every occasion, represent the New England troops as cowards, running away perpetually, and the Southern troops as standing bravely. I wish I could know whether it is true. I want to know for the government of my own conduct, because if the New Englandmen are a Pack of Cowards, I would resign my place in Congress, where I should not choose to represent poltroons, and remove to some Southern Colony, where I could enjoy the Society of Heroes and have a chance of learning some time or other, to be part of an Hero myself. I must say that your amiable general [Washington] gives too much occasion for these reports by his letters, in which he often mentions things to the disadvantage of some part of New England, but seldom any thing about any other part of the Continent."

Washington repeated his requests to Congress for a dependable regular army—they did provide at this time for a force of eighty-eight battalions—and asked also that they strengthen the Articles of War, improving the positions of officers and furnishing bounties, among other requests. For the most part Congress complied. Day after day, courts-martial tried cases of mutiny, stealing, cowardice and desertion. Washington felt that neither public nor private property was safe from many of his soldiers. In addition, the army was in need of virtually every necessity, from kettles to tents.

There followed now a lull of almost a month while both Howe and Washington wondered what to do next. The Continental lines were too strong for a frontal assault; besides, Howe reasoned, he did not have to hurry. If he waited till November and December, the enlistment terms of many of the Americans would expire.

On October 12, Howe made his move. Some eighty ships carrying his army sailed through Hell's Gate in Upper Manhattan. A fire had broken out in the city and had been raging for two days almost unchecked. No one knew (then or now) who started it. Each side blamed the other. Wash-

ington, however, must have taken grim satisfaction in realizing that the enemy's Tory stronghold was seriously
damaged. It was at this time that Nathan Hale, a young
American spy, was caught and summarily sentenced to death
by General Howe. Washington was to remember this well.

Howe landed his men on Throg's Neck, in the southeast
Bronx, in the hope of trapping Washington's army below.
But a small number of revolutionaries held a bridge over
which the redcoats needed to pass. This slowed the enemy
advance. Soon the twenty-five riflemen who had stopped the
British were reinforced to almost two thousand, and both
sides dug in. Howe saw that progress through the creeks
and marshes that lay ahead would be difficult if not impossible. On October 18, he moved his forces and put them
ashore at Pell's Point, not far below New Rochelle. Here
Colonel Glover and a few hundred men attempted to slow
him. Howe easily overcame this opposition and pushed on
to New Rochelle, where strong Hessian reinforcements
joined him. After a few days, the British moved again, to
the Bronx River, near White Plains. Here thirteen thousand of them settled down to await their baggage and supplies.

With his army now in danger of being flanked, Washington called a council of war on October 16 to make plans.
General Charles Lee had arrived from the Carolinas; characteristically he urged a general retreat, which was voted
down. Washington decided to reorganize his army, this time
into seven divisions. Two thousand remained in Fort Washington on the Hudson, some four thousand across the river
at Fort Lee. The main force moved slowly and tediously
northward west of the Bronx River to White Plains. Because of the shortage of wagons and horses, the journey,
which ordinarily required one day, took four.

Washington chose a strong position at White Plains. It
was on a series of heights. One division was placed on

Purdy Hill, another on Hatfield Hill and Washington himself in the center at White Plains Village. Two defensive
lines were erected from the Bronx River on the right to a
millpond on the left, the ends receding to defend the flanks.
Howe attacked on October 28, four thousand redcoats moving up against sixteen hundred Americans on Chatterton
Hill. The redcoats were met with such heavy fire that at
first they were forced to withdraw. They did rally and carried the hill, but at great cost. American soldiers were awed
at the sight of the British. "The sun shone bright," one of
them wrote, "their arms glittered, and perhaps troops never
were shown to more advantage." Their "appearance was
truly magnificent. A bright autumnal sun shed its luster on
the polished arms; and the rich array of dress and military
equipage gave an imposing grandeur to the scene as they
advanced in all the pomp and circumstance of war."

British and Hessians advanced to the top of the hill and
began to place their artillery in position. Washington saw
that his own position was hopeless. On October 31, he withdrew by night to higher and safer ground at North Castle
Heights. He correctly reasoned that the enemy would not
wish to move farther north with winter approaching.

Howe instead turned his attention to the Americans' forts
in Upper Manhattan. A line of vessels had been sunk across
the Hudson to prevent the passage of British ships up the
river. Fort Washington's mission was mainly to defend the
New York end of this line. Fort Lee, opposite, guarded
the western end.

Washington was doubtful that the forts could be held,
but some of his subordinates disagreed. Congress urged that
the bastions be held—not being in a position to know much
about it—a council of war had agreed and even Nathanael
Greene was optimistic. For some reason (perhaps as he said
in later years because of the conflicting opinions), Washington left the decision to Greene. Even so, Washington

must share in the responsibility for the outcome; he could have given Greene orders to evacuate had he so chosen.

By the middle of November, Howe had brought his troops within striking distance of Fort Washington. He then demanded a surrender. Colonel Robert Magaw, commander of the fort, replied that he intended to hold at all cost. Next morning, after a conference, Washington, Greene, Putnam and General Mercer set out from the Jersey shore to take another look at Fort Washington and make a final decision about holding it. Just as they arrived, however, the British and Hessians attacked. Washington, not wanting to interfere with Magaw's command, returned to Fort Lee.

Eight thousand attacked Fort Washington under the command of Generals Knyphausen, Cornwallis and Percy. For hours, the stubborn Americans held off the massive assault but finally had to capitulate. They then ran the risk of being bayoneted by the Hessians, who had sustained most of the 450 casualties on their side. The rebel loss was 59 dead, 96 wounded and 2,813 captured. Great quantities of artillery and ammunition were also taken. It was one of the major disasters of the war.

For once, William Howe did not hesitate after this victory. Two days later, he sent Cornwallis over to the Jersey coast eight miles above Fort Lee. The British soon took possession of it, the defenders losing 100 more men plus 146 cannon and thousands of rounds of ammunition. It was a terrific double blow to the Patriot cause. Greene himself barely escaped to join Washington, who by now had moved his troops from Westchester to Hackensack and planned to retreat across New Jersey. Howe probably could have cut him off, but for some reason did not try.

Washington himself underscored the dire situation when he wrote his brother that if the army were not increased very soon, "I think the game will be pretty well up."

V TRIUMPH
IN NEW JERSEY

MORALE was at its lowest point. The retreating, disintegrating army faced frosty nights and chill November downpours, and winter was fast approaching. There was a serious shortage of tents, blankets and essential clothing. Many soldiers had neither shoes nor stockings. Small wonder that they looked forward to the termination of their enlistment periods at the end of December 1776.

The British now had a substantial force on the west side of the Hudson. Washington assumed that General Howe would occupy part of New Jersey and perhaps even take the colonial capital at Philadelphia before winter impeded operations. He asked New Jersey and the Congress for reinforcements. He also requested that General Charles Lee move his troops, which had been left at North Castle to oppose Howe, westward across the river into New Jersey. Lee's slowness in complying has been the subject of historians' speculation ever since. Whether Washington stood in awe of him or was simply trying to be tactful with him is hard to say. Doubtless it would have been better if he had given Lee a direct order to move. Then there would have been no mistaking his meaning or Lee's reaction. As it was, there was indirection on both sides. An aide of Washington's, Colonel William Grayson, wrote to Lee: "His Excellency thinks it would be advisable in you to remove the troops under your command on this side of the North River." On the next day, Washington himself wrote: "I am of the opinion that the public interest requires your coming to this side."

One less vain than General Lee would probably have responded more actively. But he chose to take the urgings as a sort of recommendation. His attitude toward Washington was not improved by a letter the commander-in-chief's own adjutant general, Colonel Joseph Reed, wrote to Lee at this time: ". . . I confess I do think it is entirely owing to you that this army and the liberties of America are not entirely cut off. You have decision, a quality often wanted in minds otherwise valuable. . . . We are in a very awful and alarming situation—one that requires the utmost wisdom and firmness of mind."

No wonder Lee did not feel he had to move, at least not quickly. He has been accused of being a traitor and a coward. It is possible that he was, but these terms were not so clear at this time of divided loyalties and uncertainty as to the status of the new nation. Fed by his vanity and eccentricity, Lee found Reed's disloyal comments encouraging and may have felt that Washington was really inefficient. Because of his recent failures, he would probably soon be relieved of his command by Congress. Hindering Washington's plans might well hasten the day. And who would be the logical successor to Washington if he were replaced? Why obviously, Charles Lee.

Despite Reed's doubting words, Washington evidently still retained confidence in his aide. According to one historian, Washington asked his adjutant what would happen if the Americans were forced to retreat to the remote interior of Pennsylvania. To which Reed answered that if the eastern counties gave up, the western counties would surrender. Then Washington, it is said, passed his hand over his throat and commented, "My neck does not feel as though it was made for a halter. We must retire to Augusta County in Virginia. Numbers will be obliged to repair to us for safety and we must try what we can do in carrying on a predatory war, and if overpowered, we must cross the Allegheny Mountains."

Sensing despair in the rebels, Howe took his time. Rather than chase the Americans deep into New Jersey he decided to spend the winter in his snug quarters in New York, with gay society and his mistress Mrs. Loring. Next spring, he would make a thrust against New England. So confident was he that he could finish Washington almost whenever he chose that he divided his army and sent Henry Clinton to Rhode Island for the winter. (Here they served no useful purpose, as it turned out.) Meantime, in order to make the way clearer for a southern advance when he chose, he sent Cornwallis to drive Washington from eastern New Jersey.

By November 28, as Washington was entering New Brunswick, the vanguard of the British arrived at Newark. To add to his heavy woes, some two thousand of his Maryland and New Jersey units left the service, their enlistment periods having expired. It did not seem to bother the New Jersey men that their own state might be laid more open to invasion by their departure.

The astute Cornwallis was conscious of the plight of his enemy. He now pushed toward the diminishing rebel force, by this time only thirty-five hundred in strength. To stop the British from using them, Washington had his men destroy the bridge over the nearby Raritan River and directed that all small boats along the Delaware River for a distance of seventy miles above Philadelphia be moved to the west bank. He joined Stirling at Princeton and was disheartened to learn that his little army had shrunk several hundred more.

There was one small bright note. Cornwallis might have

crossed the Raritan and finished off the revolutionaries, but under orders from Howe, he remained in New Brunswick for six days. Thankful for this respite, Washington now moved his force to Trenton, staying with his rear guard while it cut down trees and destroyed bridges to prevent pursuit. Cornwallis arrived in Trenton early in the afternoon of December 8, just as "the old fox"—as he had called Washington—was moving his men westward across the Delaware. After reaching the shore, Knox's artillery men found the redcoats too tempting and lobbed a few shells back into their midst.

Around two thousand militia from Pennsylvania now showed up, bringing Washington's troop strength to almost five thousand.

Lee and his four thousand men finally crossed the Hudson. When Washington heard the news, he urged Lee to join him at once. Lee moved westward, at a snail's pace, undertaking no action against the enemy whatever. In another inexplicable move, he and a small detachment decided to spend the night in a tavern. He left his troops under the command of General Sullivan and billeted three miles away. At the tavern, Lee found time to write his friend Horatio Gates a letter criticizing Washington. But this cozy interlude was short-lived. On the morning of December 13, a detachment of British cavalry under the command of their best mounted officer, Lieutenant Banastre Tarleton, rode up and surrounded the hostelry. Lee and his party were ignominiously captured. Washington was shocked and regretted the loss, even though he had begun to lose confidence in Lee. But Sullivan did bring the men who were left, about two thousand, into Washington's camp.

American military fortunes had reached a new low when the Continental Congress met at Philadelphia at this time. From the reports of losses in New York and New Jersey, the members were gloomy about any chance of success. In desperation, they passed a resolution giving Washington full power to direct the operations of the war, which of course did not mean much under the adverse circumstances. His own despair is reflected in letters he wrote to Congress during this period. He deplored the unfortunate policy of short enlistments. If they continued to expire as scheduled, he would have only about fourteen hundred men by 1777. Unless better fortune intervened, he predicted, the war would soon be lost. The Howe brothers had issued a proclamation pardoning all Americans who would take an oath of allegiance to the British Crown during the next sixty days. Washington, commenting on the many citizens who took advantage of the opportunity, gave vent to sorrow and sharp disappointment.

In the middle of December, John Honeyman, a Trenton butcher who posed as a Tory, informed Washington about the Hessian brigade stationed there under the command of Colonel Johann Rall. Numbering about fourteen hundred, there were Rall's and Lossberg's men in blue, Knyphausen's in somber black.

The presence of these mercenaries gave Washington a new and intriguing idea, and it came none too soon. "I saw him in that gloomy period," wrote James Wilkinson, "and attentively marked his aspect; always grave and thoughtful, he appeared at that time pensive and solemn in the extreme." This is understandable—the weary and discouraged commander was about to stake his own fortunes and those of his new nation on a big gamble. Two days before Christmas, Washington called his generals and key colonels together and outlined his scheme: he would attack Trenton. It was a daring plan. Where would he get the power to attack the powerful British legions? Even with the armies of Sullivan and Gates, his actual strength was less than six thousand. These were spread thin over twenty miles above

Bordentown. And only about half of them were Continentals, the rest being untried militia.

The words of Tom Paine's newly published pamphlet, *The Crisis,* were ringing in his ears. But this was not his only impetus. Washington knew that he had to have a victory or the game would really be over. He must electrify the country with a dramatic success or else go home and await probable capture and defeat. He needed a triumph, too, to encourage reenlistments. If he could strike a successful blow at Trenton, he might then raid the main British supply center at New Brunswick and obtain uniforms and badly needed ammunition and gold.

He issued orders that three days' rations and precious ammunition were to be distributed. On Christmas Eve, 1776, he called another council of war. His plan was to cross the Delaware on Christmas night at McKonkey's Ferry, nine miles above Trenton. Twenty-four hundred men—most of his Continental troops—and eighteen cannon under Knox's command would make up the main thrust. Lieutenant Colonel John Cadwalader with about two thousand Continentals and militia was to cross the river near Bristol, south of Trenton, to divert the enemy's attention from the main attack. Brigadier General James Ewing and about seven hundred Pennsylvania and New Jersey militia were to cross the river at Trenton Ferry, a bit south of the town, and hold a bridge over Assunpink Creek to cut off the escape of the Hessians if they should flee that way.

Washington had had all the boats moved from the east to the west bank of the Delaware; his foresight now paid off. They were sturdy Durham boats of about fifty feet in length capable of carrying about fifteen tons each. John Glover's Marblehead Mariners, who had so capably evacuated the Americans from Brooklyn, manned them.

It was a tense occasion for the rebel troops when they gathered on Christmas afternoon in a kind of hidden val-

ley west of the ferry. Besides his rations, each man had forty
rounds of ammunition, a blanket and his knapsack. As they
marched in front of their commander, they seemed to have
caught some of the spirit of the occasion. Though their
faces showed the lean look of hungry and weary men and
their clothing was ragged—many of them were barefooted
and only a few had overcoats—they marched tall and with
courage. Enough for Washington to note in his diary:
"Christmas, 6 p.m. It is fearfully cold and raw and a snow
storm setting in. The wind is northeast and beats in the
faces of the men. It will be a terrible night for the soldiers
who have no shoes. Some of them have old rags tied around
their feet, but I have not heard a man complain."

The embarkation began. First the Virginians of Adam
Stephen's brigade slipped into the waiting boats and shoved
off for the Jersey shore. The Delaware was jammed with
large cakes of ice that thumped against the boats as they
were poled and made the crossing fearful and uncertain;
new snow was beginning to fall, too. Next came General
Hugh Mercer's Continentals followed by Stirling's force.
All these were under the divisional command of Nathanael
Greene. The other main division was commanded by Sullivan. Washington felt he could depend on all his major subordinates, and this time he was right.

By evening there was a full moon, but the sky, fortunately
for the Americans, was darkened by heavy clouds. By 11 p.m.
the snow changed to sleet, which made the going even
harder for the ill-clad soldiers. Even with the skill of the
Marblehead Mariners, progress was slowed and the schedule
was lengthened. Much time was lost in getting the heavy
guns aboard and then unloading them on the slippery shore.
Transporting the horses caused more delay, so that the operation, which it had been hoped would be completed by
midnight, was at least three hours behind schedule. This
worried Washington as it might lessen the element of sur-

prise on which he had counted. But come what may, he was determined to push on.

He stood quietly on the bank as the last cannon was pushed past him and harnessed to a waiting team of horses that Knox had efficiently arranged for. Then he strode to where Sullivan and Greene were readying their columns for the move southward. He appeared stern and haggard, but they too were caught up in the stress of the situation; they doubtless expected their commander to be no less concerned. Those in charge realized that now it would be daybreak before the attack could begin, a delay that might well mean the difference between victory and defeat.

An officer noted that Washington seemed more determined than he had ever seen him. He stood calmly wrapped in his cloak. When a messenger came from Sullivan to say that the storm was wetting the muskets and making them unfit for firing, he replied that he wanted the men to use their bayonets, that he was resolved to take Trenton whatever the price.

At 5 A.M. at the Birmingham crossroads, some four miles below the landing, the men stopped briefly for a hasty breakfast of the rations they carried. The rain and sleet still were falling; many of the soldiers keeled over into sleep, being aroused with considerable difficulty. Washington watched as they were shaken awake by their officers. His expression saddened when two of the men did not respond. In the chilly dawn, they had frozen to death.

There were two roads to Trenton. The one on the right ran parallel to the curving Delaware and entered the town at its southern end. The other, Pennington Road, swung left and approached Trenton from the northwest. Each was about equal in length. Greene's division took Pennington Road and Washington chose to accompany him. Sullivan's units took the river road. Orders were given that strict silence was to be observed by all men; any man breaking ranks without permission would suffer death.

There was the sound of Christmas revelry in Trenton. Colonel Rall and his Hessians had carried on their holiday celebration all day and far into the night. Rall was an efficient officer, but he had the reputation of playing as hard off duty as he fought during battle. He had scoffed at warnings that he might not be safe here and had been supported in this view by General James Grant, commander of the British forces in New Jersey. So Rall continued to celebrate.

At about 7 A.M., near Trenton, Greene's advance guard sounded an alarm and spread out across the road. With the column halted, Washington and Greene galloped up to the forward point and saw a small number of men coming toward them. They turned out to be a detachment from the brigade of Adam Stephen. Washington had lacked confidence in Stephen, and now he learned with chagrin that the brigade had crossed the river the day before, carried out scouting raids around Trenton and shot up a Hessian outpost during the night.

This was a blow to Washington. Now, he reasoned, the surprise element was completely gone. He logically expected that the Hessians would be deployed outside the town waiting for him. Momentarily he gave vent to his emotions and strongly rebuked Stephen for sending men across the river without permission. But his fears were unfounded. Even though six Hessians had been wounded and troops had been called to resist the attack on their picket guard, the Hessians had returned to their quarters—and Rall had gone on with his drinking.

Rall was at the home of a wealthy merchant, who was giving an all-night party. At midnight, a visitor knocked at the door and asked to see the colonel, but a servant refused to admit him. The caller then wrote Rall a note saying that the American army was about to attack Trenton. Rall apparently never read it but put it into his pocket; it was found there after the battle.

At 8 A.M., though regular pickets had been posted, the Hessians seemed unaware of imminent danger. The weather was so bad their sentries evidently did not keep a careful watch. The town of Trenton was virtually asleep, the soldiers in a stupor from their heavy Christmas celebration of food and drink. Then a German lieutenant stepped out of his tiny house in the midst of the picket guard and saw coming toward him a small detachment of men some two hundred yards away. His sentinels sounded the alarm, but it was late. Greene's and Sullivan's divisions swept down upon them. The guards fired a few volleys and then retreated. Over the hard snow, the thin-clad Continentals, the smell of game in their chilled nostrils, now raced toward the mercenaries. The Germans withdrew in professional manner, keeping up a running fire. Though this slowed the advance, it did little to stop the numerically superior invaders.

The two main streets of Trenton, King and Queen streets, ran north and south. At the southern end of town, a number of cross streets intersected. Here the Hessians were quartered, close together. Hessian Lieutenant Jacob Piel heard the firing and rushed to the house where Colonel Rall was staying, beating loudly on his door. Rall, groggy with sleep, appeared at an upstairs window in his nightclothes. Soon he was in his uniform and astride his horse, forming his own regiment at the foot of King Street.

Henry Knox had quickly placed his guns at the head of both main streets; by this time, cannonballs were streaking down them, disabling horses and men. The artillery ammunition had been carefully kept dry, the gunners covering the touch holes with their hands to prevent the icy rain from dampening the powder chambers. Two Hessian cannon suddenly appeared in King Street. Leading a rifle charge, Captain William Washington—a cousin of George's —and Lieutenant James Monroe were both wounded as their Virginians captured the German guns and then turned them against the enemy.

Those Americans whose weapons were too wet to fire made their way among the houses with fixed bayonets, being careful to stay out of the line of artillery fire. Washington noted that the mercenaries were beginning to form east of Trenton. He ordered Greene to block their escape route toward Princeton. Stephen was on the left, Stirling pushed down King and Queen streets and Mercer joined with Sullivan's left flank to move into the town from the west. For Washington it was an ideal military situation: the Hessians were blocked off from three sides with the swollen Assunpink Creek at their rear.

Colonel Rall, by this time somewhat sober, ordered his band to strike up a march. Stirred by the martial sound of it, the colonel valiantly tried to lead his veteran regiments in a countercharge, leaving the Knyphausen regiment in reserve. But it was too late. Americans were all over town, the houses full of them, their muskets and rifles now dry and going into action from doors and windows. Over and above the small-arms fire, Knox's big guns dominated the scene, shells bursting devastatingly among the demoralized Hessians.

His officers and men were falling all around him, but in characteristic fashion, Rall ordered a charge. Some Hessians obeyed, others hung back; those who attempted the advance fell before they could get close enough to the Americans for a bayonet thrust. With Sullivan's force now holding the bridge, there was no way to retreat to the south, so Rall ordered a withdrawal to an orchard in the southeast part of Trenton. Hardly had he spoken when two bullets struck him in the side and he went down. At the orchard his men, overwhelmed, surrendered; Rall died soon after.

By 9 A.M. the battle was over. It had lasted just over an hour. Twenty-two Hessians were dead, 948 captured, including 92 wounded. About 430 had escaped. As for the Americans, the casualties consisted of only two officers and two privates wounded. It was a remarkable victory. Washington ordered the forty-eight hogsheads of captured rum staved in and spilled on the ground—very disappointing to his troops.

But there was no time to tarry or celebrate. Washington was aware that within a few hours British and Hessians could move against him from Bordentown and Princeton. Their numbers would doubtless be many more than his twenty-four hundred exhausted men, who right now had neither ammunition nor energy to fight. (Cadwalader and Ewing had never managed to cross the Delaware.) Washington must leave the scene of his triumph without delay.

The weather was still bad. As they returned to McKonkey's Ferry, snow and hail beat upon them from the northeast, and the roads were just as slippery as they had been before. Now they had the job of escorting prisoners as well as hauling captured ammunition and cannon. While they lay in the boats on the return trip across the Delaware, three more Americans froze to death. By early evening, however, the men had reached their huts, though some of them did not arrive until morning.

They had marched and fought for as long as fifty hours, some going as far as fifty miles in the stormy cold. But they were happy with the flush of victory. Next day, over a thousand of them could not report for duty. The historian, Trevelyan, said about the battle, "This was a long and severe ordeal, and yet it may be doubted whether so small a number of men ever employed so short a space of time with greater or more lasting results upon the history of the world."

On December 27 Washington gave his men a hearty if belated Christmas dinner. Two days later, he crossed the Delaware for the third time in four days and reoccupied Trenton, asking Generals Heath at Peekskill and McDougall at Morristown to come and join him. He realized that he must not rest on the laurels he and his men had just gathered. His follow-through would be in some ways as important as his victory.

On the last two days of 1776, Washington visited each of the Continental regiments in Trenton and made earnest, personal appeals for them to reenlist. Added to the argument that they remain because of patriotism was an offer of a ten-dollar bounty each. More than half responded favorably, no doubt encouraged by the outcome of their recent battle. By the final hours of the year, Washington had sixteen hundred veterans plus new militia from Philadelphia, bringing his total strength to almost five thousand men.

Adding to his elation was a resolution just passed by Congress that reached him on December 31. Not only did it approve of his use of bounties—something he had not previously been sure of—but asked him to "use every endeavor, by giving bounties and otherwise, to prevail upon the troops whose enlistments shall expire at the end of this month to stay with the army." The resolution further stated that after having closely considered the current crisis and "having perfect reliance on the wisdom, vigour and uprightness of General Washington," he was given for six months full and complete powers to raise sixteen battalions of Continental infantry, artillery, cavalry and engineers. Furthermore, Washington was empowered to commandeer whatever supplies he needed, to appoint and promote officers and to fix rates of pay. In other words, he was given virtually dictatorial powers.

The genial English official in Maryland, William Eddis, wrote his wife on January 1, 1777, that "The provincial forces, who were only enlisted for a stipulated time, discouraged by a succession of unfavorable events, were so greatly reduced in their numbers, that it is asserted, on the day preceding the affair at Trenton, the muster roll scarcely exceeded three thousand men; and the greater part of those were anxious for the expiration of their term that they might return to their families and their accustomed vocations. The Congress, from a well-founded apprehension of danger, retreated with precipitation to Baltimore; and many who had been most zealous in promoting hostile measures began to avow sentiments of a conciliatory nature; in a word, the general disposition of the colonies tended to a reconciliation, and even the submission of some of the provinces was daily expected.

"Affairs were in this promising train when the American general planned and executed the late important enterprise. Trifling as this maneuver might have been considered in the prosecution of a regular war, it has been in this instance attended with the most prejudicial and alarming consequences to His Majesty's arms. It has given spirit to those who showed the utmost despondency; it has recruited the enfeebled ranks; and it has enabled the enthusiastic leaders to magnify in the most exaggerated terms the advantages that must inevitably arise from the success of this brilliant exertion."

And it was high time. Since the Battle of Long Island, Washington's military reputation had been slipping. There is nothing like victory, the commander-in-chief found, to revive the spirits of the people and to bring in the militia.

The effect on the British was electrifying too. Lord Cornwallis, who was about to depart for England to see his sick wife, was ordered to stay and set right the British positions on the Delaware River. On January 1 he arrived at Trenton, just a few miles away from the Americans, with some eight thousand regular British troops. Washington sent General Roche de Fermoy and his brigade to engage the British advance he expected from Princeton and dispatched Sullivan and his force to another delaying position near Trenton. Before daybreak on January 2, Cornwallis began his attack, and despite the rebels' efforts and the muddy thawing roads he was soon within sight of Trenton. Fermoy was not effective, but Colonel Edward Hand, who took his place, did better, holding the advance of the redcoats somewhat in check until dark.

Had Cornwallis pushed on at once, he might well have ended the war. His Brigadier General Sir William Erskine did suggest that Washington had better be attacked that night or he might not be there next day. For once, Cornwallis hesitated. He felt he could assault the American forces more effectively the next morning. He was in for a disappointment.

In the early evening, Washington sent his baggage down to Burlington and then called a council of war. There is some question as to what occurred during this conference but it seems clear that Washington himself had plans in mind and pressed them rather strongly.

At 1 A.M. the next morning, with light infantry from Pennsylvania leading the van, Washington began his march. The Continentals filed out of their trenches in the darkness and made their stealthy way around the British left flank. Little-used and difficult roadways had been selected by Washington so that the movement would stand less chance of detection. The sleepy soldiers and their horses slipped and stumbled on loose rocks in the roads; the large guns caught between trees and logs and had to be freed by hand.

But the way led on to Princeton and that was what counted.

Knox had muffled the sounds of his artillery wheels by wrapping rags around them. Washington, the strict disciplinarian, now issued one of his sternest orders: no soldier was to break the silence by talking or other noise on pain of court-martial. No man under the rank of a brigadier general was to know the destination or the purpose of the American advance.

Living up to his British-bestowed name of "the old fox," Washington had left some four hundred fifty men behind to work noisily on entrenchments. The sounds of their picks and shovels could be heard plainly in the enemy camp. They were also to pile wood high on the blazing campfires, thereby appearing to patrol near the river. When daybreak came, they were to break away and join the main force as quickly as possible.

The ruse worked. Even the elements seemed to favor the rebel cause. Around midnight, the weather had turned cold, freezing the muddy roads and making them more passable. The men were weary and sleepy, but buoyed with recent victory, they were remarkably cheerful and eager—just what Washington wanted. The Continentals as well as the militia kept up a steady march. Just before dawn, when the forward troops reached a point south of Princeton, they paused to rest briefly. Then they resumed their march on an out-of-the-way road that ran alongside Stony Brook for about a mile until it reached Princeton.

Washington now ordered Mercer's brigade to cover the left flank and destroy a bridge over the brook, across which he assumed Cornwallis's redcoats might retreat. The main part of the American army, led by Sullivan, pushed up another old road toward the town just as the sun came up to shimmer on the frosty landscape. Nassau Hall, today much as it was then, proved a welcome sight to the tired soldiers.

The day before, Cornwallis had left at Princeton a strong

brigade under Lieutenant Colonel Charles Mawhood to protect the British communications line. But when Cornwallis discovered the revolutionary army in trenches before him along the Assunpink Creek, he ordered Mawhood to join him. As Mawhood began to comply Mercer's men appeared. Both sides were surprised. Each deployed quickly along the brook, trying to gain a position on the high ground between the two old roads. Although the Americans reached the crest first, Mawhood immediately attacked.

Washington was to the south at a place called Quaker Meeting House when he heard gunfire from the direction of the high ground. He sprang to his horse and galloped up the road to see what was going on. Mercer's unit was outnumbered, so Washington called for some nine hundred Associators of Philadelphia who were stationed nearby. But they did not have time to arrive before Mawhood began a heavy attack of infantry supported by artillery against Mercer's brigade. His horse having been hit in one leg, General Mercer dismounted to carry on the fight. But as he and his officers tried to rally his men, who were terrified by the sight of oncoming British bayonets, a blow from the butt of a musket knocked Mercer to the ground. Rising to his feet, he endeavored to defend himself with his sword but soon fell with seven bayonet wounds, not to rise again.

Seeing the death of their commander, the men fled in disorder, pursued by the British. Two of Knox's guns located in an orchard to the right of Mercer's line now opened up on the redcoats. This bombardment caused Mawhood to halt; he was preparing to turn his men about and increase his own artillery fire when he saw Cadwalader's militia emerging from nearby woods. They rashly came within fifty yards of Mawhood's line and then had to fall back. After withstanding one volley from the British regulars, they took to their heels and ran helter-skelter toward the woods.

Just at this moment, Washington arrived. Mercer's and

Cadwalader's soldiers were in riotous retreat. As he passed the groups of bewildered and frightened men, Washington sensed their desperate fear and waved his hat to them. He shouted that they should stand their ground, that all would be well. Onward he galloped to the very front of the firing, until he was within thirty paces of Mawhood's line.

The British soldiers looked up from their muskets and stared at him on his huge white horse. They could not help but pause in admiration of his courage. Then a sharp volley crackled from the redcoat line and the smoke hid Washington from view. One of his staff officers thought he saw him fall. But when the smoke had blown away, the general was still there, not harmed and calling loudly for his men to fight, that there was but a handful of the enemy and the Americans soon would dispose of them.

At first, the Continentals stood for a moment as if paralyzed. Then the presence of Washington electrified them into action; they rallied and returned the enemy fire. Seeing this, the militia from Philadelphia also turned around and re-formed ranks again. A two-gun battery of rebel artillery on a ridge close by flung grapeshot at the British; from behind stacks of hay and buildings American marksmen gave support. The effect was to make the enemy think a much larger force was attacking them.

Mawhood's men were firmly situated behind a fence on the opposite ridge. They gazed with surprise at the troops they had just routed, who now turned to fight with renewed spirits. Just then Washington galloped across the field right between the two opposing forces, waving his hat and shouting at his soldiers to follow him. Again his words were magic. Again the militia and Continentals sallied out and advanced across the fields. Less than fifty yards from the British, Washington suddenly reined in his horse and commanded his men to halt. They obeyed, lifted their muskets into position and awaited his orders. But the redcoats fired at the advancing troops with a heavy volley. The Americans answered the fire in a reflex action, and again Washington was caught between the two sides. And again he survived.

Colonel Daniel Hitchcock's men and those of the fallen Mercer enveloped both flanks of the British, forcing Mawhood to leave his guns and order a retreat. To do so, he had to drive through the opposing ranks with a bayonet charge. He and his men escaped across the bridge and sped toward Trenton, dragoons covering their rear. Washington, with a troop of light horse from Philadelphia, pursued them. At first, the British maintained an orderly withdrawal. They soon broke, however, and scattered into the fields adjoining the road. As they fled, the American foot-soldiers raced after them. Washington paused for a moment and ordered an aide to collect the British baggage and have the bridge destroyed. Then he jubilantly resumed his pursuit, crying out, "It's a fine fox chase, my boys!"

When he was certain there would be no more fighting from Mawhood's men, Washington reluctantly gave up the chase. Cornwallis, he surmised, would soon be arriving from Trenton, so he ordered his cavalrymen to turn back and move on into Princeton. The fields appeared almost covered with British muskets and other abandoned equipment, lying among wounded redcoats. Washington spied a thief trying to rob a wounded British soldier who was stretched out on the ground. He chased the thief away, saying a comforting word to the surprised soldier. Then he rode on hastily to Princeton, which he found in control of his troops under General Sullivan.

Almost half the English force had taken refuge in Nassau Hall. Captain Alexander Hamilton ordered one of his artillery pieces to fire upon the structure. A cannonball crashed through the wall—its point of impact may still be seen there—and tore through a painting of King George II, taking off his head. (Washington's portrait hangs in the same spot today.) The hall was soon surrounded, and the British, over a hundred of them, decided to surrender. The remaining redcoats fled from Princeton toward New Brunswick.

Washington had the British stores collected. His famished, ragged men were fed and shod. Then, as Cornwallis led his troops toward Princeton, the American general was conducting his men safely inland toward Morristown. The Battle of Princeton had lasted less than half an hour, the British losing about 100 dead and wounded and 200 captured. The Americans lost some 40 dead and wounded.

The small engagement that climaxed the most brilliant campaign in Washington's career as a soldier had national significance. The British had been driven from most of New Jersey, and the victories greatly raised the spirits of the American people. They believed now that they had a general who could stand up to the British at their best. The Revolution could go on, could be won. Cornwallis later stated that this was Washington's greatest triumph.

The English historian George Trevelyan wrote that "From Trenton onward, Washington was recognized as a farsighted and able general all Europe over—by the great military nobles in the Empress Catherine's court, by the French marshals and ministers, in the King's cabinet at Potsdam, at Madrid, at Vienna and in London."

Soon after the Trenton and Princeton victories, the sometimes irascible John Adams, the man who had dreamed in vain of becoming a soldier, told Congress: "I have been distressed to see some members of this house disposed to idolize an image which their own hands have molded. I speak here of the superstitious veneration that is sometimes paid to General Washington. Although I honor him for his good qualities, yet in this house I feel myself his superior. In private life, I shall always acknowledge that he is mine. It becomes us to attend early to the restraining of our army."

VI PORTENTOUS WITHDRAWAL

MORRISTOWN, NEW JERSEY, has always had a welcoming appearance, and so it had when Washington and his tired troops entered it in early 1777. Then the town consisted mainly of a church, a tavern and about threescore dwellings. It was set on a plateau having high declivities on both sides and seemed an ideal place for recuperation. Washington had taken this into account and had noted that it could be approached from the east only by way of gaps in a series of hills. Supplies could be obtained from the west through defiles; these passages could be also used for retreat if it should be necessary.

Washington established his headquarters in Freeman's Tavern on the village green, while his men were comfortably placed in log cabins in and around the hamlet. His purpose in coming to Morristown, he said, was to draw the Patriot forces west of the Hudson River together, to observe the actions of the British and to avail himself of any favorable circumstance that might take place. At first, he expected to be at Morristown for only a few days; he was there almost half a year.

Had he reasoned deliberately, he doubtless would have concluded that more time was necessary. But apparently it required several months to relax after the pressures of Trenton and Princeton. He saw then that the army needed a period of inactivity. The enlistments of the men were running out; in addition there were numerous desertions.

Early in 1777, when the strength of the army had sunk to one of its lowest points, Washington planned a deception he hoped would fool the British. The shivering little army totaled about three thousand men, and its desperate commander strung them out in houses around Morristown so that even many of the townspeople thought there were nearer forty thousand.

A New York merchant—actually a British spy—posing as a refugee, had been sent to Morristown to obtain a true estimate of the American strength. Instead of arresting him, as some aides wished, Washington allowed the agent to remain undisturbed. He ordered his brigade commanders to prepare false returns showing a strength of twelve thousand men. These he let fall into the hands of "the merchant," who soon gathered them up and fled to New York, where he was warmly welcomed by Howe. According to Colonel Elias Boudinot of the American forces, the false information nonetheless "convinced General Howe that we were too strong to be attacked, and saved us through the winter."

By the end of January, Washington told Congress that unless he soon had substantial reinforcements, he would have virtually no army at all. By the middle of March, he did indeed have fewer than three thousand men, most of whom were short-term militia. How he was to face a strong enemy, he did not know. His troops were in dire need of the mere necessities of life, perishing for want of clothing, cold and hungry for want of food. Washington was compelled to resort to the extreme powers granted him by Congress in late 1776 to commandeer beef, pork, flour and liquor from the inhabitants of New Jersey.

As if this desperate state of things were not enough, the army was plagued by an epidemic of smallpox. Having already had a serious case of this dread disease, Washington was well aware of its possible consequences. He immediately separated the affected troops, placing small numbers in homes in the surrounding area. He issued orders that both the local populace and his soldiers receive inoculation for smallpox. At this time, the measure was a novelty; many people came to dread the prevention as much as the disease. Nevertheless, despite the protests of the surprised civilians, Washington succeeded in getting the job done and thereby saved many lives. At one time, a third of his men were sick from the ailment.

Understandably, recruiting under these circumstances was at a low ebb. Even the veterans who had been in for some time had endured, they felt, enough of the hardships of cold, hunger and squalor. Their attitude was naturally communicated to the younger men, and this made matters even worse. The states, perhaps unintentionally, were competing with the army by offering more attractive terms for men enlisting for service within their borders. Washington protested but to little avail. Congress had urged men to join the army, but when it came to serving more comfortably near home, the choice was usually obvious.

But the sun shone now and then through the clouds. From France in March came a ship bearing thousands of muskets, barrels of powder, gunflints and clothing. As spring wore on, men began to arrive; forty-three new Continental regiments showed up at the Morristown encampment. Each regiment, however, averaged only about two hundred men including officers. Washington could now count almost nine thousand men, two-thirds of them fit for duty. He quickly organized them into five divisions under his major generals, Nathanael Greene, Adam Stephen, John Sullivan, Benjamin Lincoln and Lord Stirling. Things were looking up again in the American camp.

General Howe had been spending the winter dallying with

his mistress in New York. There was hardly any military action in New Jersey during the cold weather. Had Howe attacked, with his professional army of nearly thirty thousand men, he could well have surrounded and captured Washington's small force of about four thousand at almost any time during the first few months of 1777. Even if Washington had dared venture from the high ground that he had chosen, the resulting fight in open country would have been just what the European-trained Howe could wish for. Fortunately for the Patriot cause, General Howe lingered while Washington and his weary men rested.

When bright spring came to the Morristown heights, the Americans bestirred themselves. Washington was afraid that Howe might march from New Brunswick to Trenton and perhaps Princeton, little more than a score of miles below Morristown; so on May 29, he made the first move. He marched to Bound Brook, only a few miles from Howe's encampment, where he hoped he might intercept the British general, using the Watchung Mountains as bulwarks from which he could watch the enemy movements. This tactical location also enabled Washington to observe the road to Philadelphia in case the redcoats decided to push in that direction.

The reaction of Howe was that two could play at the game of maneuvering: he went into motion, marching to New Brunswick in two main columns. In this way, he hoped to get Washington out of Middlebrook, as Bound Brook was then called, and onto an open field of battle where the British were patently superior. But Washington shrewdly saw what Howe had in mind and declined to expose himself. He skillfully positioned his men so as not to be trapped. He did not allow Howe enough leeway to execute his plans, which, if applied on a customary European field of battle, would have doubtless been all too effective. The English professional and the American amateur thus sparred with each other in New Jersey, neither coming off to great advantage, and a stalemate followed.

Washington was worried about Howe's next move. It was known that General John Burgoyne had arrived in Quebec in early May and was planning an expedition southward by way of Lake Champlain and along the Hudson down to Albany. "Gentleman Johnny," as Burgoyne was called, did set forth with some eight thousand British, Canadians, Tories and Indians, and to Washington, the logical next step would be for Howe to sail up the Hudson and meet Burgoyne in Albany. On the other hand, Howe might choose to proceed to Philadelphia or even Charleston, South Carolina. In a dilemma, Washington sent only Varnum's, Poor's and Sullivan's brigades up the Hudson to be on the alert. He and his main army remained at Morristown.

The summer wore on, and so did Washington's patience. By late August he started south himself and formed his troops near Germantown, Pennsylvania. Because of the general feeling of doubt and discouragement in the colonies, he astutely concluded that it would be good public relations to parade his forces through the streets of Philadelphia in as ostentatious a manner as possible. Tories and neutral Quakers in Philadelphia had exerted a disproportionate amount of influence, Washington felt; here was his chance to offset this bleak atmosphere by a show of American military prowess.

Washington's preparations for the display in Philadelphia were detailed and typical of his careful planning. His men were to look as decent as possible, to carry their arms properly. Any man who had the audacity to quit ranks would receive thirty-nine lashes at the next place they halted. Drums and fifes were to play music for a moderate quickstep. The only generally identifying item they could wear was a sprig of green leaves in their hats.

George Washington rode at the head of his motley army.

Tall and dignified, his graceful form astride his big horse, General Washington wore his impressive blue uniform. Followed by some sixteen thousand men, it was an awesome spectacle, even for John Adams, who was among those looking on. "They marched twelve deep," he wrote his vivacious and appreciative wife, Abigail, "and yet took above twelve hours in passing by. They were extremely well armed, pretty well clothed and tolerably disciplined, yet did not have quite the air of soldiers. They don't step exactly in time. They don't hold up their heads quite erect nor turn out their toes exactly as they ought. They don't all of them cock their hats; and such as do, don't all wear them the same way."

But on they came past Front and Market streets in the city of Philadelphia that William Penn had established for more peaceful purposes. Their drums were beating and their fifers were shrilling "Yankee Doodle" and "The White Cockade"; some were ragged and some wore British or Hessian uniforms taken from the captured or dead on the field of battle. Some were farmboys in homemade jackets carrying squirrel rifles from home. Some were lean and tired, some quite young, others middle-aged and old. Though their gait was not always that of the smart military man, they moved purposefully and seemed inspired. The raw recruits could not keep step simply because they had not been in the army long enough to know how. These men had no uniforms, but on they came, following the big figure astride his huge horse, who could plainly be seen by all. There were those more used to drinking and carousing than to patriotic activity, but this did not seem to matter on this day of parade. Some were barefoot; others had tied their tattered shoes to their feet as best they could, bound and twisted them with leather thongs until it was remarkable that they stayed on.

There were also horsemen, who were more impressive

because of their sabers and pistols, though some of these were so rusty they could have been of little immediate use. Brass and iron cannon spotted the procession—bulky but energetic Henry Knox led his artillerymen with understandable pride. The new army, which many of its own supporters had not believed in, was now on display to convince the doubters that they did have fighting men, many of them, who could stand up and be counted on to defend their new country in a brave tradition. Soon Washington was to say, "The fate of unknown millions will now depend, under God, on the courage and conduct of this army. We have therefore to resolve to conquer or die."

The march through Philadelphia had been a sort of quiet success for Washington, but this unfortunately was short-lived. On to Darby the American army went, then approached the picturesque country around Wilmington. Washington and his staff officers entered the town and established headquarters on Quaker Hill. It was here that the commander-in-chief learned with anxiety that the British had landed that very morning some six miles below the head of the Elk River, a northern extension of Chesapeake Bay near the present town of Elkton, Maryland. At once, Washington tried to gather all the troops he could, asking urgently for Greene's, Stephen's and Sullivan's divisions.

The commander was up early next morning, and in the pleasant summer sunshine set out with Greene, Lafayette and a strong body of horsemen to reconnoiter the area. From the summit of Gray's Hill, they could see the tents of the British camp two miles away but could not determine the enemy's strength, even at this close distance, with their crude field glasses. To make matters worse, as the day wore on, a harsh thunderstorm struck and thoroughly wet the mounted officers. Finally, drenched and disgusted,

Washington found shelter in a farmhouse and decided to spend the night there. His aides warned him they were risking danger of capture, especially since the house belonged to a Tory. When he looked out upon the stormy night, however, Washington decided—foolishly as he later admitted—just to remain there, come what may.

Fortunately nothing happened, and the American high command was able to resume its activities refreshed by a good night's sleep. Washington sent Colonel Daniel Morgan and his corps of expert riflemen northward to join the northern army under General Horatio Gates to support the struggle at Saratoga. These hardy frontiersmen from his own Virginia were not easy to replace, but Washington tried, by detailing seven hundred and twenty soldiers selected from various brigades and placing them under the command of Brigadier General William Maxwell of New Jersey. They were to constantly watch and harass the enemy. Maxwell was warned by his superior that the British would soon be on the move. Washington, it seemed, was now continually keeping abreast of enemy movements. Because of crude communications, however—these conditions existed, in fact, even through the Civil War—it was difficult at times for a commander to know the movements not only of the enemy but also of some of his own men.

Action was not long in coming. Two hours before daylight on September 8, the entire British army began an advance that was lighted by "a remarkable borealis." It would seem that having sensed their intentions, Washington would have been glad of this anticipated action. But Howe was hard to fathom. He wanted Washington to expect him to strike as seemed logical; so the astute British leader sent a detachment to a point west of the Americans and at the same time marched his main forces to the north. Washington, confused, thought the enemy was trying to flank him and cut him off from Philadelphia. He withdrew his men after midnight the next day to Chadd's Ford on nearby Brandywine Creek and placed them along the road leading to Philadelphia, while the redcoats also headed for this position.

The maneuvering of Washington and Howe against each other inspired an English writer to state in the magazine *The Gentleman's Observer,* "It should not be denied that all things considered, Washington really has performed wonders. That he is alive to command an army, or that an army is left him to command, might be sufficient to insure him the reputation of a great general, if British generals any longer were what British generals used to be. In short, I am of the opinion that any other general in the world than General Howe would have beaten General Washington; and any other general in the word than General Washington would have beaten General Howe." Whether such speculation was true or not, the two generals were certainly allowed the opportunity to test one another.

It seemed to Washington that the best site for an advantageously defensive battle with Howe was along the banks of Brandywine Creek, a stream that feeds the Delaware River and from slightly north of Wilmington flows southeastward. The creek, as Washington noted then, flows through a narrow bed that broadens into meadows on each side, stretching outward to hills as high as two hundred feet and almost a mile from the Brandywine itself. Here and there the hills slope gradually to the water's edge and at other places they drop off sharply. Although the creek was considered a natural defense line, it had several fords by which it could be crossed. But from the eastern bank, the Americans could see across the far side of the valley and observe the British if and when they used the fords in advancing.

From Philadelphia southward, the main road passed

through Kennett Square and then crossed the Brandywine at Chadd's Ford. Here Washington planned his main defense. The American army arrived at the ford on the clear morning of September 9, 1777. On top of a rise slightly above the ford, the usually dependable brigade of Anthony Wayne was placed. Opposite the ford and in the center of the line was Greene's division; Sullivan's held the right flank. Behind these, Washington placed Stephen's and Stirling's divisions as reserve supporting units. Picket guards were stationed along the upper reaches of the creek. It would have been better if more reconnaissance had been done along the northern parts of the stream, as was shown later. Perhaps there was little opportunity. Washington set up his headquarters in a house a mile east of Chadd's Ford.

That Washington was not fully aware of the military situation is strongly suggested by the following incident. Sullivan had taken his position on the afternoon of September 10. It was late in the day before he was established, and he had had little opportunity to reconnoiter the area. He went, therefore, to Washington's headquarters to inquire about the enemy position and was given the incorrect information that there were no fords above where he was stationed for more than ten miles—as a matter of fact there were three.

The next morning dawned damp and foggy through the Pennsylvania countryside, but by noon the sun had come out and turned the murky air hot. Maxwell's corps had been sent back along the road to find out what the British were doing, and when they arrived at Welch's Tavern near Kennett Meetinghouse, the advance troops tied up their horses and went into the bar to refresh themselves, although it was still early in the morning. About an hour later, one of the Americans happened to look unsteadily through a window and saw redcoats coming down the road not far away. What he happened to see was a crack detachment of Tory troops, the Queen's Rangers, led by Major Patrick Ferguson, the intrepid marksman and inventor of a breech-loading rifle, who was later to go down fighting at the Battle of King's Mountain. The Americans frantically fired one understandably ineffective volley and took off.

Behind the Rangers were two British brigades led by General James Grant; dragoons, heavy artillery, provisions, baggage and cattle; and a battalion of Scotch Highlanders, some five thousand men in all, who had been marching since daybreak without even being detected by the Americans. The formidable column continued unopposed until it reached a cemetery. There, suddenly, from behind the stone walls, a burst of fire from Maxwell's corps greeted them. This officer had finally rallied his veterans of the tavern bar. The British formed and fired back, and Maxwell and his men retired down the road toward Chadd's Ford, where he reinforced his troops, placed them on high ground and resumed firing at the enemy.

Here General Maxwell held for a time, while Ferguson's riflemen were being reinforced by a detachment of Hessians. Two heavy guns and a pair of smaller ones took positions behind Ferguson and backed his own fire, the Queen's Rangers meantime moving to the left to flank Maxwell, who was finally driven out of his strong position and back across the ford. After a brisk cannonading from both sides, the combat, by late morning, had simmered down to spotty activity. That this could be a lull before a storm, no one on the American side, especially Washington, seemed to realize. Historians have pointed out that the lesson of Long Island had not yet been learned. There, General Grant had held Lord Stirling by using the same delaying tactics while the main British army was moving in another direction for a big assault. Here, instead of feeling out the intentions of the enemy, Washington and

Greene were at least a mile behind the front lines at the ford, apparently waiting for the redcoats to make an expected frontal attack.

Then word came to Washington that beyond Welch's Tavern to the west, a large British column was moving northward along the Great Valley Road, which ran parallel to the creek. He sent a dispatch to Colonel Theodorick Bland, on the west side of the Brandywine, asking for "a continuance of your vigilant attention to the movements of the enemy and of the course they are pursuing. I wish you to gain satisfactory information of a body confidently reported to have gone up to a ford seven or eight miles above this. You will send an intelligent, sensible officer immediately with a body to find out the truth." This Bland did, and the report should have had the desired effect.

As if this information were not enough, another report, marked 11 A.M., now came from Lieutenant Colonel James Ross of Sullivan's division, telling of a large force of the enemy, about five thousand in strength with nearly a score of field pieces, marching along Great Valley Road. The double-barreled reports astounded Washington and his staff. They could hardly believe that General Howe would so divide his forces in the face of the American strength. Even so, it was time to act. Washington ordered a counter-attack across the Brandywine to take advantage of this "terrible error" in British tactics. Generals Greene, Wayne, Maxwell and Sullivan were to advance across the creek while Stirling and Stephen remained in reserve.

Some of Greene's troops were already across the stream when another note arrived, this time from Sullivan, that a Major James Spear had been on the Great Valley Road but had heard nothing of the enemy and was convinced they were "not in that quarter." For some reason, Washington accepted this latter report as correct without verifying it. Orders to cross the creek were rescinded. Greene was called back. Then a breathless man on horseback, without hat, coat or long trousers dashed up to Sullivan's headquarters and asked to see General Washington at once. Being an uncouth-looking individual, the man, who gave his name as Thomas Cheyney, was at first refused permission. But Cheyney insisted. He had important news, he said, and he was a squire and a good Patriot, one of the few, he believed, in this part of the country. Finally he was interrogated. He revealed that he had been watching the movements of the armies since early that morning—he had gotten up so early that he did not even wait to put on his stockings, hence his bare legs. He then had ridden to the crest of a hill and had sighted the British forces less than a hundred yards away. They had even sighted him before he could flee and had fired on him as he dashed away on his horse.

Squire Cheyney was taken to Washington and there repeated his story to the astonished commander-in-chief. At first Washington suspected the man was a Tory; there were so many in Chester County. But the squire persisted and swore that if Anthony Wayne were there he would vouch for his veracity. While the officers were deliberating, another dispatch came from John Sullivan confirming that the British were on the east side of Brandywine Creek and coming down fast on Washington's rear. Cheyney was telling the truth.

It later became known that Howe and Cornwallis, before daylight that morning, had marched along the Great Valley Road, crossed the creek and now were in the rear of the American lines only about two miles away. Washington immediately ordered Sullivan to shift his division to the right, while he remained with Greene. Wayne, Maxwell and one of Knox's artillery detachments were to hold fast to the position at Chadd's Ford. The American line was formed on the slope of a hill south of Birmingham Meetinghouse, a strong position that drew the admiration of even the British. Having made these hasty dispositions, Washington went north to examine the situation, accompanied by Greene and two brigades of his men.

By the middle of the afternoon, the British forces had gone into position on Osborne Hill, about four miles north of Chadd's Ford. About four o'clock, they began their advance toward the oncoming Americans. Bright were the red uniforms; their firearms gleamed and their bands played "The British Grenadiers." As these veteran European troops marched down the slope and across the valley, they displayed the self-assurance and aplomb that characterized their training and experience. Then over the whole landscape, there was an ominous quiet. Suddenly from an American outpost in a nearby orchard, a volley of musketry crackled, and the redcoats returned the fire. Now the battle was joined.

As the British and Hessian infantry coolly turned and advanced on the Americans, they did not fire, just thrust their shining bayonets into the Patriot ranks. This was more than the latter could stomach; many broke and ran. Sullivan rushed in reinforcements, but as fast as he could form one unit another broke and fled. Soon the left flank of the American line was shattered. The arrival of a brigade from Greene helped to stem the retreat but not for long. Meanwhile, Washington was in the rear waiting to see where the main attack would strike. It came from General Knyphausen across Chadd's Ford and was signaled with a great roar of artillery.

Evidently Washington was confused about what to do in the early stages of the Battle of the Brandywine. If this hesitation can be explained by his lack of information about the enemy, some justification can be made for the results. But judging from military axioms, he should have made it his business to know the movements of the British. Not being so informed, he had to suffer the consequences. Howe was all too often a mystery to him.

As it was, Washington did not even know how to get to the scene of the forward action toward Philadelphia. He ran across an old man named Joseph Brown and commanded him to lead the way, although the elderly fellow had to be persuaded by the sword of one of Washington's aides. As they dashed across the countryside, the commander was so anxious to hurry that he kept saying, "Push along, old man! Push along!"

Aided by heavy artillery fire, Lord Cornwallis advanced across the Brandywine and then pursued the Americans. For almost two hours, the raw troops of the British colonies resisted the onslaught, fighting muzzle to muzzle. In five charges by the British the Americans were driven back, and five times they returned. Finally the order to retreat was given. Nathanael Greene—who always seemed better in retreat than in attack—stood calm and allowed those who were drawing back to enter his ranks and re-form in the rear, while his men held a protecting line to their front. One by one the American units had to give way in the face of overwhelming British power. Knyphausen at Chadd's Ford pounded with his artillery and blasted the Americans there into a rout. But they withdrew in good order on the whole and felt they had stood up rather well to the veteran redcoat divisions.

Washington lost about 200 dead and 750 wounded, with some 400 prisoners taken by the British. The English counted 90 dead, 480 wounded and 6 missing. The local amateurs had lost to the seasoned professionals. In the Battle of the Brandywine, Washington did not exercise good intelligence supervision, failed to distinguish true from false information and relied too much on subordinates. But he did manage to retain his army and lived to fight another day.

In typical forthrightness, Washington, after busying himself with administrative details far into the evening, sent, at midnight, a dispatch to Congress about the outcome of the battle. He added a cheerful note when he stated, "Notwithstanding the misfortune of the day, I am happy to find the troops in good spirits." The impressionable John Hancock, who had once wanted the American command himself, received the news at 4 A.M. and at once roused the members of the Congress out of their beds to gather at six and learn the unfavorable tidings. Alarmed, that legislative body frantically called for troops from New York, New Jersey and Maryland to join Washington. Then as if to cushion the blow of defeat, they donated thirty hogsheads of rum to the army.

It was not only rum that sustained the men. They found that they had stood up quite credibly against the well-trained British and German soldiers, although the Americans believed the enemy had sustained more casualties than they actually had.

Washington retreated north from Chester on the morning of September 12 to the falls of the Schuylkill River, where he encamped on the outskirts of Germantown. He realized to his satisfaction that his army was still between Philadelphia and Howe's forces, which was what he desired. Congress had just granted him dictatorial authority for a period of two months and for as far as seventy miles in radius from his headquarters. This, however, does not seem so generous on the part of the lawmakers when it is considered that they had become increasingly alarmed at the proximity of the British and were about to take off for Lancaster and York after a hurried departure from Philadelphia.

By this time, Washington lacked most important supplies

and fortunately was able to replenish them from depots north of the Schuylkill. He recrossed the river on September 15 in order to prevent the British from entering Philadelphia. But again, as at New York and elsewhere, Howe's delay favored Washington. In five days, the British general had moved only ten miles to the north. Also, to Washington's delight, the British army was strung out in a long, thin line that seemed right for attacking. Accordingly, he prepared to do just this. Howe learned of the plan and hastily marshaled his forces in defense. As both sides got ready to fight, nature intervened with a tremendous downpour that flooded the countryside. The heavy rain drenched uniforms, wet muskets and ruined ammunition on both sides—an occurrence that especially saddened the eager Knox. The wind increased; with water in their faces and mud up to their ankles, the British could not even use their bayonets effectively.

Washington suddenly realized that his low ammunition left him all too vulnerable to the redcoats, whose cartridge boxes were better protected than those of the Americans. He hastily withdrew to Warwick, where he awaited expected supplies. As a precaution, he left Anthony Wayne and a brigade of fifteen hundred men hidden in the woods near Paoli, Pennsylvania. This turned out to be one of the most dramatic episodes of the Revolution.

Wayne—who had been nicknamed "Mad Anthony" because of his ardent but impulsive nature—was in his home territory. Not only was he a systematic and efficient general during the war, but afterward was the commander who finally defeated the western Indians at Fallen Timbers. His defeat of the Indians followed two disastrous attempts by Generals Harmer and St. Clair, both of them bitterly disappointing President Washington and Secretary of War Knox.

Wayne assured Washington at Paoli that he knew this

country, could hold his own against the British and would be able to hide from them successfully enough to surprise them and attack their rear as they crossed the Schuylkill River. But the idea of surprise proved to be ironic here. With his men and four pieces of artillery Wayne stationed himself on a wooded hill about a mile north of Warren Tavern. Under ordinary circumstances, the position would have been unknown to the enemy. But there were numerous Pennsylvanians about who had never lost their loyalty to the King, and these Tories reported Wayne's movements to General Howe. That doughty commander forthwith ordered Major General Charles Grey to make a surprise night attack.

Grey gathered together the 40th, 42nd (the "Black Watch"), 44th and 55th regiments of foot, the 2nd battalion of light infantry and a few of the 16th dragoons and was on his way. He ordered his men to remove the flints from their muskets so they could not fire and make noise and ever after was known as "No Flint Grey." At ten o'clock on the dark evening of September 20, Grey's men advanced stealthily along the road leading to the tavern, capturing every inhabitant who showed his face, in order not to have an alarm spread.

Wayne had posted his guards and instructed them to keep constantly on the alert. Otherwise, what happened might have been much worse. As it was, the British, expertly led by local Tory guides, swept silently toward Wayne's line, brandishing their bayonets and dashing toward the American soldiers, who unfortunately for them were all too clearly silhouetted against the evening sky by their campfires.

Upon seeing the advancing enemy, Wayne's sentries fired and fled, but most of them were already so close to the redcoats that they were killed by bayonets before they could escape. Wayne ordered his men to form and fight, and he took a position with his artillery on the right. General Grey ordered a full charge with bayonets and the surprised Americans managed to get in a round of musket fire before they became confused by the sudden and overpowering rush of their opponents. They ran from the sharp and deadly weapons in a headlong retreat. Some of Wayne's men stood valiantly, but they were no match for the charging enemy. Their crestfallen leader did succeed in drawing off his four cannon to a considerable distance in the rear, where he re-formed those of his men who had not run away.

Grey was now satisfied with what he had accomplished and ordered his troops to return to the British camp. He took with him some seventy-five prisoners, ten loaded wagons and a thousand muskets his men gathered from the ground where the fleeing Americans had thrown them. Wayne lost about one hundred and fifty men killed, wounded and captured, to say nothing of the cost in prestige and confidence. Word of the "Paoli Massacre" spread rapidly among Washington's other units, especially the militia, many of whom as a result "soon found pressing business at home."

The crafty Howe meanwhile had moved north, no longer fearing an attack on his rear. This was another surprise for Washington, who had thought the British might advance south instead. Actually Howe was edging toward Washington's supply depot at Reading Furnace. In order to offset the maneuver, Washington marched his men up the Reading Road to what is now Pottstown; but evidently the British general had other objectives in mind. Having drawn Washington out of his way, Howe crossed the Schuylkill River and placed his forces between the Americans and Philadelphia, continuing for the next few days to occupy the city, which was already half-deserted.

Washington found that his men were in sad condition. They had marched some one hundred forty miles in less than two weeks, lacked tents, shoes and clothing for the coming winter and also were in need of proper food. Many of them had left their blankets at Brandywine; when Washington asked Congress to supply replacements, they replied by giving him authority "to take wherever he may be, all such provisions and articles as may be necessary for the comfortable subsistence of the army under his command, paying or giving certificates for the same." When Washington sent Alexander Hamilton to Philadelphia to make the necessary purchases, this young financier-to-be found to his dismay that the Patriots had already given what they could spare and the Quakers and Tories hid their goods in order not to lose them.

William Howe, with eight thousand of his troops, was now in Germantown, a hamlet of houses enclosed by rail fences that was located northwest of Philadelphia. The British were encamped slightly south of School House Lane where Wissahickon Creek emptied into the Schuylkill River, Howe's headquarters being not far to the rear of the camp. For some reason he had decided not to entrench his men, perhaps feeling it would be a sign of weakness. Besides the main army of eight thousand, Howe had another three thousand under Cornwallis in Philadelphia and almost the same number strung out along the Delaware River for the purpose of aiding the fleet of his brother, Lord Howe. Opposing this force of some fourteen thousand British, Washington had about eleven thousand men, a third of whom were militia.

But the American commander felt he knew this region well and that he might seize the initiative and attack successfully, especially since Howe had not strongly fortified himself at Germantown and had divided his forces. This time, learning a lesson from Brandywine, Washington had seen to it that his intelligence reconnaissance was working well. With accurate information regarding the British positions, he and his staff laid plans for a night march and surprise assault.

The plan called for dividing the American forces into four columns, each to approach Germantown on different roads leading into it from the north and northwest. General Sullivan, frequently active but not as often victorious, was placed in command of a column composed of Wayne's, Conway's, Stirling's, Nash's and Maxwell's units. Their route was along the Bethlehem Road for the purpose of hitting the British left flank. Nathanael Greene, who had changed from a peaceful Quaker into an able military leader, commanded the second column, which comprised about two-thirds of the American army and was composed of Stephen's division and McDougall's brigade. It was to make its approach by way of the Limekiln Road. The third column was under Smallwood and Forman and was to strike the right wing of the British. General John Armstrong and his Pennsylvania militia made up the fourth column and were to move down on the right along Manawatamy Road to get in behind the left flank of the enemy.

In itself, the plan was a classic. All four American columns were to arrive at the British lines by four o'clock on the morning of October 4, and then simultaneously attack the enemy outposts at 5 A.M. with bayonets—a page out of the book of No Flint Grey. Apparently, however, Washington did not sufficiently take into consideration the roughness of the terrain over which his men had to run or the number of rail fences in their way. The overall plan was to be a wide pincers movement with Greene and Sullivan crushing the main British army and Smallwood and Armstrong folding up the left and right wings, to some extent similar to the attack on Trenton, though larger. The plan resembled the grand tactics of Hannibal when he succeeded in a double-enveloping movement against the Romans at Cannae in 216 B.C., where his force of forty thousand Carthaginians fought seventy thousand Romans and killed fifty thousand of them by pulling in their center and then surrounding the whole army, capping the great victory by breaking the Romans up into small and comparatively defenseless units.

Whether Washington had studied the Battle of Cannae is not known. Certainly Knox, the former bookseller, had; and it may have been that Greene had also, since he, along with Knox and Wayne, had made a considerable study of military history. Later, Daniel Morgan was to use the Cannae idea with brilliant success at the Battle of the Cowpens. But while the jaws of the pincers both in the ancient and modern battles referred to were strong, this was not so in the case of Germantown, as will be seen. Washington's flanks were made up mainly of militia, which he often found undependable.

The march along the Bethlehem Road began at 7 P.M. on October 3, with the respective columns moving along the planned routes. There had been much criticism in Congress of John Sullivan, who was held largely responsible for the defeat at Brandywine, but evidently Washington still had confidence in him. As an extra precaution, though, and in order to be on hand if needed, Washington accompanied Sullivan. For identification in the darkness, the men wore pieces of white paper pinned to their caps.

Timing was most important and coordinated precision of almost equal value. But though Washington had allowed what would seem to be plenty of time for the approach— two hours—it was not enough. Green troops led by officers lately recruited from civilian ranks, marching fifteen miles in separate units with little communication between them, could hardly be expected to execute the action perfectly. The roads were rough, the men's shoes badly worn, and they were still tired from so much marching in the preceding months. It was dawn when they reached the first British outpost, located at Mount Airy, about an hour later than they had hoped. To add to the difficulties, Greene's guide had lost his way, and Washington did not even know about it for some time.

The sun was rising over Chestnut Hill when Conway's advance company of light horse came upon the enemy outpost. Under the leadership of the dashing Captain Allen McLane, the Americans charged the pickets with bayonet and sword; but the intended silence was broken by a loud return fire from two field pieces the redcoats discharged as they fled, and thus the British army was alarmed. Almost before the chagrined Americans realized what had happened, Howe's 2nd Light Infantry formed and gave vigorous support to the threatened pickets. As if this were not enough, Lieutenant Colonel Thomas Musgrave threw his 40th Regiment of British Foot against the Americans, who by this time were reeling in surprised dismay. With Conway now forced to a standstill, Sullivan was compelled to throw the rest of his division and his artillery into the fight. Still the stubborn Musgrave would not give way. Sullivan called for Wayne's brigade, which soon came up from the rear and charged the British with bayonets. Washington later noted that Wayne's men must have had memories of the Paoli Massacre in their hearts as they drove so bitterly against Musgrave's troops.

The British line gave way, but very slowly, the redcoats pausing at every fence and wall and firing at their pursuers. Refusing to be stopped, the Americans—who at this position were superior in numbers—pushed on and drove the enemy for at least a mile. General Howe himself became aware of the onslaught and rode out to learn what was happening. Observing that his light infantry were retreating, he shamed them by crying out that he had never seen them run before, especially from a scouting party. Just then a burst of grapeshot from Knox's guns tore through the leaves of the chestnut tree under which the general sat astride his horse, and some branches fell on his shoulders, to the gratification of his scolded men. Howe, realizing that this was an attack in strength, galloped off to his headquarters to make preparations for it.

There had been mist in the early morning. Now the mist thickened into a fog that grew more dense until men could see for only about fifty yards. To the inexperienced Americans, fence posts and low trees loomed up like men, and many musket shots were wasted by those who were nervous and trigger-happy. This haphazard firing grew so extensive and noisy that Washington became concerned about the expenditure of ammunition and sent a message to Sullivan to do less shooting. This effort was only partly effective. Wayne's brigade was shifted eastward and, in the fog, swerved off their approach to the British left and moved toward the center of the British camp.

In the meantime, the resourceful Colonel Musgrave came upon a huge stone mansion a mile north of Germantown and hurried one hundred and twenty of his British troops into it. Called Cliveden, the structure was known locally as the Chew House, after its owner Benjamin Chew, one-time recorder of the city of Philadelphia, later attorney-general of Pennsylvania and eventually, in 1774, its chief justice. Chew had been suspected of being a Tory and was at the time of this battle under arrest in Virginia. The house was like a sturdy fortress. It was built of extremely hard gray stone and had a slate roof. As Americans raced past the house on both sides, Musgrave and his men slammed the heavy shutters closed, fastened the thick doors and cluttered the halls with pieces of furniture. Then they scampered to the windows of the second floor and from there poured a hot fire on Wayne's and Sullivan's men.

The problem of the Chew House was brought to Washington's attention. As he usually did, he called a staff conference. From Adjutant General Timothy Pickering came the opinion that the house could be left to itself and could be skirted by the Americans. Others were for leaving a regiment to immobilize the garrison inside it, while some were in favor of demanding of the British that they surrender and, if they refused, storming the house itself.

General Henry Knox, the young artillery chief, whose judgment in such matters Washington trusted, contended that since they were within enemy country they should not leave an occupied fortress in their rear. Washington agreed with Knox and ordered that a summons be sent to the Chew House to demand its surrender. Lieutenant Colonel William Smith volunteered for the mission. As a reward for his gallantry Colonel Smith, who proceeded under a white flag, was shot as he approached the house and died soon afterward.

Washington now ordered his reserve troops to keep away from the Chew House and Knox to shell it. The artillery hurriedly formed a circle around the structure and pounded it with round shot, grape and canister. Soon the strong roof was pierced and the glass in the windows shattered. But the sturdy walls held out, smoke and bits of flying material filling the air as the maddening episode delayed the main American advance. Knox then turned his three- and six-pounders loose on the house, but the cannonballs bounced off the surface like tennis balls. Here was a situation the military textbooks had not covered. The doors and windows had given way, but in the hallway a barricade of furniture protected the stubborn British, who held out with bayonets.

Someone suggested the house be burned. Colonel John Laurens and the Chevalier de Mauduit du Plessis from France offered to try. Laurens seized straw from the stables for kindling, and the Frenchman slipped up and forced open a window shutter, then climbed on the sill. Suddenly, du Plessis was confronted by a British officer holding a pistol, who asked what the intruder was doing there. He replied that he was only taking a walk. The redcoat demanded he surrender, but before du Plessis could reply, a British soldier rushed into the room and took a shot at him. It hit the British officer instead. The Frenchman managed to get away unharmed, but Laurens, nearby, received a bullet in his shoulder.

The American artillery now resumed its furious fire, but, like the musketry of Maxwell that joined it, the results were futile. Wayne and Sullivan, some distance away, finally heard the noise at the Chew House and, reasoning that their comrades were having a hard time of it, separately ordered their men to charge toward the noise. In the confusion that resulted, they fired on each other.

By this time, Washington realized that he had made a mistake. A rumor spread through the ranks that the Americans were being attacked in the rear by a hostile force. Before their officers could reassure them that the rumor was unfounded, they fled from the field in confusion. Washington tried in vain to halt the retreat, but it was like trying to hold back the heavy fog. Yet he did not blame Knox or anyone else, only himself. Historian J. T. Headley wrote, "Although Washington attributed the failure to win the battle to Providence, Providence will always be found against such bad management as that halt at the Chew House most indubitably was. Knox and Providence are by no means one and the same, and had the opinion been less scientific and more practical, the course of Providence would have taken a far different and more satisfactory direction."

Washington must have received mixed consolation from the report of the *Independent Chronicle* about the Battle of Germantown: "Alas! We have fled when no man pursued. Our troops behaved with bravery becoming veterans. Never was an attack better managed—until the retreat. But our people are in high spirits to find that the old English veterans can run with as much precipitation as Americans. Our reinforcements come in fast, and we shall soon be ready for them again."

Meanwhile, as he galloped forward to see what was going on, Washington was met by General Sullivan, who insisted that he move out of British musket range. This Washington reluctantly did, still hoping for a victory. But by now, the main army of the British, still intact, began an attack and drove between Wayne's and Greene's front lines. These Americans, as well as Sullivan's men, joined in the general retreat, holding up their empty cartridge boxes to Washington and Sullivan to show them why they ran. In vain did the officers try to halt them.

Here was a battle that was well prepared. Had it gone according to Washington's plan, the results would undoubtedly have been drastically different. Proper timing and coordination among his commanders might well have assured a success instead of a defeat, but the fog, the Chew House incident and the unexpected panicking of his troops resulted in a dire disappointment for the Americans.

As nearly as can be determined, the British counted 70 dead, 450 wounded and 15 missing at the Battle of Germantown. American losses were 152 dead—53 of these at the Chew House—521 wounded and some 400 missing. Much English opinion, however, showed admiring surprise at the extent of the American success. The historian George Trevelyan pointed out that European courts were impressed that a young army had attacked a victorious enemy in its own quarters and were repulsed only with great difficulty.

One grievous disappointment was Washington's when he discovered General Adam Stephen, an able officer, drunk and lying in a fence corner during part of the battle. This may have been owing partly to exhaustion, for General

Conway and Count Pulaski, a Polish volunteer officer, though sober, were also found asleep.

During the next two weeks, the armies of Washington and Howe were virtually inactive, remaining about twenty miles apart. Then, on October 18, 1777, General Howe decided to leave Germantown and enter Philadelphia, which he intended to fortify. Washington learned that Howe was also trying to clear the Delaware of American fortifications and warships, which blocked the river's channel from Chester to the mouth of the Schuylkill. Washington had placed much store in these defenses. "If they can be maintained," he wrote, "General Howe's situation will not be the most agreeable; for if his supplies can be stopped by water, it may easily be done by land. The acquisition of Philadelphia may, instead of his good fortune, prove his ruin."

On the New Jersey shore halfway between Chester and the Schuylkill River, there was an unfinished American redoubt at Billingsport. This faced a double *chevaux-de-frise,* a heavy-timbered line of rock cribs filled with stones and sunk in the water, with iron-tipped beams projecting upward and threatening any seagoing ship that tried to pass. Some three miles north were three more lines of this French-named impediment, protected by the artillery of Fort Mercer and Fort Mifflin. The former was on the New Jersey shore and had fourteen guns, the latter was on Mud Island and had strong walls on its river side. Between these forts and Philadelphia were several units of the small American navy, including the thirty-two-gun frigate *Delaware,* which ran aground and was forced to surrender.

Sir William Howe was of course aware of these land and water hindrances. He sent a couple of regiments across the Delaware River to attack the Billingsport redoubt. Seeing the formidable British assault, the small American garrison spiked their guns and left, thus allowing the enemy ships to pass unmolested. On October 22, Fort Mercer was attacked by Colonel von Donop's Hessian brigade, which advanced under the protection of a heavy naval bombardment. In this small fortification were only four hundred Americans under the command of Colonel Christopher Greene, a cousin of Nathanael's.

The Americans waited until the Hessians were at short range, then poured a murderous defensive fire on them until they withdrew, their commander Donop fatally wounded. Three British ships ran aground or were burned, and it took three weeks for the enemy to recover sufficiently to resume their attack against the forts.

But recover they typically did, and they gradually intensified their cannonading, mainly with the help of H.M.S. *Valiant,* whose sixteen heavy guns pounded American defenses from a distance of less than a hundred yards. Lord Cornwallis, the ubiquitous redcoat leader, crossed the river with two thousand troops and knocked out Fort Mercer, so the Howes were now secure, for the time at least, in their possession of Philadelphia.

VII REST AND RESURGENCE

WHILE WASHINGTON was fighting in Pennsylvania, the fortunes of war took a turn for the better for his side elsewhere. A dispatch from George Clinton at Albany, dated October 15, 1777, told of the "capitulation whereby General Burgoyne and his whole army surrendered themselves as prisoners of war." This defeat of a major British army was great news, even though Washington himself had not played a personal part in it. Nonetheless, Washington rejoiced, telling his troops, "Let every face brighten and every heart expand with grateful joy and praise to the Supreme Disposer of all events who has granted us this signal success." He ordered a salute by thirteen cannon and directed the chaplains to deliver to their various corps "short discourses suited to the joyful occasion."

The commander-in-chief had another cause for rejoicing. Though he was criticized in some quarters for his losses in Pennsylvania, the *Freeman's Journal* of Portsmouth, New Hampshire, took a different view. While flattering, the article at this particular time must certainly have been heartening to the struggling general. "At a crisis when America is invaded," the newspaper rhapsodized, "by one of the most powerful fleets and armies that ever the world beheld, turn your eyes to that bright luminary of war [here the article compared Washington to Fabius, Hannibal and even Caesar and thanked the Almighty that] we are blessed with a Washington for a leader."

General Horatio Gates, at Saratoga, had not even officially notified Washington of the victory. But the commander-in-chief took the omission magnanimously and was heartily gratified over the victory that was much needed. He had long wanted a success in the north, and this was it, decisive and important to the American cause. In June Burgoyne had come down from Canada with a large force and captured Fort Ticonderoga without a struggle. The flamboyant British general was supposed to have been joined by Colonel Barry St. Leger with a smaller group of Loyalists and Indians from the Mohawk Valley, but these were dispersed by the resistance at Oriskany and then turned back. Disappointed and needing supplies, Burgoyne sent a detachment to Bennington, Vermont, to obtain them, but General John Stark and his raw militiamen soundly defeated the British invaders, most of whom were German mercenaries. Burgoyne now decided to press on to Albany, where he hoped to be joined by General Sir Henry Clinton and an army from New York City, but Gates stood in his way at Saratoga with over six thousand men. On September 19, Burgoyne attempted to overcome Gates at Freeman's Farm but was thrown back with heavy losses. Again on October 7, at Bemis Heights, Burgoyne tried to pierce the American lines but again was repulsed, Benedict Arnold and Daniel Morgan leading the Patriot forces. So, outnumbered and outfought, the British general surrendered to Gates on October 17, 1777, and the Battle of Saratoga was over. Actually, Gates agreed to allow the defeated troops to be sent back to England under a "Convention" agreement, but this was never honored by the American Congress. About one-fourth of the King's soldiers in America thus laid down their arms.

General Horatio Gates was to figure with significance in Washington's military career. Gates was born in England, the son of a duke's servant. Though handicapped by his somewhat lowly birth, he became a captain in the British army and saw service in the Braddock expedition. Gates resigned from the British army in 1772 and came to Virginia. Here he settled on a small estate and renewed his acquaintance with Washington, which had started in the Braddock campaign. Gates joined the American cause and Washington made him the adjutant general of the army with rank of brigadier general. In this job, which was mostly paper work, Gates was excellent. He was later promoted to major general; however, he was not a good field commander. In the victory at Saratoga he was fortunate in having able subordinates such as Morgan and Arnold. Gates wore glasses, and these gave him a kind of old woman's appearance that won for him the nickname of "Granny."

After the Burgoyne surrender, the *Continental Journal* and *Weekly Advertiser* reported that "General Gates invited General Burgoyne and the other principal officers to dine with him. The table was only two planks laid across two empty beef barrels. There were only four plates for the whole company. There was no cloth, and the dinner consisted of a ham, a goose, some beef and some boiled mutton. The liquor was New England rum mixed with water, without sugar; and only two glasses, which were for the two commanders-in-chief; the rest of the company drank out of basins. An officer remarked, 'The men that can live thus, may be brought to beat all the world.' After dinner, General Gates called upon General Burgoyne for his toast, which embarrassed General Burgoyne a good deal; at length, he gave *George Washington;* General Gates, in return, gave *the King.*"

But such tributes to Washington at this time were few.

It was obvious to many that though Washington had recently lost two battles, Gates had won a glorious one and had captured some six thousand men, including seven generals. All the British garrisons in the north were now in Canada; on the eastern seaboard, where Washington was in direct command, the New York City area as well as that of Rhode Island and Philadelphia were still in the hands of the British. No one was more cognizant of this situation than Horatio Gates.

Congress, as well as some of his fellow officers, had also criticized Washington's conduct of the war. Typically, instead of stopping to pay attention to the grumbling, Washington chose to devote himself to obtaining food and clothing for his hungry and threadbare army and to keeping an eye on the British in Philadelphia. But in November, Washington received a report he could not ignore. One of his most loyal generals, Lord Stirling, called attention to information he had received that Brigadier General Thomas Conway had been slandering Washington in some correspondence with General Gates. An Irishman who had previously served in the French army, Conway was under Stirling's command. Stirling, a major general, had incidentally also been criticized by Conway, so that Stirling had more than one motive in his report. Criticized by some for heavy drinking at times, Stirling has nonetheless emerged in modern historical appraisal as an effective officer.

Conway had had thirty years' experience in the French army and was insisting that he not only be promoted to major general but be given the post of inspector general of the army as well. When his demands reached Congress, the other twenty-three American brigadiers, all senior to Conway in rank, were greatly incensed that such a brazen request would even be considered. Another affront to many of the officers, especially to the colonels, was the early promotion of James Wilkinson, a lieutenant colonel, to brigadier general in one jump. He was aide-de-camp to General Gates, who had made a special request for the promotion. The fact that it was successful shows Gates's influence at the time with Congress; it was even greater than that of Washington, who would never have countenanced such an unusual step. The clever and wily Wilkinson, who later was to figure in serious intrigues, may have had a hand in his promotion himself.

Conway was trying to have Washington replaced by Gates. In this he was probably aided by General Thomas Mifflin, the quartermaster general, who had fallen out with Washington because of supply difficulties the preceding summer. But whether there ever was a Conway Cabal, as the affair has been called, has never been established. There seems to be no doubt, however, that Gates would have liked the supreme command and was aware of the activities of Conway and Mifflin, as well as some members of the Congress including Richard Henry Lee, Samuel Adams and Benjamin Rush, who tried to disparage Washington during this trying period.

So despite Washington's low opinion of Conway, both officially and personally, the latter received his promotion to major general and inspector general of the army. Horatio Gates was made president and Mifflin a member of the Board of War. These two felt that since this board was directly responsible to Congress, it was independent of if not superior to Washington. Hence, the slandering campaign went on and the harsh comparison of the 1777 battles involving Washington with the glorious victory at Saratoga increased. For his own sake, it would have been well if Washington had forthwith spoken out against his enemies. But he felt he had good reason not to. To do so, he believed, would show the British both the weakness of the American forces and their internal dissension, which might encourage them even more. The plotters against him typically mis-understood his attitude at first. They apparently felt that if badgered enough, he would become so disgusted with the situation that he would resign.

The tide of events was at a low ebb for George Washington. He told his friends privately that he had been discouraged before and had often wished to leave his strenuous post; that he would be glad to do so now if the people felt that someone else could do a better job than he. He would even be willing to assume a lesser position and act in it conscientiously if he were asked to officially. Until that time, no amount of abuse, difficulty or reverses would swerve him from the course on which he had embarked.

To some extent this feeling was shared by others in the American army. Washington had plenty of friends there—sturdy and persistent Nathanael Greene, emotional and devoted Lafayette, impulsive and brilliant Alexander Hamilton and able and loyal Henry Knox. They declared their warm attachment to Washington as soon as they heard of the "conspiracy." In their letters can be traced a note of strident condemnation of the men who supported Gates. Although Washington has often been described as a cold individual, it is hard to see how such a person could inspire the ardent devotion shown by many of his military associates.

By waiting until the right moment, Washington found that his enemies played into his hands. Gates had been corresponding with Conway and at length felt that he must do something to justify all this communication. So he wrote Washington stating that he and Conway were being slandered by some officers on Washington's own staff and accused them of intercepting letters and then misquoting their contents. Overconfident, Gates sent copies of these letters to Congress, apparently hoping to appear justified and open-minded. In this way he also attempted to put himself offi-

cially on an equal basis with Washington. Now Washington
sent to Congress copies of some impudent and presumptuous
letters of complaint he had previously received from Conway. And just before his birthday, Washington dispatched
a masterful, cutting letter to Gates and sent a copy of this
to Congress. In this letter, Washington set forth an astute
appraisal of General Conway, not only showing that he
understood him and his motives but revealing an august
contempt for him as well. He also showed that he was perfectly aware of what had been going on behind his back
and even of the amount of progress the attempt to under-
mine him had made. The eloquent missive made clear that
if General Gates should continue to support the contempt-
ible Conway, those in responsible and official positions could
have no other alternative than to judge Gates a culpable
scoundrel.

Washington's letter to Congress was a bombshell. Gates
and his followers were caught completely off guard. The
plotters found that whatever support they had had in the
army quickly faded away. The scheme collapsed and Gates
felt compelled to write an obsequious letter of apology to
Washington.

Washington's triumph over Gates did little to help the
physical situation of his army. He had to get his men into
some kind of quarters for the winter. During the early part
of December, 1777, through days and nights of the snow
and sleet, he led his weary and discouraged soldiers toward
a resting place. En route, the badly dressed and exhausted
men tried to keep warm by crowding around small, smoky
campfires, futilely endeavoring to cook their slim provisions;
sleep was impossible when they had few blankets and the
freezing rain had severely drenched their already wet and
tattered uniforms. When, bleary-eyed and numbed, they
staggered out along the primitive roads, their ill-shod feet

slipped on the rough surface, furrowed by the newly formed ridges of ice. Later on, Washington wrote, "You might have tracked the army from White Marsh to Valley Forge by the blood of their feet."

Their arrival on the slopes of a ridge above the Schuylkill River some twenty miles northwest of Philadelphia did not mean surcease or even respite from hardship. About the best that can be said about Valley Forge was that it was near enough to Philadelphia for Washington to keep an eye on Howe and that it was a rather good defensive position.

In general orders dated December 17, 1777, Washington explained the bad news to his men. He thanked them for the fortitude and patience with which they had sustained the fatigues of the recent campaign. "Although in some instances we unfortunately failed," he said, "yet upon the whole Heaven hath smiled upon our arms and crowned them with signal success; and we may upon the best grounds conclude that by a spirited continuance of the measures necessary for our defense, we shall finally obtain the end of our Warfare: Independence, Liberty and Peace. These are blessings worth contending for at every hazard. But we hazard nothing. The power of America alone, duly exerted, would have nothing to dread from the forces of Britain. Yet we stand not wholly upon our own ground. France yields us every aid we ask, and there are reasons to believe the period is not very far distant, when she will take a more active part, by declaring war against the British Crown."

Washington expressed his wish that he could take his men to better quarters but added that to go into the interior of the state would crowd the people already there, including many refugees and leave a large section of the country open to the enemy. So his army must take a post near Philadelphia where it could protect its friends and prevent the British from living off the surrounding countryside.

According to his new efficient quartermaster, General

Greene, half the American troops were still without breeches, shoes or stockings. Thousands were without blankets, and many had to be classed as unfit for duty because they were barefoot or partly naked. Some supplies there were, but many of these were scattered along the roads for want of a coordinated effort to bring them into camp.

Nevertheless the hungry, unsheltered and freezing troops did arrive at their destination. Washington knew that if Howe had attacked him then, the war would have been speedily over. Along the southern border of the slope of Valley Forge—so named because wrought iron was once made there—a line of entrenchments was built, the western end being guarded by a series of abatis, redoubts and redans. Here, brigade villages of log cabins were hastily built along the wooded hillside, one row of huts facing another, with streets running between. Washington supervised the construction of the cabins and would not have any kind of shelter for himself other than a homespun-linen tent with open sides. After a week, he established his headquarters in a stone house which may still be seen today, on the western edge of the encampment. It is not as large as that of General Henry Knox, some distance away.

Ever the detailed planner, Washington set forth in general orders the specifications for the huts. They were to be fourteen by sixteen feet in size, the log walls six and a half feet high, daubed with clay in between. Fireplaces and chimneys were to be built of wood covered with clay and the sharply sloped roofs to be made from slabs. In each log hut were to be twelve men. Astutely, Washington offered a prize of twelve dollars to the group of soldiers who would finish building their hut in the quickest and most workmanlike manner. The men worked as had those whom John Smith had driven to labor at Jamestown under the stress of necessity. Their axes rang through the woods. As soon as the trees fell, they were sawed into the right lengths, properly notched at the ends to fit the corners of the tiny houses and then pulled through the snow by hand. Some of the straightest logs were split into boards for roofs and doors.

One zealous group finished their hut in two days and won the prize, but it wasn't until Christmas that most of the men completed their shelter. Green wood soon shrinks, so it was not long before cracks appeared in the huts; through these openings the frigid winds of the Pennsylvania winter hissed and froze the occupants. Smoke from the crude little fireplaces was wafted by the drafts back into the cabins and into the eyes of their occupants. Most of the huts had no floors except the wet earth, on which the men tried to sleep, their mattress, if any, being a sparse layer of old straw.

If the shelter of the soldiers during that 1777–1778 winter at Valley Forge was bleak, the food supply was worse. Nothing seems to cause complaints among military men so much as lack of good food. Washington was touched when he heard, all too often, his men crying out that they had no meat. Some even had no bread. In late December, Washington reported to Congress that the scarcity of provisions had caused "a dangerous mutiny" which was difficult to put down. He added that a few days of bad weather would prove to be disastrous and could not foresee how his forces could survive the winter, much less be ready for any fighting in the spring. On December 23 he wrote to the president of Congress, "I am now convinced beyond a doubt that unless some great and capital change suddenly takes place, this army must inevitably be reduced to one or other of these three things. Starve, dissolve or disperse, in order to obtain subsistence in the best manner they can."

This was the winter of Washington's discontent. The fact that he kept an army together at all at Valley Forge must be acknowledged as one of his greatest accomplishments. Lieutenant Colonel Henry Dearborn observed that "God knows, we have very little to keep with, this being the third day we are without flour or bread, and are living on a high, uncultivated hill, in huts and tents, lying on the cold ground. Upon the whole, I think all we have to be thankful for is that we are alive and not in the grave with many of our friends."

As if such dreadful conditions were not enough, Washington received word on the morning of December 22 that a sizable British force had left Philadelphia and was moving in his general direction. Almost automatically, he issued orders for his army to prepare to move against the redcoats. The response he received shocked him; it was the first of its kind he had encountered in two and a half years of command. The men could not stir from their huts. They were either too ill or were suffering from want of food and clothing and were too weak to move. This realization shook Washington. Had Howe not been dallying in Philadelphia, he could have defeated the Americans almost at will. Instead, he hung on to his comfortable quarters. All Washington could do, he reported to Congress, was to send out a few light parties to watch and harass the enemy. A few others, of those who were able to walk, were dispatched to forage for whatever provisions they might find. But he had little confidence in the results. A few days of bad weather would prove to be the destruction of Washington's army— or rather what was left of it.

To those who criticized him, Washington retorted, "I can assure those gentlemen that it is a much easier and less distressing thing to draw remonstrances in a comfortable room by a good fireside than to occupy a cold, bleak hill and sleep under frost and snow without clothes or blankets. It adds not a little to my other difficulties and distress, to find that much more is expected of me than is possible to be performed, and that upon the ground of safety and policy, I am obliged to conceal the true state of the army from public view and thereby expose myself to detraction and calumny."

What food there was at Valley Forge was hardly nourishing. Clothing was so scarce that throughout the correspondence and other reports runs the word *nakedness*. It was true not only of the enlisted men but of the officers, many of whom requested separation from the service because they were ashamed to be seen in public in such disgraceful apparel (or lack of it). Even water was in short supply, the high hills of the encampment having few springs. Water had to be carried in buckets from Valley Creek, the Schuylkill River or a brook half a mile away. So many troops used the brook for washing that it became quite muddy.

Pestilence moved in. Virulent and devastating typhus, that serious and contagious fever transmitted by body lice, characterized by eruption of red spots on the body, prostration and cerebral disorder was the worst invader. It would have been bad enough had there been proper knowledge of and means for treating this serious ailment. Virtually no medicine for it was at hand, and doctors were almost as scarce. Smallpox was another ravager, though it was not as prevalent as typhus.

At Bethlehem and other nearby towns hospitals were established. Even with their limited facilities, these would have been more helpful had they not already been crowded with ill and wounded men from the battles of Brandywine and Germantown. Patients had to be placed in tents in the freezing weather. One disadvantage to being ill in those days was the practice of cupping or drawing blood from the patients, which was practiced by the best doctors, even the eminent Benjamin Rush of Philadelphia. It was thought that draining a few pints of blood "relaxed" the patient. Beds were bundles of dirty straw used over and over again, as many as five men, perhaps, dying on the same pallet before it was changed. This was especially bad in the cases of typhus that came in from Valley Forge, men sick with a contagious disease and clothed in rags that were full of the infecting vermin. Doctors, nurses and attendants caught the disease and became its victims. A regular army historian has observed: "During that terrible winter, nearly 3,000 men died from starvation, exposure or disease. It is amazing that the army held together at all. That it did can be attributed only to the amazing influence of Washington's strength of character, will and determination. This austere man was truly loved by his devoted officers and men."

Despite heavy losses from illness, death and desertion, there still remained at Valley Forge over six thousand men, about two-thirds of them regarded as fit for duty. These were put to work to try to relieve the dire conditions. Anthony Wayne dashed across much of neighboring New Jersey, Henry Lee made incursions into Delaware where he found some fat cattle, and Allen McLane scurried about ubiquitously, in characteristic fashion. Not only did McLane take food from farmers but he delighted in surprising small British parties and relieving them of their provisions. Washington found to his dismay that many of the farmers around Philadelphia preferred to sell their crops to the British, who paid them in sterling instead of the virtually worthless Continental currency.

In an attempt to remedy this serious situation, Washington called on Nathanael Greene. General Thomas Mifflin, who had distinguished himself in the early part of the Revolution, had proved a failure as quartermaster general during the dark days of Valley Forge. Washington had put in his place the genial and capable Greene, the crippled Rhode Island Quaker who had become an outstanding officer in the Continental army. Greene did not really want the job, which was comparatively sedentary compared to field command. But he accepted. He sent men out into the country in rapid-fire fashion, telling them to forget small scruples and take cattle, horses, sheep and hogs whenever they saw them. Wagons too were to be procured indiscriminately. Whenever provisions were found and could not be brought in because of transportation or other circumstances, these were to be burned to prevent their falling into the hands of the enemy. "Forage the country naked!" he enjoined. Receipts were given, with promise of payment in the future. Even so, the results were meager. The British had been there before, and what was left was often concealed by the owners.

Not only humans suffered as a consequence. Horses starved to death. Henry Knox reported that he had lost at least five hundred in his artillery department. For lack of places to bury them in the frozen earth, their reeking carcasses decayed around the encampment, endangering the health of the soldiers.

On February 16 Washington commented, "For some days past there has been little less than a famine in the camp. A part of the army has been a week without any kind of flesh and the rest three or four days. Naked and starving as they are, we cannot enough admire the incomparable patience and fidelity of the soldiery, that they have not been ere this excited by their suffering to a general mutiny and dispersion."

Right in the middle of February, the worst month of the winter, Martha Washington arrived at Valley Forge. Martha may not have been very pretty or alluring according to conventional standards, but she was a wholesome and loyal wife who could brighten her husband's life when he needed it most. She gave a party for him on his forty-sixth birthday, for which she engaged the army band and personally paid fifteen shillings for its appearance.

Nor did she confine her attentions to her husband. She could see that the soldiers at Valley Forge were in great need of things to comfort the body as well as brighten the spirit. She organized morning gatherings of the ladies of the encampment, who assembled in her living room to

sew, knit and mend. Many a warm sock and repaired gar-
ment emerged from these informal sessions of work and
gossip. In the afternoons, the wives visited the hospitals,
distributing their improvised wares and cheer.

In the cold evenings, there was a warm spirit within the
Washington headquarters, which still stands in the memo-
rial park at Valley Forge. Card playing had been forbidden
by Washington, who felt that it led to gambling and to
the ruination of many good young officers; there was no
room large enough for dancing, but there were other festivities. Tea and coffee were served, and sparkling conver-
sation often lightened the otherwise lonely evening hours.
Martha was a superb hostess and had the knack of bringing
out not only the social part of her husband but the affability of others. Anyone who could sing at all was urged
to do so. Socially her equal, Mrs. Henry Knox—the former
Lucy Flucker of Boston, daughter of a prominent Tory—
assisted Martha in sewing as well as in social activities.
Lady Stirling was a blithe and comely addition to the
group as was Mrs. Nathanael Greene, who had come to be
with her husband (although it was rumored that she and
the general did not always get along well). Polly Wayne
was hardly ever with her Anthony, though they did not
seem to be hostile to each other.

Mrs. Greene had studied French and thus was able to be
helpful to the lonely and homesick French officers. Knox,
Hamilton and Laurens were the only American officers
who could speak French. The Marquis de Lafayette was
of course outstanding among the Frenchmen now allied
with the colonies. He was a great favorite of Washington's,
who loved him like a son, and next to Henry Knox, could
be called the personal choice of the commander-in-chief
among all his staff. He was a natural ladies' man as well.
Marquis de la Rouerie, formerly of the French King's

guard, was another welcome addition to the social gatherings, as was the able Duportail, an engineer who was to become minister of war under Louis XVI. Lower ranking but affable was Pierre Charles L'Enfant, who was to lay out the city of Washington. The youthful Pierre-Étienne Duponceau, secretary to Baron von Steuben and later a prominent Philadelphian, expressed in ardent terms his opinion of Washington: "I could not keep my eyes from that imposing countenance; grave, yet not severe; affable without familiarity. Its predominant expression was calm dignity, through which you could trace the strong feelings of the patriot and discern the father as well as the commander of his soldiers. I have never seen a picture that represents him to me as I saw him at Valley Forge and during the campaigns in which I had the honor to follow him."

As the first hint of spring fell across the cool Pennsylvania slopes, new hope accompanied it. The strenuous efforts of Greene and of Jeremiah Wadsworth, the commissary general, began to pay off. Wadsworth concentrated on getting food and clothing, Greene on transporting them and on obtaining horses and wagons, on fixing bridges and roads so that what was available in the way of supplies could be brought into camp and used. Soon each man received daily a pound and a half of bread; a pound of beef, fish or pork and beans; and a gill of whiskey. The springtime run of shad coming up the Schuylkill to spawn brought many of them into the waiting nets of the soldiers. The faces of the men regained some color from the sun, their muscles filled out and a new verve in their step was noticed by gratified and weary supply officers.

Washington began to look ahead not only to new battlefield tactics but to overall strategy, as is evident in his correspondence of the time. He believed firmly that his officer corps needed much strengthening. The need for recruits, especially for his regular infantry, had become shockingly apparent. He had little cavalry and had had limited experience with mounted troops. Probably his greatest problem was logistics, the procurement and transportation of supplies.

He felt that good officers should be rewarded with half-pay when discharged and that their widows should have adequate pensions. Congress sympathized with the latter provision but was wary of the half-pay proposal. He stuck to it, however, and eventually mainly prevailed. Having experienced the lack of voluntary enlistments when needed, he advocated a draft much like that of today, and later General Henry Knox established the modern draft system.

Howe and his forces, it was reported, were experiencing an enjoyable winter in Philadelphia, then the largest city in the colonies. Witty Benjamin Franklin, upon being told that Howe had captured Philadelphia, replied that this was not the case, "Philadelphia has captured General Howe." This was the city where Benedict Arnold was to flourish and marry a fair Tory. Filled with loyal Tories and well-to-do citizens without strong convictions about the new nation, Philadelphia took Howe and his officers to its social bosom and made the season of 1777–1778 a festive one.

An American inventor, David Bushnell, designed a naval contact mine that was ignited by a fuse attached to a floating barrel of gunpowder. Hoping to sink British vessels, he released several hundred of these mines in the Delaware River above Philadelphia in early 1778. But the kegs stuck in the floating ice and were discovered and sunk by the English sailors before they struck any vessels. This somewhat humorous situation caused Francis Hopkinson to write his famous ballad, "The Battle of the Kegs," which contained the popular stanza:

Sir William, he, as snug as flea,
Lay all this time a-snoring;
Nor dreamed of harm, as he lay warm,
In bed with Mrs. Loring.

Even so, Howe had already applied to the British government to be relieved of his command. In typical lethargy, the London officials took from October to February to approve the request and then named as successor to the slow Howe the even slower Sir Henry Clinton. Howe had often puzzled Washington; so did Clinton. Washington, as a matter of fact, respected Clinton enough to refrain from attacking New York City while the British general held it, which he did till the end of the war.

By this time, Washington had learned what the English could do, given anything like an even chance on the field. He had come to respect the professional precision, well-ordered discipline and obvious experience of the foreign soldiers. They might well have won the war already had it not been for the vague indecision and poor leadership of some of their officers. Prospects for an American victory had not been bright before the winter at Valley Forge; now they were bleak, despite the improvement in the health of the men and the advent of spring, which at last was bringing some comfort to the dreary coldness of the encampment.

Washington had had time during the long winter to reflect on his needs. Outstanding was the lack of leadership. He had some good officers, but they, like himself, had little or no professional military experience. Their strength was in their stout hearts rather than in their heads; their knowledge of warfare for the most part had been derived from reading books and from their few campaigns against the Indians, French and British. American military methods were of the irregular, guerrilla type. These tactics were effective in special situations, as had been demonstrated by Daniel Morgan and his expert frontier riflemen. They were the exception. The pitched battles in the open against more highly trained and seasoned men were what Washington feared. In order to be ready, his officers and men must have more knowledge of discipline, drill and maneuver.

One of Washington's prayers was answered in late January of 1778, when he received a letter from Benjamin Franklin, then in Paris, introducing a Prussian soon to come to America: Lieutenant General Baron Friedrich von Steuben. This officer with the imposing-sounding name was offering his services as a volunteer in the army, asking no particular rank or pay beyond his expenses. This last bit of generosity must have appealed particularly to Washington since he himself had asked for no pay except his expenditures. So with some doubts—he had come to mistrust a number of foreign officers—Washington welcomed von Steuben, with what proved to be fortunate good judgment.

Perhaps it was a good thing that von Steuben's credentials were not too well examined. Anyway, at this low point, American officials could not afford to be particular. The newcomer was not a lieutenant general. His highest rank in the Prussian army had been that of captain. It seems ironic now that Washington felt compelled to accept a member of that elite corps, which symbolized German militarism. But strictness and organization were just what was needed at Valley Forge, and von Steuben furnished them. As usual, when America had needed something badly, Franklin had supplied the need. He was impressed with von Steuben and was sure that Washington would be also. Von Steuben had served on the staff of Frederick the Great during the Seven Years' War. Forty-seven years old, he was solidly built, with heavy features. He immediately impressed Washington as being a true soldier.

But before he could assign von Steuben, Washington was confronted with an obstacle. The baron could speak no English. This could have proved formidable had it not been realized that French, long the international language, could be utilized by both von Steuben and two of Washington's favorite aides, Alexander Hamilton and John Laurens. They were given the job of interpreting for the new officer.

As an expert taking his first look, von Steuben's impressions of Valley Forge are revealing. "The men were literally naked," he observed, "some of them in the fullest extent of the word. The officers who had coats had them of every color and make. I saw officers mounting guard in a sort of dressing gown made of an old blanket or woolen bed cover. With regard to military discipline, I may safely say no such thing existed. There was no regular formation. A so-called regiment was found of three platoons, another of five, eight, nine and the Canadian regiment of twenty-one. The formation of the regiments was as varied as their mode of drill, which consisted only of the manual exercise. Each colonel had a system of his own, the one according to the English, the other according to the Prussian or the French style. The greater part of the captains had no roll of their companies and had no idea how many men they had. . . . The arms were in a horrible condition, covered with rust, half of them without bayonets, many from which a single shot could not be fired."

Instead of trying to deceive Washington, von Steuben was frank in his appraisal. This candidness was appreciated as was the glowing report that Hamilton and Laurens gave of their guest's qualifications. The baron was also offered the warm attention and friendship of Henry Knox and Nathanael Greene. By now Washington began to feel confirmed in his favorable judgment. Von Steuben's infectious personality, his soldierly bearing, fine horsemanship and gracious sense of humor added to his attractiveness. Washington made him inspector general pending Conway's departure from that post. For his part, von Steuben realized that though the Americans were not well trained, they did possess courage and strong devotion to their duty. He remarked to Washington that no European army would have held together under such an awful lack of food and clothing.

Washington asked von Steuben to formulate steps for training the army. This was not difficult for von Steuben except for his language handicap. So he wrote the directions in French and had them translated by his aide, Pierre Duponceau. Today it would be a simple matter of mimeographing, but then hundreds of handwritten copies had to be prepared for distribution to the officers. No regular drill regulations existed, no uniform way of operating weapons nor even a generally used method of marching. Whatever precedents had been observed had been based on British practice. Even then, a lack of veteran sergeants greatly handicapped the training.

To the credit of the new drill supervisor, he decided not to leave the main effort to subordinates. He determined to drill the men himself. First he organized a model company of a hundred men selected from different regiments. Facing this company, von Steuben picked out a squad and began teaching its members. In a kind of pantomime he demonstrated various positions, then called on each man to imitate him. He taught by example and corrected mistakes as soon as they were made. He showed the men how to form in straight line, march in unison and proper cadence, do an about-face, march to the rear and other such movements. As von Steuben drilled his model group, thousands watched; this group was then divided into similar units and assigned officers to teach them. Next he took up the manual of arms, basing it on the Prussian practice. He showed the men how to load and fire a musket, how to carry it, how to fix a bayonet quickly and how to charge against an enemy.

Von Steuben found a difference in European and American troops. "The genius of this nation," he wrote, "is not in the least to be compared to that of the Prussians, Austrians or French. You say to your soldier, 'Do this' and he does it; but I am obliged to say, 'This is the reason why you ought to do that'; and then he does it."

Apparently the newly arrived officer understood men. And in turn, they instinctively understood him. His lack of knowledge of English had provided an amusing incident. One of his orders was misunderstood, and some of the men marched one way, some another. Again he tried but to no avail. Finally he gestured frantically and in utter disgust cursed the soldiers in guttural German. The encampment rang with laughter, and from that time on, von Steuben was popular with the men. Captain Benjamin Walker of New York offered to interpret von Steuben's commands to the troops, and consequently was made his aide.

By late March, a drill program for the whole army had been established. Von Steuben wrote the regulations in French and then at night learned the English translations from Hamilton and Laurens so that he could bark them out at the men the next day. Now the use of the bayonet was stressed for the first time. The Americans, who at one time had feared the power of the British bayonet almost more than their bullets, became fierce fighters with the silent, cold steel and at times were a match for their adversaries. Instead of marching in single file like Indians, the soldiers learned to advance in compact formation, thus aiding orderly discipline, saving time and preventing straggling on the march.

Delighted with such progress, Washington asked von Steuben to choose one hundred and twenty men from the various regiments, to be Washington's bodyguard. An officer was also selected from each brigade as an inspector, and von Steuben himself drilled the bodyguard and inspectors, having by now picked up enough English to make himself fairly well understood. Again the special drill became a spectacle, almost all five thousand men gathering around to see the much-decorated foreign "general" putting small units through smarter and smarter paces. One could almost see the improvement materialize; at the end of a week of solid drill, the special company showed remarkable precision and soldierly bearing. The brigade inspectors returned to their commands and put into active instruction what they had learned.

Von Steuben also inaugurated a system of periodic inspection of all clothing and equipment. These had to be laid out and checked against the records that were set up in each company. In a notable step, von Steuben stressed the importance of the enlisted men. He emphasized that officers should be responsible for the welfare and readiness of their men, pointing out that their love would be gained by kind and humane treatment.

A lower-echelon officer at Valley Forge eloquently described the results: "The army grows stronger every day. It increases in numbers and there is a spirit of discipline among the troops that is better than numbers. Each brigade is on parade almost every day for several hours. See the regularity and exactness with which they march and perform their maneuvers. Last year it was almost impossible to advance or retire in the presence of the enemy without disordering the line and falling into confusion. That misfortune, I believe, will seldom happen again, for the troops are instructed in a new and so happy a method of marching that they soon will be able to advance with the utmost regularity, even without music and on the roughest ground."

The propitious combination of events seemed to grow with the warming of the spring sunshine. By late March, new recruits began to flow into the army at Valley Forge; by April this force greatly increased. Fitted into their proper organizations, aided by Greene's improved supply system and trained by von Steuben's discipline and drill, these new men, by the middle of May, became an army that Washington felt for the first time really deserved such a name.

One morning, to add to his enjoyment, a mass of white dogwood blossoms seemed suddenly to spring forth at Valley Forge. Through the harsh winter, the tough, small dogwood trees had stood out bleak and scraggly against the cold landscape. But now they were transformed, the trees bursting into thousands of big white blossoms. To the lonely men weary of winter and homesick for their own hearths, these flowers seemed a kind of symbol of the reawakening of hopes. Soldiers are not usually sentimental; but even to Washington, the blooming of the dogwoods at Valley Forge seemed a harbinger of better things to come.

And he needed such inspiration. Little has been written about the health of Washington. True, he was tall and impressive and, when in the saddle, the dynamic personification of the majestic man. He rarely complained and was fearless in battle. But some, like his wife, could look closer at his weatherbeaten face and see the pockmarks, a reminder of his smallpox before inoculations had begun. He had gotten not only the childhood diseases but had suffered from malaria in his teens and, after returning from Barbados, had contracted pleurisy. At the height of the Braddock campaign, he was quite ill from what seems to have been influenza and dysentery. Though it is not reported that he was ill at Valley Forge, the winter took its physical toll on him. Washington was blessed with a remarkably strong physical constitution and his early employment surveying in Virginia as well as his experience as a young soldier had hardened him in the trying situation in which he found himself. At any rate he ordinarily said or wrote little about his illnesses, apparently not wishing to trouble others with his personal ailments. He would sound off in anger about some problem, but these rare storms would soon calm down. He even dictated letters to several secretaries while he was indisposed, but the idea that he could, like Julius Caesar, keep them all busy at once is doubtless untrue. Another pastime of his was map making, which he regarded as being very important. He needed to keep up with the excellent maps he knew the British had. In fact, some of our most valuable military "scenes" of the Revolution have been preserved for us not by American but by British maps.

It is generally admitted that although Washington was deficient in several important ways as a general, a strategist, a tactician or even at times as a leader, there was no other man of his time who combined so many good qualities. He was thus able to cope with his situation as no one else could have done. Robert Morris was a practical man, a financier who had few illusions about human nature. Yet he wrote Washington that "Heaven blessed you with a firmness of mind, steadiness of countenance, and patience in suffering, that give you an infinite advantage over other men."

Washington was, too, a practical man. He owned an immense plantation and had had experience in providing for the daily needs of hundreds on his beloved farm. He treated his slaves kindly and was to take steps toward their eventual freedom. For all men he believed in strict discipline and was saddened at the sometimes unruly conduct of Martha's son. Washington was hard but fair, strict but understanding, and stern only when he had to be.

Obviously many among his men did not care who ran the country, King George or Parliament or the Continental Congress. But most were loyal to a cause led by a great man who was willing to share equally in their ordeals, treat his enlisted men with respect and consideration and even place himself in front of them in the most dangerous places on the field of battle.

When his men left—which they too often did, especially if the army happened to be encamped near their homes—they spread their impression of their leader. He soon became a symbol, not only of leadership but of the cause for which they were fighting. Washington was the new America personified. He was capable of associating with and dealing with prominent people and political leaders, such as governors and congressional figures. His background was more aristocratic than that of most; he was wealthier, he had had experience as a legislator in Virginia and he was beholden to no man for his appointment as commander-in-chief. Yet he could be friendly with the common man, sharing his views and winning his respect at the same time, a rare quality for any leader in the history of the world.

France, as had been expected, was now coming into the war on the side of America. Washington should have been kept better informed on foreign affairs by Congress, but that body was so busy with routine affairs—and with keeping at some distance from the British—that it did not get around to corresponding with him sufficiently. Of course Washington knew efforts had been made to bring France into the war on the Patriot side, possibly Spain too, but he was suspicious of the intentions of European courts and therefore dubious of the results. Visitors to Valley Forge now told him of reports that France was about to take an important step.

At the end of April, Washington received unofficial information that France had recognized the new American nation and that as a result Great Britain was in a state of excitement. Characteristically wishing to be certain before he announced the news to his troops, he wrote Congress asking for official notification. Five days passed and no word came from that "august aggregation." Then someone brought in a copy of the *Pennsylvania Gazette* that contained a whole section devoted to the French treaty. Washington thereupon added to his general orders: "It having pleased the Almighty ruler of the Universe propitiously to defend the cause of the United American States and finally by raising us up a powerful friend among the princes of the earth, to establish our liberty and independence upon lasting foundations, it becomes us to set apart a date for gratefully acknowledging the divine goodness and celebrating the important event which we owe to his benign interposition."

Next day the celebration was held. Ammunition may have been in short supply, but there was enough to make highly audible this *feu de joie,* a sort of salute for the entire army. Promptly at 9 A.M., cannon shot signaled the soldiers to fall into line at their respective parades for formal ceremonies conducted by clergymen. Washington and his staff rode out in dress uniforms to hear a minister read a summary of the treaty with France, then with warm eloquence rendered praise to the King of France. For once, even Catholic aid was welcome! Over an hour of such tribute went on, then the cannon roared again and the men returned to their huts to arm themselves for the military pageant, under the direction of Baron von Steuben.

Washington, astride his horse, rode past the white dogwoods lining the road to the center of the parade. Smart military commands were given by the newly trained officers. Quickly the officers lined up their troops, the several brigades marching to their posts in order of battle, their lines being formed rapidly and with precision. The artillery then boomed out three hearty salutes of thirteen guns each, and the infantry troops fired the climax of the *feu de joie.* This was a volley of musketry starting at the right of the front line and progressing one shot at a time to its left and back again along the rear rank, which was carried out "to perfection and gave a sensible pleasure to everyone present." Washington was delighted. "The exactness and order with which their movements were performed," he stated in general orders, "is pleasing evidence of the progress they are making in military improvements."

After the last shot of the celebration had been fired, the officers led several cheers such as "Long live the King of France!" "Long live the friendly European powers!" and "To the American states!" As the echoes reverberated against the surrounding hills, the men marched back to their encampment, where each of them was served a gill of rum. A simple repast followed. A band played martial music, and Washington and his officers graciously greeted each other, their ladies and some visitors from Philadelphia. To those who had never been close to him socially, this was a new Washington, a friendly, human man who was not above mixing with others. In turn, they warmed toward him, and in Laurens's opinion, at least, he received much proof of the affection and attachment of his officers.

Another of his officers observed, "I was never present where there was such unfeigned and perfect joy in every countenance. The entertainment was concluded with a number of patriotic toasts attended with huzzas. When the general took his leave, there was a universal clap, with loud huzzas, which continued until he had proceeded a quarter of a mile, during which time there were a thousand hats tossed in the air. His Excellency turned round with his retinue and huzzaed several times."

But still the war had to go on.

VIII A DIFFICULT TIME IN NEW JERSEY

As WINTER WORE AWAY, Washington had time for more reflection on what had happened at Valley Forge. Though he was never to forget the image of the place—sentries at their post freezing in the snow, shivering men starving around a tiny campfire and some pitiful soldiers dying because of lack of proper food and medicines—he began to realize that the weather was not the worst factor. In fact, he was to face a worse winter during his second year at Morristown. The real obstacles were man-made. Pennsylvania farmers chose to sell their goods to the British in Philadelphia for real cash. In New York there was even a surplus of grain, but this too was sold either to the British or to civilians in New England, instead of going to the needy American army. Boston merchants refused to sell clothing except for high cash profits. Pork in New Jersey spoiled because there was no way to transport it to Valley Forge. These conditions, plus the Conway Cabal, must have made Washington wonder which were more detrimental, his enemies or his friends.

He also received reports of atrocities American Tories were committing against their neighbors, many of which were true. But although he once declared that some should be hanged, his usual attitude was one of moderation, and he recommended lenient treatment. He realized too that the Patriots committed similar offenses against the Tories in an often bloody and less publicized type of internecine warfare. When he had time, he haggled with General Howe about the cruel treatment of American prisoners in Philadelphia and elsewhere and urged the exchange of a number of them, especially high-ranking officers. There was also the problem of preventing harsh reprisals by his own men against the redcoats in their hands.

In the spring came news of a very welcome exchange. A veteran field commander, General Charles Lee, in whom Washington long had much confidence, was exchanged for Major General Richard Prescott, a British officer who had been captured the previous summer in the arms of his mistress. Lee arrived at Valley Forge full of his usual boastfulness, but this was overlooked in the hope that he would be of help.

On May 11, 1778, General Sir Henry Clinton arrived in Philadelphia to assume command of the British army, replacing General Howe. Although Howe had asked to be relieved, he was now reluctant to go because he was having such a good time. Gala dances, colorful performances at theaters, horse racing, cockfighting and conviviality had filled the winter season. Despite inflationary prices the people had fun. Evidently no one had more fun than General Howe himself; Mrs. Loring was still with him.

The concerned Tories wanted Howe to take his twenty thousand men and march out and defeat Washington, which he could well have done. One writer expressed it in rhyme:

> Awake, arouse, Sir Billy,
> There's forage in the plain,
> Ah, leave your little Filly,
> And open the campaign.

On the seventh of October, 1777, Washington had dispatched a courier to Philadelphia under a duly honored flag of truce who presented this message to British headquarters: "General Washington's compliments to General Howe—does himself the pleasure to return to him a dog, which accidentally fell into his hands, and by the inscription on the collar, appears to belong to General Howe."

Soon afterward, a wildly festive extravaganza was given in Howe's honor by the British just before his departure. It was called a *Mischianza*, meaning, in Italian, a brilliant medley. Brilliant it was, directed by the artistic and talented John André, who was assisted by the local Tory ladies, especially the beautiful Peggy Shippen, friend of André and later Mrs. Benedict Arnold. An outdoor celebration of parading, dancing and dining by British officers and social elite of loyal Philadelphia, it was held on the verdant lawns of the gentry. The climax was a jousting match between the Knights of the Burning Mountain and the Knights of the Blended Rose. In the evening, there was an uninterrupted flight of rockets and bursting balloons, with some twenty bands playing "God Save the King." Supper was announced at midnight, and dancing continued until 4 A.M.

Washington reacted with understandable relief to reports that the British army would soon be moving out of Philadelphia. He would have been happy to end the war at any time, provided the new nation obtained its avowed independence. So when ships began to sail down the Delaware River loaded with British baggage and supplies, apparently bound for New York, Washington rejoiced.

Washington knew that the young Marquis de Lafayette longed for military action. The two had first met at a dinner in Philadelphia. Lafayette was impressed by the majestic figure and deportment of Washington, as well as "the noble affability of his manner." For his part, Washington immediately liked the slender and handsome young Frenchman, in whom he sensed a kindred soul. He invited Lafayette to become a member of his close military family, something achieved only by a few. Lafayette wrote to his wife that the relationship between him and Washington was like that of attached brothers, with mutual confidence and cordiality.

As for Lafayette, he was little impressed with the American army, which he felt was poorly armed and clothed. To him it was a strange spectacle for soldiers to wear hunting shirts and linen coats. Lafayette was accustomed to European formality and uniformity, and American military tactics seemed to him unorthodox, though he thought the American soldiers were effective and their officers zealous.

Lafayette was directed by Washington to conduct a reconnaissance in force toward Philadelphia, with a brigade of Continental and militia troops. In all, including some irregulars under the command of Captain Allen McLane, there were about two thousand men. In this plan Washington's heart rather than his head seemed to prevail, for the project was senseless and dangerous. Obviously, he wanted to give the young and likeable Frenchman his chance to have a field command. Lafayette moved to Barren Hill, just east of the Schuylkill River about midway between Valley Forge and Philadelphia, taking up a good defensive position and posting sentries along all the roads of approach. Of course a movement with this many troops could not be made without it becoming known to the British. Accordingly apprised, General Sir Henry Clinton, not the most dynamic but one of the ablest enemy commanders, decided to make an example of this audacious operation. Before daylight on May 20, he sent ten thousand redcoats converging from three directions against Lafayette's new position. He almost succeeded. Only a last-minute warning of the British approach by Captain McLane kept Lafayette from disaster and, using the order and discipline infused by von Steuben, the young Frenchman and his force successfully withdrew.

By the end of May, 1778, American intelligence reported

to Washington that the British in Philadelphia were preparing for some kind of movement. Even so, it was difficult
for Washington to figure out just what his adversary was
going to do—a problem that haunted him for the rest of
the Revolution. At first he thought it might be an offensive
against him or part of his forces, such as those at Wilmington under General Smallwood. British ships laden with
baggage were sailing down the Schuylkill every day; his intelligence operatives had brought word also of a big wagon
train being prepared by the redcoats as if in readiness for a
prolonged march. As these reports and rumors continued,
Washington gained the impression that Clinton intended to
move back to his favorite city, New York.

Directing Maxwell and his men to cross the Delaware
and watch the British, Washington also sent word of the
expected movement to General Philemon Dickenson of the
New Jersey militia. But Clinton might go elsewhere. Sup-
pose, reasoned Washington, that the British commander
went by water up the Hudson River and took possession
of that important valley. But no, the enemy did not possess
enough transport vessels and so surely must go by land
across much-traversed New Jersey. So Washington sat down
and studied a map that would not only inform him of possible enemy routes but might suggest a way he himself
could approach the northern theater of the war.

Meanwhile, in a plan put forth by Lord North and his
government, a peace commission headed by the Earl of
Carlisle came to Philadelphia to suggest terms to Congress.
The commission had been authorized by the English government to offer an almost autonomous dominion status to
the colonies. Had it come earlier in the war it might well
have been accepted. But now Congress, buoyed by the
French alliance and some military success, refused to deal
with the Carlisle commission on any terms except those of
absolute independence.

By the middle of June, the military situation had become clear to Washington. Even so Washington, as was his custom, called a council of war to consider possible courses of action. Most of his generals favored action of some sort against the British. Not so the erratic Charles Lee, who insisted that the Americans should not try to oppose Clinton's movements and by all means not risk a general engagement. Others believed that the Patriot army should lose no opportunity to hit the British while they were in motion and not well prepared for action.

On the bright morning of June 18, before daybreak, the British army started across the Delaware and moved northeastward. Washington noted that big quantities of supplies, horses and wagons and artillery were underway, as well as some ten thousand British soldiers. In addition, a third as many Tories—men, women and children—felt they had to leave Philadelphia and were transported in ships that could well have been used by the military. The Tories were supposed to be of significant assistance to the British army in most of the important phases of the Revolution but all too often proved a hindrance rather than a help.

A courier from Philadelphia confirmed to Washington that the British had left, and he at once put his own forces into motion. It was now a quite respectable army of trained men, some twelve thousand in all. General Lee was to command the right wing and Lafayette the left, the fine work of Greene as quartermaster general showing in the improved condition of the uniforms and equipment of the men as well as in their better physical prowess. In addition, the drilling and discipline that von Steuben had contributed made them more maneuverable and dependable. Washington, still fond of Benedict Arnold and admiring his dash and fire in battle, wanted to have him as a division commander in the coming campaigns, but the wound Arnold had received at Saratoga—coincidentally in the same leg that was hit at Quebec—had still not healed. As a result he was made commander of the American troops that occupied Philadelphia after the departure of the British. This situation, seemingly insignificant at the time, was to be of lasting importance, for here Arnold was to meet and win the lovely Peggy Shippen, whose Tory tendencies were to influence the vulnerable Arnold to such an extent that he became a traitor.

By June 23, the forces under Washington had crossed the Delaware River at Coryell's Ferry in their march northward and were soon about fifteen miles west of Cranbury, New Jersey. Clinton's army was encamped at Allentown, some twenty miles to the south. He had had his men move in two parallel columns in order to be able to form quickly in case of an attack. At the time, New Jersey was in the grip of a wilting heat wave, during which the temperature was around one hundred degrees for most of the month of June. Though occasional thunderstorms took place, the relief from the muggy heat was only temporary. Clinton's men were alternately scorched and soaked along the road from Philadelphia. When the weather was dry, the dust rose; when it was wet, mud puddles impeded the progress of the slow-moving army. Most of the bridges along the route had been destroyed by the Americans and had to be rebuilt. The roads were clogged with fallen trees, and causeways had to be constructed over swamps in order for the artillery to get through. Hundreds of wagons slogged forward in a serpentine procession, so that it required a week for Clinton to travel the thirty-four miles to Allentown. Of course the Americans encountered the same difficulties, but their packs were light compared to the eighty-pound loads borne by the British and Hessians. Bridges on their route were more often intact and their wagon trains easier to maneuver. As a result, Washington's men moved forty-seven miles in the same week of Clinton's slower march.

It was a new role for Washington. He was now the pursuer and was watching for an opportunity to attack. He asked General Philemon Dickenson of the New Jersey militia to hover on the British left flank with his eight hundred troops, while Daniel Morgan and his crack riflemen were dispatched to the east to harass the right. Washington correctly believed that Clinton was determined to reach New York at all costs and was determined to stop him if possible or, if not, to impede his progress in a way he would remember. On the morning of June 24, Washington called another council of war and asked his generals for advice. Lee strongly advised that the Americans should refrain from attacking the seasoned British regulars, while others urged prompt action. Washington typically took the middle position and announced that he would not attack the British—who outnumbered him by some three or four thousand men—unless a definitely favorable opportunity presented itself. If it did, he would quickly take action. In the meantime, he would make a cautious pursuit.

By now it was learned that Clinton had changed his mode of march as well as his approach to New York. Instead of going by New Brunswick, the usual route, he decided to combine his forces into one column and go by Monmouth Court House (now Freehold) to Sandy Hook, where his troops would be taken on board ships to sail to New York. But on the road to Monmouth, almost a third of his heavily clad Hessians were overcome by the one-hundred-degree heat and fell by the roadside, numbers of them dying of sunstroke. Not until the evening of June 26 did the weary British straggle into Monmouth Court House, where they tried to rest despite a heavy thunderstorm. The next day Washington found that the British were immobilized at their new location.

With circumstances favoring him, Washington decided that despite the lukewarm sentiments expressed at his last council of war, it was time for action. He thereupon doubled the strength of his advance guard, placing the leading echelon under the Marquis de Lafayette, who had favored attacking, and the second one under Charles Lee, who had opposed it. As the senior officer, Lee now had charge of both. Washington has been roundly criticized by historians for allowing Lee to have any major part in these operations in which he apparently did not have any faith. But when it is considered that Lee was greatly admired and respected by virtually all the mature American officers because of his reputation and self-confidence the arrangement is not so strange.

Even now, Lee vacillated. When the separate command was first offered to him by Washington, he demurred, muttering that it seemed "a more proper business of a young volunteering general, than of the second in command of the army." This hint was aimed directly at Lafayette, and the youthful Frenchman was anxious to have such a post; he seized upon the proffered opportunity. But when Lee learned that the advance force was to consist of more than six thousand men, nearly half the army, he asserted his prerogative of rank and asked for the command, which he received. In hindsight this was a mistake on Washington's part, who probably, again, did what any other conventional commander would have done.

Now Lafayette had to be consoled for the loss of the prize so recently bestowed upon him. But so warm was the personal relationship between him and Washington that this was not difficult. Lafayette was ordered to combine his force with those of Lee at Englishtown, about five miles west of Monmouth Court House. Washington and the main army were concentrated between Englishtown and Cranbury. Here, on the evening of June 27, 1778, Washington felt that the time to attack had come. Clinton's men lay motionless at Monmouth and would doubtless soon be spread out in a long column of march on their way to New York. What did it matter that Lee did not appear to have his heart in the project? The combined forces could hardly miss. At least the chance of success seemed so propitious that Washington would have felt himself greatly remiss if he did not take it.

Washington called Lee to his headquarters and in the presence of Generals Wayne, Lafayette, Maxwell and Scott told him of his plans and directed him to attack the British as soon as they were on the road on the following morning, assuring him that he would bring up the main army in support promptly if and when it was needed. For those who condemn Lee for what happened later, it must be pointed out that Washington did not prescribe any special plan of his own, but asked Lee to call his own general officers together that afternoon in order to make specific plans for the attack. Washington also requested that his other generals temporarily waive their respective precedence of rank and place themselves under the orders of Lee, cooperating with him when he requested it. Lee then called his conference for five o'clock. When the generals were assembled, he simply stated that since the strength and various locations of the enemy were not yet clearly known and the land been insufficiently reconnoitered, he would formulate no definite plan for the time being but would move ahead with caution and depend upon his subordinates to use their best judgment and act according to the circumstances. Lee, however, failed to obtain adequate intelligence of the enemy that night.

Later during the evening, Washington, not having word of any definite preparations on Lee's part, sent him instructions to station an observation party near the British to watch and report any suspicious movements. This order was received by Lee soon after midnight, but it was daylight before the party, under Colonel William Grayson, was formed and active in its mission. Meantime, Washington had received word from Dickenson that Clinton, who apparently had suspected the American intentions, was already on the move. General Knyphausen and part of the army and wagon train were in the lead, Clinton, Cornwallis and the rest following in line, the whole making up some of the finest troops in the British army. Dickenson and his New Jersey militia had been watching the enemy all night; in fact, he had already skirmished with some of Cornwallis's men.

As soon as Washington received word of this activity, he sent a message to General Lee asking him to "bring on an engagement or attack the enemy as soon as possible, unless some very powerful circumstance forbid it, and that he would very soon be up to his aid." Washington seems to have wanted Lee to move and let the enemy know that the Americans were aggressively present, while still not running any risk of becoming dangerously involved. So Lee may have misunderstood Washington. At any rate, Lee started out at 7 A.M. and ground to a halt within an hour. This was because an aide to von Steuben arrived with information that the British had not yet begun to march. What was meant was that Cornwallis had not yet gotten underway, although Knyphausen had. So by the time General Dickenson arrived at Lee's headquarters, Lee, an unstable man at best, was already irritated and gave Dickenson a "good bawling out" for sending "false information" to which Dickenson replied indignantly.

The events that followed in the Battle of Monmouth from this point on somewhat resembled a comic opera, with Charles Lee playing the lead in buffoonery. One historian has described the bizarre engagement as "the most confusing in its movements and the most difficult to present or follow in detail of any of the battles of the Revolutionary War." In the early phases, Lee appears to have accepted Washington's advice and orders without question. But for some reason that has never been satisfactorily explained, he adopted a fatalistic attitude toward the success of the battle and became certain that the Americans would lose. Whether Lee was secretly determined to do what he could to assure such a defeat has never been established. Historians differ in their conclusions, describing Lee with adjectives ranging from treasonous to stupid. Two things are certain: Lee had no real plan for an attack, and up to the very climax of the engagement he was trusted by Washington.

What Lee did was to march his men in a slow and somewhat disorderly manner in the general direction of Monmouth Court House without keeping in enough communication with his officers to bring about any kind of effective coordinated action. Lee did notify Washington that the rear guard of the British seemed quite vulnerable and that he intended to attack it. But no follow-up orders to carry this out seem to have been given, and the result was more confusion. Finally, after becoming aware of the American pursuit, some of the British units turned and fired on them. Still Lee gave no orders to close in and fight. Instead, he is supposed to have indicated somehow to a few of his brigadier generals that they should fall back. With so many Americans milling around Monmouth like a huge swarm of grounded bees, those retreating soon conveyed this order to the others, and Lee's whole force started to retreat in great disorder.

General Sir Henry Clinton, now engaged in one of the few major battles in which he took part in the war—although he planned for and dreamed of many—could not mistake this obvious chance for a victory. He directed Cornwallis to counterattack and ordered Knyphausen to halt and send back three thousand troops. By thus pressing upon the Americans filtering to the rear, the British turned the retreat into a tumultuous rout. Outstanding among the withdrawing Americans were Anthony Wayne's men, who fell back in good order, intact, and were ready to form a badly needed delaying position; this undoubtedly saved the retreat from becoming a disaster. But most of the fleeing force, some in good order, some disorganized, fused into a motley mass scurrying backward in heat that reached one hundred degrees. Among the retreating throng, riding coolly beside the hot, tired and thirsty men, was General Charles Lee who, according to the description of some officers, appeared to be quietly exulting in the failure of a movement that he himself had opposed. But these opinions were formed in the midst of dismay and disgruntled withdrawal and may have been overdrawn. Lee did conduct the retreat effectively enough to get his men out of the clutches of the redcoats, which he contended was necessary to avert capture by Clinton.

Where was George Washington during all this melee?

He was with the main army a few miles to the rear and was approaching Freehold Meeting House in order to come to Lee's aid. In fact, he had been on the move from the time he heard of Clinton's departure from Monmouth Court House. Having made clear what he felt were good general plans—though Lee insisted afterward that they were not—Washington stopped at a farmhouse on the way to the front and ate a late breakfast. He received Lee's message of assaulting Clinton's rear guard and thought this sounded reasonable. But he began to be alarmed when, for some time after this message, he heard no sound of battle. Then just before noon the noise of some light and irregular firing reached his ears and made him wonder more. Waiting no longer, he and his staff spurred their horses forward to see what was going on. Near the meeting house, Washington met some stragglers, one of whom told him that Lee's forces were retreating. This news seemed incredible, and Washington ordered that the informant be placed under arrest for spreading a false report.

The report proved all too true. Not far from Freehold Meeting House, Washington met Lee riding blithely along with his staff officers, headed toward the rear with as much aplomb as if he had been leading a charge.

"What, sir," Washington demanded angrily, "is the meaning of this?"

"Sir, sir?" answered the flabbergasted Lee, apparently taken completely off guard. Again Washington inquired what was the reason for the retreat.

Regarding the remainder of the confrontation, there are several versions. Probably the most often quoted are those of Washington Irving, who seems more imaginative than accurate; Lafayette, who was not even present but who said that Washington called Lee "a damned poltroon"; and General Scott, who fancifully waxed eloquent, stating that Washington "swore until the leaves shook on the trees."

Not often cited is the testimony of General Henry Knox at the later trial of Lee. Said Knox: "His Excellency and General Lee were together. His Excellency expressed much displeasure to General Lee on the subject of affairs, and though I cannot ascertain the precise words, the sentiment was that either he or General Lee must take command of these troops, speaking of the troops that were present, and that it must be an instant determination. 'If you will take the command,' continued His Excellency, 'I will go to the rear and form the army.' General Lee replied, 'I will do everything in my power, and Your Excellency may rely on it that I myself will be one of the last to leave the field!' "

This seems more believable than Scott's account, since there has never appeared a well-documented report from any witness who heard George Washington ever swear a double-barreled oath of real profanity. That he had a temper is a matter of record, that he lost it upon occasion is also established and that he used strong language is a natural assumption.

On the day of the confrontation, Washington made an impressive appearance. He was mounted on a large white horse, a recent gift from Governor William Livingston of New Jersey. Lafayette recorded his impression of how Washington's arrival affected the men. "His presence stopped the retreat," the Frenchman wrote. "His fine appearance on horseback, his calm courage, roused to animation by the vexations of the morning, gave him the air best calculated to excite enthusiasm. He rode all along the lines amid the shots of the soldiers, cheering them by his voice and example and restoring to our standard the fortunes of the fight. I thought then, as now, that never had I beheld so superb a man."

So the troops, heartened by the presence of a commander who faced forward, not backward, turned again toward the enemy. Washington went along, galloping on his majestic horse toward Monmouth Court House, where he crossed a bridge and met some Pennsylvania and Maryland troops. They were the last to retreat, and hard on their heels, only about two hundred yards away, were the exultant redcoats hot in pursuit. Quickly, the Americans faced the British, the steadfast men of Anthony Wayne being the ones who were nearest and most exposed. Washington told them to hold the line until he could form reinforcements behind them. True to the drilling they had had under von Steuben and even more to the real spirit of the Pennsylvanians under a fighting leader, Wayne's troops stood and held.

This gave Washington an opportunity to gallop a few hundred yards to the rear to the crest of a ridge that overlooked a winding stream flowing through a slight defile. At this desperate point, as he tried to round up whatever men he could, to his great delight the dependable Nathanael Greene arrived on the scene with the main body of the army. Washington was so heartened by his appearance that he ignored the fact that Greene was now a staff officer—in military theory ineligible for field command—and at once placed him in command of the army's right wing. He ordered Lord Stirling, in the rear, to come up as quickly as possible to protect Greene's left, while Washington and Lafayette tried to organize the scattered remains of Lee's force as a reserve. All this had to be done in minutes, for Wayne's men were by this time under heavy attack by British dragoons and grenadiers.

Fortunately for the Americans, the artillery under Henry Knox was stationed on both of their flanks, especially on the right atop a rise known as Comb's Hill. Here, under able command, the heavy guns were in a position to enfilade the enemy, which they did with enough telling effect to repulse a charge of redcoats. As it would in later wars, American artillery had already learned to fight tactically as well as from a strategic position.

The British under Clinton and Cornwallis meantime pressed forward against the Americans as rapidly as heat and exhaustion would allow them. So strong was their impact that Wayne and his regiments were forced to give way. This worried Washington, although he was not surprised. He had been keeping an anxious eye on the British even as he tried to form his men for a counterattack. By now, he had learned the hard way that two sides function in a battle and a successful commander must be ever aware of this. So he sent up two additional regiments under Brigadier General James Varnum to reinforce Wayne. Washington, confident that Wayne was among his most reliable commanders, now ordered him to fall back and form another delaying position, leaving Varnum in charge of the first covering force. Wayne soon discovered a hedgerow between Greene and Stirling, and behind it he placed what scattered men he could assemble from his own and southern units.

With both sides now somewhat stabilized, the battle became an artillery duel. Excited at the opportunity, Knox threw his heaviest pieces into position on the American side of the ravine and proceeded with a bombardment such as he had not been able to achieve thus far in the war. Years later, his wife was to say that this hot day at Monmouth with its physical strain shortened the life of her corpulent husband. The two sides were separated now by less than a hundred yards across the ravine. The British brought up their own formidable field pieces as well as the famous Black Watch and other foot regiments. In addition to the artillery roar, a continual volley of musket fire flew from both sides, new units arriving at the line bringing their own firepower into play. For an hour, the guns pounded away, the noise was deafening and the weather was as hot as the engagement. General Sir Henry Clinton ordered his very best men into the fray and called for a victory. English and Hessian grenadiers as well as the fabled Coldstream Guards made valiant attempts but were thrown back repeatedly. Lord Cornwallis, in some ways Britain's best general, personally led the assault but found to his dismay that the once-green Americans now held their line in the manner of the best European soldiers.

And well they might. Washington and von Steuben saw with as much delight as a hot battle could allow that the results of the training at Valley Forge now bore martial fruit. Alexander Hamilton said that until he saw what the Americans did at Monmouth, he never had realized the value of military discipline. The raw recruits who had fled at the first musket shots now wheeled into line in orderly fashion much as if they were at a parade. They stood firm, Washington noted, as they repelled attack after attack and returned the enemy fire as steadily as it was delivered. Twice the British assailed Wayne's tough infantry line; twice they were thrown back with serious losses. Lieutenant Colonel Henry Monckton of the English Sherwood Foresters formed his men so close to the American line that they could hear him telling his grenadiers to move forward.

Anthony Wayne exhorted his troops and asked them to wait for "the king birds" before they fired. They did, and as Monckton and his men came on, the gallant British officer dropped right in front of the Patriot ranks.

But the determined Clinton still would not give up. He had sensed a conquest and meant to have it. Just as determined, however, was Washington. The fourth British assault was made in overwhelming numbers, and the heavy impact forced the Americans back. But they were in good order, and it was not a retreat but a strategic withdrawal. Wayne, Greene and Stirling all withdrew a short distance into strong positions. The enemy mistook the withdrawal for a retreat and came charging on, cheering with loud shouts. Then, as the redcoats were trying to re-form their onrushing tide, Wayne counterattacked and smacked them hard, driving them down a slope and back through a marsh they had just crossed.

By this time, Washington was thirsting for a victory and in his ardor hastily planned a final assault on the British. He cast about for fresh troops and thought for the moment that some Virginians and North Carolinians might simultaneously attack the enemy on its flanks. But then he realized that it was near the end of the day and wisely called off the attempt. Meanwhile, Clinton also became conscious of the time of day and decided that he could not force the Americans from their positions. He withdrew his men to a safe location out of range of the American artillery and bivouacked—so Washington thought—for the night.

Now that the sun was dropping and twilight coolness came to the sweating and tired combatants, Washington could begin to relax for the first time in many anxious hours. After seeing that his army was well encamped and alert, he slumped down under an oak tree and drew his big cloak over him as he fell asleep, having given orders for a dawn attack and for plenty of food and ammunition to be brought up during the night. He and his leaders felt that they had won some kind of victory; at least they had stood off the British. Now both sides must rest.

But when he awoke next morning, Washington could see no redcoats anywhere. Clinton had taken a leaf from Washington's book when he had escaped from Cornwallis at Trenton, and at midnight had stealthily slipped away. By the end of June the British were at Sandy Hook and within five days more were in New York City. Reports of the Battle of Monmouth stated that the Americans had sustained 360 casualties, including 40 dead from sunstroke. The British suffered about the same number lost, with even more dying from the heat. Subsequent estimates place the losses at about twice the reported number on both sides, with many of the British and Hessians having deserted while on the march from Philadelphia.

Washington could claim a victory but so could the British. The Americans had showed that they could withstand the best the British had; the English were disappointed that they had not gained more. Both sides had displayed courage and bravery. In more ways than one, this was the "hottest battle of the war," as it was the longest and also the last major engagement fought in the North.

Washington got off a brief note to President Laurens of the Continental Congress: "I have the honor to inform you," he wrote, "that about 7 o'clock yesterday morning, both armies advanced on each other. About 12 o'clock they met on the grounds near Monmouth Court House, when an action commenced. We forced the enemy from the field and encamped on their ground. They took a strong post in our front, secured on both flanks by morasses and thick woods where they remained until about 12 at night, and then retreated. I cannot at this time go into a detail of matters . . ."

Even if he did not go into detail, Washington gave a succinct account of what happened, slightly colored from his viewpoint. But not only Washington was happy about the outcome. Henry Knox wrote his wife Lucy: "Indeed upon the whole it is very splendid. The capital army of Britain defeated and obliged to retreat before the Americans." The dynamic Anthony Wayne, one of the heroes of the fray, wrote that he wanted Philadelphians to know "the heavenly sweet pretty Red Coats, the accomplished gentlemen of the Guards and Grenadiers, have humbled themselves on the plains of Monmouth. The Knights of the Blended Rose and the Burning Mountain have resigned their laurels to the Rebel officers."

But not untypically, the Americans overcelebrated. Some of them were accused of stealing articles that residents of the vicinity had hidden from the British, and Washington threatened death to any man convicted of such thefts. Then he and his staff rested and picnicked at Passaic on cold ham, biscuits and clear water from a nearby spring.

Lee was still smarting under his tongue-lashing and communicated his feelings to Washington, writing that he had been accused unjustly and demanding "some reparation." Washington replied at once that he would soon have such an opportunity. Lee asked for a court-martial. It was forthwith granted, and Lee was found guilty of disobeying orders, of making an unnecessary and disorderly retreat and of disrespect for the commander-in-chief. He was sentenced to be suspended from the army for twelve months and the verdict was approved by Congress. Lee might have been reinstated, however, but months later he wrote a letter to Congress which contained insults to that body, whereupon he was suspended.

Confidence in his troops and himself now restored, Washington could look ahead with growing hopes and plans for a more definitive advantage over the enemy. Fitting opportunities were not long in coming.

IX VARIETY IN THE NORTHEAST

AFTER THE BATTLE OF MONMOUTH, Washington, exhausted, realized that his men must feel the same way. He therefore allowed Clinton to proceed on his way to New York without bothering him. Clinton soon arrived at Sandy Hook, where Lord Howe's transport vessels were waiting to take him the rest of the way. For a few days, the American army relaxed at Englishtown. Then Washington issued orders for the men to wash themselves in order to appear as decent as possible; he asked them to "publicly unite in thanksgiving to the Supreme Disposer of Human Events for the victory which was obtained on Sunday over the flower of the British troops." He was determined to consider Monmouth a victory and wanted his troops to feel the same way.

On July 1, they started northward by way of New Brunswick, Scotch Plains, Paramus and went on to the Hudson River, where they crossed and encamped near White Plains. The journey required about two weeks. Upon his arrival Washington stated: "It is not a little pleasing, nor less wonderful to contemplate, that after two years of maneuvering, both armies are brought back to the very point they set out from and that which was the offending party in the beginning is now reduced to the use of the spade and pickaxe for defence." He may have been relieved at the turn of events and given much credit to Providence, but several years were to pass before he would be victorious.

Meanwhile, more good news ensued. It was proclaimed in a kind of biblical way, reminiscent of the killing of the fatted calf. Washington asked his commissary department for "Fifty of your best bullocks and two hundred sheep, if they can be procured, and a quantity of poultry." These were to be presented to Charles Henri Théodat, otherwise known as the Count d'Estaing, admiral of the French navy. This new help from France—first of all an enemy of Great Britain and still smarting over its defeat in the French and Indian War—was to mean more in troops, money and morale than Washington could know.

If the count had arrived just ten days sooner and had swung into Delaware Bay in time to cut off Howe's fleet before it left Philadelphia, the war might have been won for the Americans years earlier. Even so, the French admiral with his twelve fine ships of the line and four fast frigates carrying 834 guns and four thousand troops lay off Sandy Hook. He was attempting to bring the British ships, with 300 fewer guns, to bay. But the water there was too shallow for the deep-draft French vessels, and despite trials guided by pilots sent by Washington, the Frenchmen could not move inward. For eleven days, d'Estaing waited outside Sandy Hook trying to find a way to get inside. He offered fifty thousand crowns to anyone who would take him over the bar and into the bight where lay the tempting target of Howe's fleet. But no one came forward.

Washington was now excited by hopes of making some use of this new addition to his forces. He suggested that Count d'Estaing sail north to Rhode Island and there capture Newport, which had been in British possession ever since December, 1776, and now held by Sir Robert Pigot and three thousand redcoats. D'Estaing agreed to the plan and sailed to Point Judith near Newport, arriving on July 29. At Providence, General John Sullivan had been in command of about one thousand Continental troops since March, and Washington now saw a chance to squeeze the British between the French fleet and his own ground forces attacking from Rhode Island. Washington urged Sullivan to gather troops from Rhode Island, Massachusetts and Connecticut. He wrote Sullivan, "You will, I am well assured, pursue every measure in your power that can render the enterprise happy and fortunate, and as success will depend in a great degree on the promptness and energy of its execution, I trust the conduct will answer the spirit and hopes of the expedition."

Sullivan was also asked to collect boats and pilots and prepare everything for an assault on Newport in conjunction with the French fleet and its troops. There certainly was no lack of preparation. Washington even dispatched a doctor and two assistants to establish a medical unit, and Sullivan asked General William Heath to send four or five "eminent surgeons with instruments and every necessity for restoring broken limbs and raising men from the dead." Sullivan was eager if not always realistic.

He wrote Washington on July 26: "Every effort of mine to prepare for executing Your Excellency's orders has succeeded beyond my most sanguine expectations and everything now promises success. I find I shall have a sufficiency of stores of every kind and I hope boats and troops enough to make the attempt with a moral certainty of success." Sullivan had already told d'Estaing that there probably would be a delay in the arrival of the Americans. But for some reason, perhaps because of his previous misfortunes in Canada, on Staten Island and at Brandywine, Sullivan seemed to want Washington to be sure that this time he would bring off a victory.

General Sullivan was not alone in his optimism. Admiral

d'Estaing caught some of it and wrote Washington later that the New Hampshire general was "full of that spirit of activity and confidence with which you inspire all those who have served under your orders." But Washington heard that Sullivan planned to storm the British position and he was wary of this. He wrote Sullivan, "I will only say, that as I would not on the one hand wish to check the ardor of our troops, so I would not upon the other put them upon attempting what I thought they could not carry but with a moral certainty of success. You know the discipline of our men and officers very well, and I hope you and the general officers under your command will weigh every desperate matter well before it is carried into execution. A severe check may ruin the expedition, while regular and determined approaches may effect the work, though perhaps they may take somewhat longer time. Upon the whole, I will not undertake at this distance to give orders. I submit everything to your prudence and to the good advice of those about you."

The foregoing letter may well express Washington's military philosophy, tactful yet definite, delegating authority but reminding his general that good results were expected nonetheless and urging that the best advice available be taken advantage of at all times—which Washington himself practiced diligently. He may have had in mind, too, that General Nathanael Greene was going to serve under Sullivan. Greene was very willing to do so, though he outranked Sullivan in seniority; but Washington always liked to have the counsel of Greene, a Rhode Islander himself, and was often falsely accused of being too much under the influence of Greene and Knox.

To back up his advice, Washington sent Sullivan two of his most prized brigades, Varnum's Rhode Islanders and Glover's skilled Marblehead, Massachusetts, Mariners, who had helped ferry the Americans so effectively in the battle for New York City and in the hazardous crossing of the Delaware on the snowy night of the Battle of Trenton. Sullivan and d'Estaing agreed that the four thousand French troops would land on the west side of Newport Island while the Americans would at the same time land on the east side, with Glover's Mariners manning the landing craft. The British had sunk some of their own vessels at the entrance to Newport Harbor to prevent the French from coming in, but this left the French in control of the surrounding waters.

The plan probably would have worked, but Sullivan, apparently overanxious, did not wait to consult d'Estaing as he had agreed, and made a quick crossing on the northern tip of the island a day ahead of the schedule. This premature action, which Sullivan thought was justified, infuriated the volatile French admiral. D'Estaing was the equivalent of a lieutenant general, Sullivan only a major general. So d'Estaing recalled what few troops he had put ashore and set out in his ships to engage the British fleet, which by this time had been reinforced and was not far away at sea. D'Estaing had the wind favoring him and would have taken on the British, but the weather took a hand in the action. A strong gale blew in and scattered both fleets before they could get into position. Both admirals, d'Estaing and Howe, withdrew their ships for needed repairs, Howe sailing back to New York and d'Estaing to Boston (to the discomfiture of Sullivan). The Frenchman did not wish to help the American any longer anyway because of what was felt to be a lack of cooperation and because of derogatory remarks Sullivan was reported to have made about d'Estaing in general orders. About a thousand New England militia left in a body, and Sullivan, after having to fight a rear-guard action against the pursuing British under Pigot, took his four thousand Continentals and left the scene. Washington heard the news with dismay.

Part of Washington's disappointment came from the fact that Americans had expected success at Newport, had even looked forward to decisive and encouraging results. At first blame for the failure was placed on Count d'Estaing, probably because he was the most conveniently available scapegoat. Sullivan was not averse to joining in his criticism and in general orders criticized the French admiral for not having stayed to help the Americans against the British. In Boston, where the French fleet was temporarily anchored, fights broke out between American and French sailors and soldiers, as a result of which a French officer died of injuries. D'Estaing wrote a stinging letter to Congress in which he showed his resentment.

But cooler heads prevailed. Washington became singularly uneasy and told General Sullivan that the French were "a people old in war, very strict in military etiquette and apt to take fire where others are scarcely warmed." Added to this figure of speech, he urged "in the most particular manner, the cultivation of harmony and good agreement and your endeavors to destroy that ill humor which may have got into the officers." No doubt at the instigation of Washington, Congress passed a resolution that "Count d'Estaing hath behaved as a wise and brave officer and that his Excellency and the officers and men under his command have rendered every benefit to these states, which the circumstances and nature of the service would admit of and are fully entitled to the regards of the friends of America." So d'Estaing was appeased, and after his ships were refitted he sailed off to Martinique with his troops, rather to the satisfaction of the people of Boston.

Now Washington turned from dismay to puzzlement. He could not figure out what General Clinton in New York was up to. In fact, Washington's Revolutionary correspondence is replete with wonder at what his opponents had in mind for their next move. Howe, Clinton and Cornwallis had him guessing so much that one marvels that he ever fathomed their intentions. After the Newport debacle, Clinton remained in New York, and his American adversary did not know whether this was from choice or chance. Just to make sure, Washington made tighter his land blockade of the metropolis by forming a belt of semiencirclement some forty miles long from southern New England to the highlands of the Hudson. Putnam was placed at West Point, Gates and McDougall at Danbury and Stirling on the heights that rose above Lake Mahopac.

With the British effort now mainly on the seas with France, the American phase of the war became for the time comparatively minor. In this summer of 1778, Washington had about 16,800 men fit for duty, most of them stationed around White Plains until the circling positions described above were decided upon. In October, a sizeable shipment of clothing arrived from France and was warmly welcomed by the ragged Continentals. Though waistcoats and breeches were similar, some coats were blue, others red and some a mixture. Washington tried to parcel these out by states so each would have a distinctive color; this plan was not very successful because of the proportion of numbers of troops and clothing involved, but at least the men's comfort was improved.

Meanwhile, there were military clashes between Patriots and Tories. Many persons were indifferent and took sides only when they felt it would save their lives. Members of the same family, Washington found, who fought against each other did so with a bitterness foreign to ordinary soldiers.

General "No Flint" Charles Grey, the British officer who had so ruthlessly led his men against those of Wayne at Paoli, won a similar victory when he ambushed a detachment of Continental dragoons known as "Lady Washington's Own" at Old Tappan in northwestern New York. In a typical bayonet attack Grey's troops killed forty men and captured even more. Several British ships entered Little Egg Harbor in New Jersey, where American privateers had a habit of gathering, and destroyed ten of the vessels and burned the village. This naval attack was supported by the Tory volunteers of Major Patrick Ferguson, one of the most colorful British officers of the war who, as we have seen, once had the opportunity to shoot Washington. With some two hundred fifty men in small boats Ferguson, during the night of October 14, rowed up the coast to Mincock Island, surprised the light infantry of Count Casimir Pulaski of the American forces and bayoneted fifty men before being driven off.

Another British officer General Washington and his men came to dread was Lieutenant Colonel Banastre Tarleton, who had played a leading role in the earlier ludicrous capture of General Charles Lee in New Jersey. Tarleton, probably the best cavalry officer on either side, was a dashing, ruthless rider who had gathered together a detachment of New York Tories, both foot and cavalry, which he called the British Legion. And no legion of Romans was more feared than this bloodthirsty crew of cutthroats. They were especially well known for their thorough training in hit-and-run reconnaissance operations. Tarleton and his men established a reputation, which lasted down to his climactic foray at the Cowpens, for giving their prisoners no quarter but bayoneting them instead.

Following in the wake of other British sallies, Tarleton made a daring attempt to surprise one of Washington's outposts located at Pound Ridge just north of White Plains. The American force consisted of Colonel Elisha Sheldon and some ninety Continental Dragoons, among whom was Major Ebenezer Lockwood, an extremely active patriot who had been such a thorn in the side of the British that they had posted a reward for his capture. Tarleton and three hundred and fifty of his men swooped down upon Sheldon's smaller force, but the Americans had meanwhile been warned by one of Washington's spies of the impending attack and were not surprised. Even so, Sheldon's men were at first pushed back, but with the help of some local militia they counterattacked and repulsed the raiders, who then retreated.

By now it was November of 1778, and the activity on both sides was cut down by both the weather and an inability to mount any major new offensive. The British under Clinton were depleted by the departure of five thousand troops commanded by General James Grant, who took this force to the West Indies, there to participate in a land and sea operation against the French on their island of St. Lucia. Another British force almost as large was sent to Georgia and Florida. Washington could now breathe easier, for the time being at least, so he turned his attention to taking his men into winter quarters and trying to prepare for the future.

Morristown, New Jersey, was the place he selected for his main army. It is a picturesque place set among the rolling hills of the midnorthern part of the state. Washington found it a desirable place for encampment. However, bad weather and other adverse conditions were to dampen its suitability. (Here, his brilliant and impetuous aide Alexander Hamilton met and courted Elizabeth Schuyler, whom he later married.)

Troops were also stationed at Middlebrook, Elizabeth and Ramapo, New Jersey, as well as at West Point and Fishkill, New York, and Danbury, Connecticut, forming a kind of half-circle with a forty-mile radius around New York City and key points in the Hudson highlands. Having learned about preparations for winter during the ordeal of Valley Forge, the soldiers were now instructed to build log cabins. As for their clothing, they were generally better off than at Valley Forge but still needed blankets, hats and shoes and of course proper food.

Washington issued a general order on October 2, 1779, which established the uniform of the Continental army. Until khaki came into use in the Spanish-American War, blue was the basic color of United States soldiers.

Occasionally, a hint of humor shone through Washington's usually austere character. On August 16, 1779, he wrote to Surgeon and Mrs. John Cochran to invite them and others to dine with him. "It is needless to promise that my table is large enough to hold the ladies," he wrote. "Of this, they had ocular proof yesterday. To say how it is usually covered, is rather more essential; and this shall be the purport of my letter. Since our arrival at this happy spot, we have had a ham, sometimes a shoulder of bacon to grace the head of the table; a piece of roast beef adorns the foot; and a dish of beans or greens, almost imperceptible, decorates the center. When the cook has a mind to cut a figure, (which I presume will be the case tomorrow) we have two beef-steak pies or dishes of crabs in addition, one on each side of the center dish, dividing the space and reducing the distance between dish and dish to about 6 feet, which would without them be near 12 feet apart. Of late, he has had the surprising sagacity to discover that apples will make pies; and it is a question, if in the violence of his efforts, we do not get one of apples, instead of having both beef-steaks. If the ladies can put up with such entertainment, and will submit to partake of it on plates, once tin but now iron (not become so by the labor of scouring), I shall be happy to see them."

Meanwhile, Washington's attention had turned to other operations taking place in the American interior, rather dramatically in northwestern New York and northern Pennsylvania, from the time Burgoyne was defeated at Saratoga until the end of the war. It was an internecine struggle, neighbor against neighbor and whites and Indians involved on both sides. One of the phases of the American Revolution most neglected by historians has been that of the Tories versus the Patriots, which has only received attention in recent years. For example, in July of 1778, Sir John Butler led a force of Indians and Tories in a bloody sweep through the beautiful Wyoming Valley of Pennsylvania, butchering the inhabitants as they went. The event has been called the "surpassing horror of the Revolution" and brought sadness to Washington. Later in the year, Butler's Tory Rangers and Chief Brant's Indians committed similar outrages in the Cherry Valley region, climaxed in the massacre of forty of the survivors even after they had surrendered.

In the meantime, George Rogers Clark, a Kentucky militia leader who had appealed to Patrick Henry for aid in fighting the British, Indians and Tories to the west, was also making his mark. During the summer of 1778, with some one hundred seventy-five men, Clark had occupied the post of Kaskia, Illinois, on the lower Ohio River, and also taken other points nearby. A few months later, Clark captured Vincennes, which had been held by British Colonel Henry Hamilton—nicknamed "the hair buyer"—former lieutenant governor at Detroit. But the Americans were not so successful in the South. In the last days of December, 1778, the British, aided by local Tories, captured Savannah.

Comparatively, there were few military operations by either side during the winter of 1778–1779. But British officials had not been idle regarding their colonies. Lord North had sent over a peace mission headed by the Earl of Carlisle that offered a settlement to the Americans almost on their own terms. But things had gone too far, and it failed. Concerned by the failure of the peace mission, Lord George Germain urged General Clinton to force Washington into a decisive engagement and defeat him. The trouble was, however, that Washington would not allow himself to be pushed into a European-style confrontation on the field. There, he rightly reasoned, he would be defeated.

If Clinton could not corner Washington, Germain advised, then he could drive him into the mountains out of contact with the British forces, while the latter would harry the coasts of New England and the South and attack the settlements on the western frontier. Clinton's reply was significant: every campaign of the war had been designed to force a general and definite action upon Washington. General Sir William Howe with the largest force of redcoats in the history of Great Britain had not been successful in bringing about a confrontation; how could Clinton? He answered that he would do his utmost but was not optimistic that he would succeed.

General Sir Henry Clinton was an odd character. Admittedly an able man, he spent much of his time complaining instead of planning and executing. So much was he concerned with real and imagined wrongs to himself by others that a recent biographer has devoted a whole chapter to a psychologist's analysis of his personality (a rather far-fetched attempt in view of the fact that the analytic material is almost two hundred years old). Even so, Clinton waited less than two weeks after making his excuses to Germain before taking steps. As has been mentioned, Washington had spread out his forces in a semicircle; through the winter and into the spring, he concentrated on building up the defenses of the Hudson River region, especially at West Point, which as yet held no military academy but was an important outpost. Washington also built two forts, one at Verplanck's Point on the eastern side of the river and another at Stony Point on a rocky promontory opposite.

Clinton was of course aware of what was going on not far from his own headquarters in New York City. If he could not split the New England portion of the new nation from its southern part, at least, he reasoned, he could make communications between them more difficult. On May 28, he assembled at Kingsbridge six thousand of his best men and placed himself at their head. They were British and Hessian grenadiers, dragoons, light infantry, Jaegers and the Tory regiments of Simcoe and Ferguson. On May 30, they embarked in sailing vessels and flat-bottomed boats and two days later landed on both sides of the Hudson at Stony Point and Verplanck's Point just below Peekskill, the gateway to the Hudson highlands. The two American forts surrendered without much of a struggle.

Their capture caused Washington some concern, but what he feared most was losing the bastion of West Point, only fifteen miles north. He concentrated his army between Stony Point and West Point, and Clinton stopped. At this time, the Americans held a favorable position in a place called Smith's Clove, a level plain of land located at the base of high mountains on the west side of the Hudson. West Point then was known as "the key to the Continent."

Clinton evidently regarded Stony Point as a kind of key also, for he immediately set about building it into what he hoped would be an unassailable fortress. It was on "a defiant promontory" jutting out into the Hudson for more than half a mile and extending one hundred and fifty feet high. The Point formed a virtual citadel with batteries commanding a full circle, rough and rocky on the river front and falling off into a rocky marsh behind. Two rings of abatis protected its base, and when the tide was high, the island could be reached only by a causeway, which connected with a road leading to King's Ferry. Here Clinton erected a double set of defense works with eight batteries joined by trenches. The garrison consisted of foot soldiers, Highlanders, Tories and artillerymen, over six hundred men in all.

How to regain Stony Point? Most of his officers thought Washington was foolhardy even to consider it now. Washington dreamed of a highly mobile, hard-hitting elite corps of light infantry that could maneuver when needed and fight hard when necessary. Daniel Morgan came to mind, a man who was to become a brilliant field general. Morgan was fresh from his illustrious success at Saratoga and wanted the assignment to take Stony Point; he felt this mission would help him be promoted from colonel to brigadier general. When he did not get the position, he resigned and went home to Virginia for a time.

But Washington had other considerations. He was personally fond of Daniel Morgan; he especially appreciated Morgan's loyalty when he had been asked to join the Conway Cabal and had replied that he would fight under no one but Washington. Anthony Wayne, however, also had a big claim. He had stood out as a combat commander at Brandywine, Germantown and especially at Monmouth, where he so distinguished himself that he was singled out for special praise in Washington's report on the battle to Congress. Also, there were political considerations Washington did not often lose sight of, though he rarely admitted it. If Morgan, a Virginian, were chosen, Washington might be accused of favoritism to his own state. Too, Wayne thirsted for revenge for the massacre at Paoli.

So the Pennsylvanian got the assignment. He was a stern disciplinarian, who was particular about his appearance and demanded the same of his men; he insisted they be "fresh shaven and well powdered." They were all veterans between twenty and thirty years of age, tall, sinewy, active and dependable, drawn from every state and especially adept in the use of the bayonet. Washington asked Wayne to select a trustworthy and able man to enter the British encampment and determine the type and strength of the garrison. Captain Allen McLane, one of the most romantic figures of the American army, was chosen. Disguised as a farmer wearing a hunting shirt, and accompanying a Mrs. Smith who wished to see her sons there, McLane slipped into the fort and obtained the information. On the basis of his report, Washington drew up a plan for attack and gave it to Wayne.

The plan was followed with ardor and efficiency. On the morning of July 15, 1779, Wayne's force of some 1,350 picked men assembled at Sandy Beach, a few miles below West Point. Promptly they set out on a march of thirteen miles southwestward, passing elevations with the euphonious names of Torn Mountain, Bear Mountain and Donderberg, making their way over circuitous roads, through morasses and narrow passes. By early evening, they were within a mile of Stony Point but behind it so as to be out of sight of the enemy. Here Wayne gave them their orders, most of the men not yet being aware of their real mission up till now.

With the exception of one battalion that was to have a special advance mission, none of the muskets was to be loaded; the bayonet was to be the only weapon. Shades of Paoli! Penalty for even taking a gun from the shoulder or trying to fire it or loitering was to be instant death at the hands of the nearest officer. Silence was imperative for success. Wayne wanted no foolishness, and anyone caught retreating would be summarily executed. A volunteer force of three hundred went ahead with axes and slung muskets to cut through hindering fortifications. Anyone found making noise in the line of march was to be taken into custody and silenced, any dogs encountered were to be dispatched to keep them from barking. A small number, called "the forlorn hope"—our modern suicide squads—preceded the axmen, dashing through openings and engaging the enemy hand to hand. For identification in the darkness and to distinguish them from the British each man wore a piece of white paper in his hat. When they got inside the fort, they were to shout loudly and incessantly, "The fort's our own!" Prizes from one hundred to five hundred dollars were to be given to the first five who entered the fort.

At midnight, the tense columns moved out in silence. One was led by Colonel Richard Butler, an outstanding and trusted officer of the Pennsylvania Line, and the other column by Anthony Wayne himself. The tide was still up, and the men had to wade quietly through water two feet deep before they reached solid ground. But they were not quiet enough. A British sentry perched alertly on a pinnacle heard the watery sounds and gave the alarm. Almost instantly the garrison sprang to arms and, catching sight of the American close-order columns moving in, opened up with grape, roundshot and musket fire. But instead of panicking, the invading soldiers simply fanned out, a result of von Steuben's training and the discipline of Washington and Wayne. They pressed forward up the slope to solid ground and then reached the abatis of the fort, just as the left assaulting column appeared on the causeway to the north.

The axmen swung at the wooden abatis and quickly opened holes in it. The forlorn hope squeezed through, some of them to be cut down by the now fully aroused British, under Lieutenant Colonel Henry Johnson. But others crowded through, those with axes reaching and chopping away at the inner ring of defenses, while the advance American party, which had been allowed ammunition, exchanged fire with the redcoats. The main force followed, their guns still silent, and rushed toward the citadel, which was by this time blazing with gunfire from the defenders. A musket ball grazed Wayne's head and he fell. He was only stunned, though blood poured from the wound. Almost instantly, however, he raised himself on one knee, was propped up by his men and ordered all to go forward. Seeing their leader wounded, they were angered and inspired to seek revenge; they drove ever harder into the fort, bounding over rocks, their bayonets shining, until they reached the parapet and poured inside. Ten minutes later, Butler's column joined them from the opposite side.

The first man to enter the fort—and therefore entitled to the first cash prize—was not an American but a French officer, Lieutenant Colonel François L. de Fleury. An example of what happened to the first contingents was Lieutenant James Gibbons, in charge of a forlorn hope. His clothes were torn to rags, he was muddy up to his neck, and his detachment of twenty men lost fifteen in the charge. But Wayne's men were giving a good account of themselves. With their bayonets they ripped into the redcoats, shouting as they slashed, and amid their cries of possessing the fort, for a time avenged the massacre at Paoli. The British must have sensed this, for they began calling for mercy and throwing down their arms. Colonel Johnson tried valiantly to stem the tide of surrender, but he too finally threw down his sword.

The two formations of Americans converging from left and right drove the defenders into huddles of frightened men. A few British inside their log barracks held out for a time, then gave up too. The attack lasted for just thirty minutes, but its results were decisive. The British lost 63 dead, more than 70 wounded and 543 captured, only one man escaping, a lieutenant who managed to swim out to the sloop-of-war *Vulture,* anchored in the Hudson. The Americans lost only 15 dead and 80 wounded. A large amount of military equipment including heavy artillery was captured. The big guns were at once turned upon the *Vulture,* which soon upped anchor and took off like its namesake.

After allowing Wayne the glory of the victory, Washington inspected the captured fort and was elated. But he soon saw it was an empty conquest from a practical standpoint. He decided "it would require more men to maintain than we could afford" and ordered that it be abandoned as soon as the guns and stores were removed and the works destroyed.

The victory gave the American cause a bright lift. It also made a special impact on Major Henry Lee, Jr., a spirited twenty-two-year-old cavalryman, who was a friend of Washington's. His nickname of "Light Horse Harry" was well chosen, and although he was to prove himself erratic and was at times dispirited, there was no doubt regarding his military ability and courage, which was to be displayed later by his son Robert E. Lee. But at this time, the envy of young Henry Lee was aroused. He liked the limelight, and now Anthony Wayne had seized it and was the toast of the colonies because of his successful storming of Stony Point. Lee looked around for an opportunity to bring himself to the fore.

The chance came as a result of the keen scouting eyes of Captain Allen McLane, that remarkable ranger whose exploits have not yet been given the general credit due them. McLane and his company had been roaming through the country from Stony Point to Paulus Hook for several weeks, riding here and there when something suspicious was reported. They then transmitted their information to Major Lee at his headquarters in Paramus, New Jersey. Lee at length suggested that the fortification at Paulus Hook be taken in the same manner as Stony Point.

Lee, having good access to his fellow Virginian and being from an aristocratic family himself, broached the idea to Washington. At first it received a cool reception. After all, Lee was young enough to be Washington's son; he was probably known to be at times somewhat brash and possibly tactless. Then, too, the risks could well be greater than the results, considering the number of men involved and the difficulty of holding the fort after it was captured—if it should be.

But because the plan was presented so persuasively and because Washington needed more victories at this time, he finally consented. Paulus Hook was described as a low, projecting point of land—now a part of Jersey City—on the west bank of the Hudson just opposite New York City, bounded on its inner side by dank salt meadows then accessible by only one marshy road. It was separated from the mainland by a creek that could be crossed at only two points and a deep ditch running all the way across the peninsula, making it virtually an island. Access was by a drawbridge across the ditch that was protected by a sturdy gate. Two rows of abatis formed a kind of defense on the land side of the fort, with the side facing the water protected by an extension of the abatis and other breastworks. Inside the enclosure were two redoubts containing heavy artillery pieces; a blockhouse guarded the drawbridge entrance, another overlooked the river. Barracks were within, and the post was defended by British foot soldiers, Tory troops, Hessians, light infantry and part of an invalid battalion. It was a position of strength, commanded by Major William Sutherland.

Lee knew of the strength and composition of the garrison, having been informed by intelligence reports. In fact, McLane had such a detailed description of the troops inside the fort that he made an appointment with Lee in order to inform him and also to conduct him safely to the objective. His plan was to take Paulus Hook with bayonets, after the manner in which Wayne had been so successful. He pointed out to Washington that success, even when emulated, is better than risk of failure because of a more original approach.

The assault force, however, would be only four hundred men, a much smaller body than that available for Stony Point. They were to be divided into three columns, the right composed of Virginians under Major Jonathan Clark, the center of men from Maryland and the left McLane's dismounted dragoons and some other Virginians, to be led personally by Major Lee. There were to be three forlorn hopes led by selected officers. The well-planned expedition left Paramus at midmorning on August 18, accompanied by several wagons so as to give the appearance of a party in search of forage. They rendezvoused at the New Bridge across the Hackensack River some fourteen miles from Paulus Hook and by 4 P.M. were over the bridge and moving eastward on the Bergen Road. At this rate, they should have reached their objective by midnight, but all did not go well. For some unknown reason, either from ignorance or on purpose, the main guide led the troops off their course and into deep woods, which delayed them extra hours. Major Clark raised the question of why he, whose rank was dated earlier than Lee's, should serve under him. As a result of the altercation, about half the Virginia soldiers abandoned the expedition. Even so, Clark remained.

Despite these unexpected setbacks, the determined Lee pressed on. But it was 4 A.M. before he reached the marshland behind the Hook, and the approaching daylight as well as the rising tide would certainly ruin his chance of surprise. Quickly he re-formed his men into two columns, with axmen and forlorn hopes heading each. Muskets were loaded but not primed, bayonets were fixed and the men had orders to move along in complete silence, death to be the fate of any man who took his musket from his shoulder until ordered to do so. As a precaution, each soldier must hold his hat in his right hand and against his thigh until the ditch was reached.

The men moved on and all worked well for a while. For two arduous miles they had to wade through the marsh in water up to their waists. Then they hit the ditch and could not help but make a splash. This noise aroused the British sentinels, who greeted the invaders with weak musket fire. Paying little attention to this, the advance units ripped into the fortifications, axes swinging at the abatis. Clark's men were the first to gain the interior. The charge carried not only through the first but the second line of defense as well, with most of the shocked garrison giving up after only a brief resistance. Not a shot was fired by the American invaders, but 50 of the British lay dead, victims of the bayonets. A total of 158 surrendered as prisoners, all except Major Sutherland and some 40 or 50 Hessians who ensconced themselves in a small blockhouse and refused to yield. The Americans lost only 2 dead and 3 wounded.

But possession of the fort at Paulus Hook was short-lived. The main object of the Americans was capture of the garrison, which had been accomplished. The post was too near the strong British army in New York, and now the aim was to get out of the place as soon as possible before the enemy could come from New York and cut off the retreat. Alarm guns were already alerting the British. A suggestion was made to Lee that he burn the barracks before leaving, but he turned this down when he learned that women, sick soldiers and children were inside the fort. So the retreat began.

Henry Lee then realized for the first time what a precarious situation he was in. He dashed for New Bridge, where a detachment from Lord Stirling was supposed to meet him with boats, but found none there. His men's ammunition was useless for it had become wet when the men had waded in the marsh. Most of his troops were worn out, so he dispatched the least fatigued to cover his retreat. Tories struck his right flank, but the arrival of a few reinforcements with dry powder enabled Lee to hold them off until he and his men were safe on the other side of New Bridge with their prisoners.

The country resounded with praise. Congress came through with a vote of thanks, a medal for Light Horse Harry Lee and fifteen thousand dollars for his troops—but in almost worthless Continental currency.

ABOVE Washington at Cambridge taking command of the Army.
Drawn by C. S. Reinhart (*Prints Division, New York Public Library*)

BELOW Washington's retreat at Long Island (*Prints Division,
New York Public Library*)

ABOVE Washington crossing the Delaware (*Prints Division, New York Public Library*)

BELOW Surrender of Colonel Rall at the Battle of Trenton (*Prints Division, New York Public Library*)

OPPOSITE ABOVE Washington at Valley Forge (*Prints Division, New York Public Library*)

OPPOSITE BELOW Washington at Monmouth (*Prints Division, New York Public Library*)

LEFT General Washington firing the first gun in the bombardment of the British works at the Battle of Yorktown, October 9, 1781 (*Prints Division, New York Public Library*)

BELOW Washington's farewell to his officers at Fraunces Tavern, New York City. He is embracing General Henry Knox (*Prints Division, New York Public Library*)

X HARDSHIP AND BETRAYAL

THE EPISODE of Paulus Hook ended the military campaigns of both armies for the year 1779. For a time, Washington had his soldiers engaged in fortifying West Point and continuing their helpful drill under von Steuben. Cornwallis came from England bringing more British troops, these making Clinton's New York garrison over twenty-eight thousand strong. On paper, Washington had just about a thousand fewer men, but actually only fifteen thousand were enlisted for as long as three years or the war's duration. In explanation, Washington wrote Congress that "it could not be supposed that the whole of the troops borne on the muster rolls were either in service or really in existence, for it will ever be found for obvious reasons that the amount of an army on paper will greatly exceed its real strength."

Until November, Washington kept most of his army at West Point in the realization that effective action was at a virtual standstill. He hoped that Count d'Estaing might do something "important and interesting" with his fleet against the British. But that French gentleman had gone to besiege Savannah, and after his assault there met with defeat, he dispatched some of his ships to the West Indies and with the rest sailed for France, much to the disappointment of Washington. Now that the British controlled the sea bordering the colonies, Washington realized there was little he could do, so he took his men into winter quarters.

Again, the place chosen was in and around Morristown. In order to guard against any northerly incursions, Washington sent a brigade to Danbury, while four others remained at West Point. The journey of the main part of the army to Morristown proved to be arduous, some of the Americans crossing a countryside that was almost unpopulated. As a result of the cold and snow, the hazardous roads and exposure to the rain and sleet, a number of them became ill; not a few died. Dr. James Thacher, an army surgeon, gave the following description in his journal: "We marched through deep snow . . . it being late at night before our men could all find accommodations in the scattered houses and barns along the road . . . reached this wilderness about three miles from Morristown where we are to build log huts for winter quarters. Our baggage is left in the rear for want of wagons to transport it. The snow on the ground is about two feet deep and the weather extremely cold; the soldiers are destitute of both tents and blankets and some of them are actually barefooted and almost naked. Our only defense against the inclemency of the weather consists of brushwood thrown together. Our lodging last night was on frozen ground."

This was to be the hardest winter of the war, far more severe than the one at Valley Forge. It was said to be the worst winter in the memories of the oldest residents, snow at times covering the roads under four-foot blankets, the harbor at New York being frozen over. Lumber for the huts had to be cut from standing trees, and this required weeks. Even in January, most of the men were still in frigid tents. Then came a tremendous snowstorm that covered not only the ground but some of the soldiers inside their tents, shivering on beds of straw with one blanket apiece. The depth of the snow through the cruel winter ranged from two to six feet, and Baron de Kalb reported that even though he was seated near the fire, the ink froze in his pen while he was trying to write.

Food was a great problem as well. In desperation, Washington wrote to governors of nearby states just before Christmas, telling them that the lack of supplies in his army was "beyond description alarming," explaining that the men for five or six weeks had been on a half-rations allowance and that now there was only a three-day supply of bread on hand. The commissary was destitute of money or credit. "We have never experienced a like extremity at any period of the war," Washington added. "Unless some extraordinary and immediate exertions are made by the states from which we draw our supplies, there is every appearance that the army will infallibly disband in a fortnight."

Harsh words but appropriate. Some states responded, but the collective result was not enough. Within a month, the sad situation was worse and the soldiers on the point of starvation and literally freezing. Hunger leads to hopelessness and then to desperation. The emaciated wretches began to take matters into their own hands. Nor could Washington blame them. "They have borne their distress," he wrote, "with as much fortitude as human nature is capable of; but they have been at last brought to such dreadful extremity that no authority or influence of the officers could any longer restrain them from obeying the dictates of their own sufferings. The soldiers have in several instances plundered the neighboring inhabitants even of their necessary subsistence."

The time had come for severe measures, and Washington knew this all too well. He divided New Jersey into eleven districts and assigned the amount of grain and beef to be furnished by each of them. Troops under selected officers were sent to collect the provisions, and there was to be no foolishness about complying. Even so, Washington insisted that the missions were to be carried out tactfully. The officers, among them Major Henry Lee, were first to approach the magistrates of the various districts and ask for their help and cooperation. "You will at the same time," Washington ordered, "delicately let them know you are instructed, in case they do not take up the business immediately, to begin to impress the articles called for . . . This you will do with as much tenderness as possible to the inhabitants."

This method worked. By the end of January, Washington was able to write to Congress, "The situation of the army for the present is, and has been for some days past, comfortable and easy on the score of provisions. . . . The Jerseymen gave the earliest and most cheerful attention to my requisitions and exerted themselves for the army's relief in a manner that did them the highest honor. They more than complied with the requisitions in many instances." He was somewhat oversanguine, however, or at least premature, for by March new appeals had to be made to the states for food for the hungry soldiers. The problem was not so much the lack of necessary provisions but the scarcity of real money in the form of specie, a problem that had plagued the colonies for many years. And too many farmers found patriotism less appealing than British gold.

On March 4, 1780, the *New Hampshire Gazette* printed this profile of Washington as he was seen during that terrible winter by an unnamed American gentleman, who was well acquainted with the general: "That, though advanced in years, he is remarkably healthy, takes a great deal of exercise, and is very fond of riding on a favorite white horse. He is very reserved and loves retirement; when out of camp, he has only a single servant attending him, and when he returns within the lines, a few of the light horse escort him to his tent. When he has any great object in view, he sends for a few of those officers of whose abilities he has a high opinion, and states his present plan among half a dozen others, to all of which they give their separate judgments; by these means, he gets all their opinions, without divulging his intentions. He has no tincture of pride, and will often converse with a sentinel with more freedom than he will a general officer. He is very shy and reserved to foreigners, although they have letters of recommendation from the Congress. He punishes neglect of duty with great severity, but is very tender and indulgent to recruits until they learn the articles of war and their exercise perfectly. He has a great antipathy to spies, although he employs them himself, and has an utter aversion to all Indians. He regularly attends divine service in his tent every morning and evening, and seems very fervent in his prayers. He is so tender-hearted that no soldier can be flogged near his tent; or if he is walking in the camp and sees a man tied to the halberds, he will either order him to be taken down or walk another way to avoid the sight. He has made the art of war his particular study; his plans are in general good and well digested; he is particularly careful of always securing a retreat, but his chief qualifications are courage, steadiness, perseverance and secrecy. Any act of bravery he is sure to reward and make a short eulogium on the occasion to the person and his fellow-soldier (if it be a soldier) in the ranks. He is humane to the prisoners who fall into his hands, and orders everything necessary for their relief. He is very temperate in his diet, and the only luxury he indulges himself in, is a few glasses of punch after supper."

So the weary winter wore on. Washington, meeting with Knox and other generals, noted with pleasure that some five hundred more enemy soldiers had deserted since the Battle of Monmouth. Then he turned his attention to methods of punishment for his enlisted men. Washington was a stern disciplinarian when it became necessary, though inwardly very humane. Apparently he based his practice of penalties on the theory that when meted out early and at the proper time punishment served as a preventive of worse actions. He explained to his staff that under the Articles of War the heaviest corporal punishment that could be inflicted upon an offender was one hundred lashes and that there was no intermediate punishment between this sentence and that of the death penalty; he had noticed that courts-martial were often compelled to adopt one or the other as punishment for all crimes. He observed that in the early days of the Confederation, thirty-nine lashes had been the maximum punishment allowed for a soldier; Washington had advised Congress that this number was not enough. The number of lashes was consequently increased to a hundred and at times was spaced out by giving the offender fifty lashes at one session, then later on administering the remaining fifty to his red and lacerated skin.

Dr. Thacher set down a description of how corporal punishment was given: "The culprit being securely tied to a tree or post, receives on his naked back the number of lashes assigned him, by a whip formed of several knotted cords, which sometimes cut through the skin at every stroke. However strange it may appear, a soldier will often receive the severest stripes without uttering a groan or once shrinking from the lash. This must be ascribed to stubbornness or pride. They have, however, adopted a method which they say mitigates the anguish in some measure: it is by putting between the teeth a leaden bullet, on which they chew while under the lash till it is made quite flat and jagged."

In his analysis of military punishment, Washington felt that there should be more grades of punishment, because lashes were "inadequate to a variety of cases" and the penalty of death was too extreme. As a result of these deliberations at the New Jersey headquarters, "severe, hard labor" was recommended to Congress as the intermediate sentence to be given between that of a hundred lashes and death. This labor was to be done on fortifications, roads and public works. These recommendations were accordingly put into effect. This meeting of Washington and his staff also laid the basis for the military prison system of the nation. The conclusion was that drunkards particularly should be sent to such prisons and while there should receive no other sustenance but bread and water.

There were less grim goings-on at headquarters. A dance was given with almost four hundred present, including some of the state's most prominent people. The festivities lasted until early morning, and Washington danced for three hours with the vivacious Mrs. Nathanael Greene.

In the artillery park an arrangement was set up that has been termed the forerunner of the U.S. Military Academy at West Point; it was a kind of military school. Henry Knox called it "the academy." The layout of the school included an elaborate platform and surrounding seats. It drew the enthusiastic approval of Washington, who always liked to see his men busily engaged in some form of productive activity.

As the summer of 1780 approached, the military situation slid into the doldrums. Washington tried to figure out what the British were up to, and they on their part were happy to hear of the sorry conditions within the American army. A principal difficulty, both military and civilian, was the depreciation of the Continental currency. It became virtually worthless to the public. Washington found morale slipping as the men realized that their meager pay was not even worth anywhere near its face value. In addition, they were also on half-rations; consistent hunger increased their discomfort and uneasiness.

On top of these worries, Washington found that many enlistments were expiring, and the men simply returned to their homes. Recruiting lagged to a trickle, so that by the end of spring, his forces at Morristown were less than four thousand active men. Their pay was almost six months behind. Adding to Washington's problems was the grumbling of the people in surrounding New Jersey who had sold food to the army, had been given promises of pay but had not received anything except worthless paper money.

The situation came to a head on May 25 when two regiments of the Connecticut line openly mutinied. They assembled under arms in parade formation and with the brisk beating of drums stated through their leaders that they intended to return home or at least obtain enough food to eat even if it required use of bayonets. With great difficulty, the men were finally persuaded to disperse.

British military leaders along the Eastern seaboard were well aware of conditions within the American camp and the spirit of disquiet among the civilians. When they heard of the near-mutiny and of the dwindling of Washington's forces, they felt it was time to move in and take advantage of the situation. In the middle of June a force of five thousand men was dispatched under the command of Hessian General Knyphausen from Staten Island to Elizabeth, New Jersey. This move must have caused Washington grave concern, for he knew too well he was not strong enough to counter it effectively. But if the British hoped for the disaffection of Americans in New Jersey, they were to be disappointed. The Tories there had held out great promise of operations against their neighbors, which would have been immensely helpful to the British; but as is known, throughout the war, their efforts were never sufficiently coordinated nor for that matter properly encouraged and organized by the British to be of much use. At times, Tory units such as Simcoe's Rangers wrought havoc among the Patriots, but this was exceptional.

Instead, there was an unexpected upsurge of volunteer

militia in New Jersey. It was not Washington's inspiration or even the American cause itself that motivated the local soldiers. It was, to a considerable extent, an incident that occurred which infuriated the whole countryside. As the British soldiers passed through the village of Connecticut Farms, one fired through a window of the house of a well-respected minister, the Reverend James Caldwell, and the shot killed Mrs. Caldwell, who was sitting in the midst of her small children. Her body was then taken from the house and the structure was set on fire and burned. After every house but one had been looted and burned—including the local church—the invaders left.

This reign of terror so aroused the local people that they turned out en masse to fight the redcoats. The militia met at Springfield and were then reinforced by detachments of Continentals from Morristown. Knyphausen thus found before him a somewhat imposing body of resistance and turned about to proceed to Elizabeth. But having second thoughts of perhaps not having performed his duty sufficiently, he reversed his route and marched back toward Springfield. There he found himself faced with Continental troops now numbering a thousand under General Greene, as well as hordes of New Jersey militia. Characteristically, Greene maneuvered his men so well in defensive positions that Knyphausen decided his was too great a risk in attacking them. Instead he burned nearly all the buildings in Springfield and again took off for Elizabeth, leaving behind him a few Americans dead and some threescore wounded. He suffered a good number of casualties himself from militia sniping that resembled that of Lexington and Concord.

This action at Springfield was typical of the engagements and raids that took place during the rest of the summer. Under the circumstances, Washington seemed afraid to attack, and Clinton glad of it.

In a letter to Washington, Benjamin Franklin reported

how highly esteemed Washington was in Europe: "Should peace arrive after another campaign," wrote Franklin, "and afford us a little leisure, I should be happy to see Your Excellency in Europe, and to accompany you if my age and strength would permit, in visiting some of its ancient and most famous kingdoms. You would on this side of the sea enjoy what posterity will say of Washington. I frequently hear the old generals of this martial country (who study the maps of America and mark upon them all your operations) speak with sincere approbation and great applause of your conduct; and join in giving you the character of one of the great captains of the age."

In early July a French fleet arrived at Newport, bringing five thousand troops under the command of General Jean Baptiste de Vimeur, the Count de Rochambeau. The ships, accompanied by several war vessels, not only brought men, but gold money, which was equally welcome.

Washington was so elated that for a time he appeared to be a new man. Now he and Rochambeau together could launch an attack against New York City. Such an assault was probably Washington's most cherished ambition during the whole war. Though it was to prove mainly fanciful, it now seemed highly possible to attack if the French fleet blockaded New York Harbor. So Washington at once sent Lafayette—whose French background and command of the language were to be extremely useful in the new alliance— to see Rochambeau in order to formulate plans for the combined operation. In his message to the French commander, Washington pointed out that "a decisive naval superiority is to be considered as a fundamental principle, and the basis upon which every hope for success must ultimately depend."

But such grand expectations were not to last long. Hardly had the French fleet disembarked its soldiers at Newport than Admiral Thomas Graves reached Sandy Hook with a British squadron of six ships of the line. This again upset the balance; once more Britain commanded the sea. With the enemy soon moving up to blockade Newport, information was received in August that the fleet of Admiral de Grasse had been shut up by the British in Brest. Even so, Washington went ahead with his plans and in late September met with Rochambeau at Hartford, Connecticut. Here the two commanders sized each other up. Each liked what he saw. Washington found that the veteran regular lieutenant general was not only able but affable, a seasoned soldier who could command respect from his men yet was affectionately known to them as "Papa." The Frenchman greeted a tall and stately colonial leader who mixed kindness with dignity, with more of the former quality. The two generals, who were to fashion the ending of the war, recognized in each other the rare trait of aristocratic background tempered with sincere appreciation of human values. Washington was then forty-eight years of age, Rochambeau fifty-four, yet the rigors of his experience made Washington look older.

Rochambeau explained to Washington through his interpreter that his government had instructed him to place himself under the orders of the American commander-in-chief. "The commands of the King, my master, place me under the orders of Your Excellency," Rochambeau said. "I come, wholly obedient and with the zeal and the veneration which I have for you and for the remarkable talents you have displayed in sustaining a war which will always be memorable." But the genial Frenchman added that his instructions also were that the French army and fleet act in concert; therefore until naval reinforcements arrived, he believed that he should remain in support of the blockaded French fleet at Newport. This left the Revolutionary War in the northern part of the country in a kind of stalemate, a condition that neither side cherished but that was often forced upon them by necessity.

One small, dramatic fight did occur, however. In the Long Island town of Brookhaven, a group of Tories had taken refuge in a large manor house and had converted it into a virtual fortress. Major Benjamin Tallmadge of the 2nd Continental Dragoons learned of this stronghold and decided to do something about it. On a fall evening of 1780 he set out from Connecticut in eight boats with some eighty men and landed on Long Island. Leaving a few men to guard the boats, Tallmadge and the rest started for the fort but had to return when a rainstorm blew up and prevented further progress. The next evening he started again and this time was more successful. As the troops approached the fort, it was found that strong blockades, a barricaded house, a deep ditch, an abatis and two guns protected the garrison. Tallmadge divided his men into three parties, had them fix bayonets and unload their muskets. At dawn they stealthily approached the small but sturdy fortress and were discovered less than fifty yards from it by a sentinel, who fired. Tallmadge's men rushed upon the stockade shouting, "Washington and glory!" The objective was taken in less than ten minutes, one part of the garrison holding out in the barricaded house until its doors were burst open, the occupants seized and unceremoniously thrown out of the windows. Tallmadge returned to his boats with only 1 man lost, while the Tories suffered 7 killed or wounded and more than 54 captured. Tallmadge received, for his success, the thanks of Washington and Congress. Such attacks were not always so effective against the Tories, who from time to time showed bravery and expertness in their war against those they sincerely felt were traitors to the Crown and its burgeoning new nation.

Washington, during this season, encountered the arch-traitor of the Revolution, Benedict Arnold, who has been described as "a conscienceless egotist inflamed to avenge a long chain of slights and affronts, some of them fancied, many real." Since Arnold was involved in what was probably the most traumatic experience Washington had during the war, it appears fitting here to describe the main actor in the tragedy and to set forth a detailed version of what happened, especially since there have been so many varying and romanticized accounts.

Benedict Arnold was born in Norwich, Connecticut, in 1741, a place not far from where the climax of his colorful life was reached. His inconsistency of conduct started early. At the age of fifteen he ran off and enlisted in a New York militia company but deserted the next year. The following year he enlisted again and once more deserted. After becoming a merchant, a horse trader and a smuggler, and after having married and had three sons in five years, he was elected captain of militia and rushed to Cambridge, where he joined General Washington, contributing his Connecticut company to the American forces ten days after the fighting at Lexington. From a contemporary drawing Arnold appears to be not tall but thick-set, energetic, with gray eyes, black hair, swarthy complexion, hooked nose, jutting jaw and sloping brow.

He was a whirlwind type of soldier, so active in so many directions that he was soon accused of mishandling funds. When he commanded the ill-fated expedition to Quebec in late 1775—a project in which Daniel Morgan was actually the real hero—Arnold spent the funds furnished by the army for the march in such a haphazard way that he was ever after suspect of having misused this money too. In fact, in May of 1777 he was accused by a Major John Brown, formerly of his staff, in the prophetic words: "Money is this man's god, and to get enough of it, he would sacrifice his country." Washington must have been aware of this charge, for a month after it was published in a handbill he asked Congress to make an investigation. But the accusation apparently had little effect on Washington, as time and events were to show.

Arnold also smarted under the fact that five brigadier

generals, all junior to him in rank and inferior in military achievement, had been promoted over him to major general. Finally, to placate him, Washington requested Congress to raise Arnold to the two-star rank. This was done and it made him senior to the other five generals.

At Saratoga, Arnold sustained a wound in the same limb that had been injured at Quebec. He must have regarded this leg as his "Achilles' heel." (The only statue in his memory at Saratoga today is a reproduction of a boot that represents Arnold's twice-wounded leg.)

In June of 1778, General Arnold was placed in command of Philadelphia after the British had evacuated that city. In a way, this was an ideal command for the society-loving officer; in another sense, it proved to be his nemesis. He never did like authority over him, especially civil authority, and here he was under not only the state but the federal government. There were many Tories, Patriots and uncommitted. With typical flamboyance, Arnold began "living it up" to such an extravagant extent that he was suspected of using money he had not earned. Soon the erratic Adjutant General Joseph Reed, himself not always loyal to Washington, became Arnold's enemy and charged him with misconduct. A court-martial resulted, and Arnold was found guilty of using public wagons for private purposes. The sentence was to be a reprimand from Washington. So tactfully did Washington word his official rebuke that it amounted to little more than a slap on the wrist, but the sensitive Arnold nevertheless chafed under any correction at all.

Washington had previously written Arnold that "Public bodies are not amenable for their actions. They place and displace at pleasure; and all the satisfaction that an individual can obtain, when he is overlooked [in promotions] is, if innocent, a consciousness that he has not deserved such treatment for his honest exertions." Doubtless, Arnold tried to console himself with this advice.

Meanwhile, Arnold, so successful at times in war, had also succeeded in love. His wife having died three years before, he had met and become infatuated with the beautiful Peggy Shippen, Tory daughter of a prominent Pennsylvania judge and a leader of local society. She and Major John André had been prominent in the presentation of the festive *Mischianza,* a splendid and colorful extravaganza given General Howe just before he left Philadelphia. Although Peggy was only nineteen and Arnold exactly twice her age, this did not seem to matter. The dashing and impetuous officer courted the winsome girl with all the ardor that he put into military campaigns—and won. The two were married. Washington had known of the courtship and did not disapprove, for he felt that women did not figure importantly in matters of war; besides, he was fond of Arnold and wanted him to be happy. But Arnold was now supporting his children, and after he added an expensive wife, his financial requirements became unduly heavy. This helped to draw him into the net of intrigue, as did his lovely Peggy, although she was always to prove faithful and loyally devoted to him.

With the aid of his wife, Arnold finally, in May of 1779, put out feelers to the British to ascertain how much they would be interested in his services. Letters were sent to Major André. These came to the attention of General Sir Henry Clinton, who of course knew of Arnold and was immediately interested in the proposition. The American general had also been approached by a Tory colonel of ability and prominence, Beverly Robinson, who had flattered Arnold by describing him as a strong man who might reconcile the colonies with their mother country.

Arnold sent for another Tory named Joseph Stansbury, a mild Philadelphian who seemed to be a logical go-between, and informed him that he was ready to deal with the British. Stansbury, through the offices of a New York City Tory, the Reverend Jonathan Odell, met with Clinton's aide, John André, and relayed Arnold's offer. It was accepted, but the British decided that it was best for the American turncoat to remain in his present post and keep abreast of developments in his army. Almost at once, Arnold began sending information that he obtained not only from Washington but from others in key positions who did not suspect him. He used the code name "Moore." But typically, Arnold became too greedy, even for Clinton. He demanded ten thousand pounds, regardless of whatever services he might be able to perform for the British, in compensation for the losses he would sustain should the Americans discover his treachery. Clinton refused to give him the money.

Meanwhile, Arnold worked on Washington, pleading physical disability when Washington considered him for command of one wing of the American army in its move to the South to attack Cornwallis. West Point was his object, and Arnold wrote Clinton on June 15, 1780, that he expected to obtain command of the highland post soon. Finally Clinton, feeling that the acquisition of such a key post would be extremely valuable, offered the ten thousand pounds Arnold had asked, if the British got possession of West Point, its three thousand men, the artillery and supplies. Prospects now looked promising to Arnold, who reported to the British that the American garrison at West Point had recently been reduced to about fifteen hundred Massachusetts militia and that these men needed every kind of supply from tents to provisions. Also, Arnold pointed out, his post covered not only West Point, which commanded the reaches to New York City, but also Stony Point and Verplanck's Point, some ten miles to the south.

On Thursday, September 14, 1780, Benedict Arnold wrote a letter to the still-trusting Washington which contained some interesting double-talk: "In answer to Your Excellency's questions proposed to the council of general officers, from the fluctuating situation of our affairs, which may be totally changed in a short time by a variety of circumstances which may happen, it appears extremely difficult for me to determine with any degree of precision the line of conduct proper to be observed."

At 4 A.M. on September 22, André, who had been slipped ashore just below Haverstraw, New York, from the *Vulture,* the British station ship on the Hudson, met secretly with Arnold for a conference in the woods. It happened that a young American commander, Colonel James Livingston, now decided to fire on the enemy ship with two cannon he had moved into position on the east shore at Teller's Point. Unfortunately for André, the skipper of the *Vulture* got the impression that he was in for a heavy bombardment from American batteries; unwilling to risk a disaster, he weighed anchor and sailed down river to Dobbs Ferry. André was left in the lurch. Although he had been instructed by Clinton not to proceed in disguise, not to enter enemy lines and not to carry any papers, both because of circumstances and probably impulse, André violated all of these commands. Arnold had given him documents at their early-morning meeting and had asked him to place them between his socks and his feet.

Though he had a safe-conduct pass from Arnold that was supposed to suffice in an emergency, André was stopped by three men near Tarrytown on the morning of September 23. At first he assumed they were Tories, but when they began to search him, he learned they were volunteer New York militia. Actually, they were probably more interested in loot than loyalty to the new cause, but they did discover the papers in his boots and knew enough to realize that here was something out of the ordinary. The suave young redcoat tried to bribe the three simple men, but it was no use. They turned him over to Lieutenant Colonel John Jameson, who was in charge of the American troops at

North Castle. The colonel was at first puzzled but decided on a compromise: still under the impression that Arnold was loyal he sent André to him, but feeling that the papers he carried were "of a very dangerous tendency," he dispatched them to General Washington.

When Major André learned that the papers had been sent to Washington, he took heart, because now, he felt, the matter was in the hands of a soldier and gentleman. He wrote Washington that he had come behind the lines to meet a person who was to give him intelligence of their activities and had "subsequently been betrayed into the vile condition of an enemy in disguise within your posts." It now seemed a question of which one, Washington or Arnold, would first receive the information and take significant action.

It so happened that Washington had been to Hartford to confer with the French and did not arrive in the vicinity until the middle of the morning of September 25. Meanwhile Arnold had learned of the capture of his accomplice. He was at breakfast with Peggy and three of Washington's officers. At once Arnold excused himself, went upstairs and called his wife, to whom he gave the bad news. She fainted, or pretended to. Coming back downstairs, Arnold was told that Washington was about to arrive to see him.

With a straight face, Arnold ordered a horse, left word for Washington that he had urgent military business he must attend to and hurried down to the river. There he entered his barge, which he kept ready, and pointing his pistol at the oarsmen, ordered them to row him out to the *Vulture*. At 10:30 A.M., Washington arrived with Lafayette, Henry Knox and Alexander Hamilton. The American general had already heard of Arnold's treachery, and astounded and sad, had turned to Knox and asked, "Whom can we trust now?"

Now it was time for Arnold's wife to take the stage, or

so it seemed. Peggy raced through the upper story of the house and accused Lieutenant Colonel Richard Varick of ordering her child to be killed. This twenty-seven-year-old aide of Arnold's had himself been sick for three days. He came into the room where Washington was and told him that Mrs. Arnold had run through the hall only partially clad and that finally he had succeeded in getting her into bed. After accusing him, she had stated that "there was a hot iron on her head and no one but General Washington could take it off." Varick asked Washington if he would see her. Washington rushed up the stairs and found her in bed, disheveled, but "showing all the sweetness of beauty, all the loveliness of innocence, all the tenderness of a wife and all the fondness of a mother."

Washington leaned over her in the solicitude he showed all ladies, but she appeared not to recognize him and said that it was not he. Instead, she seemed to think that he was someone who was going to help the unfortunate Varick kill her child. Finally she seemed to recognize Washington but then lamented the fact her husband was not there to protect her. "General Arnold will never return," she cried. "He is gone. He is gone forever there"—she pointed to the ceiling—"the spirits have carried him up there." Washington was at a loss to know how to handle the bizarre situation. He tried again and again, but as Mrs. Arnold dissolved in tears and clung to her child and then the bed, he eventually went back downstairs in confusion and consternation.

Dinner was served to the officers present, but no one seemed to have much appetite, especially Washington himself. After reluctantly placing Arnold's aides under arrest —they were later acquitted of the charges of any treasonable action—Washington proceeded to examine more closely the papers that had been found on André. They were important indeed. Included was a summary of the strength of the American army, a description of the troops stationed at West Point and the vicinity, an estimate of the necessary forces for proper defense of the post, a record of the ordnance, a plan of how the artillery was to be deployed in case of an alarm and even a copy of the minutes Washington had sent Arnold of an important council of war held on September 6.

Astounded and shocked, Washington nevertheless was galvanized into action. At once he sent Hamilton down to the Hudson River to try to intercept Arnold before he could reach the *Vulture,* but of course it was too late. Even before the return of his aide, Washington was handed a letter from Arnold that had been written aboard the British ship. It brazenly stated: "Love to my country actuates my present conduct"—but it did not specify which country he meant. In a long apology, Benedict Arnold emphasized that Peggy was as "innocent as an angel" and added the truthful statement that his aides, Varick, Franks and Smith were ignorant of any action of his which might be construed as improper.

Arnold's letter was audacious, but Washington had more important things to deal with. He ordered the military detachments stationed at Fishkill to repair to West Point, instructed Nathanael Greene to send his most available division at once to King's Ferry and alerted the rest of the American army for possible movement to meet the crisis. Then he ordered that Major John André be placed under heavy guard. To Washington's aides it seemed that Arnold had planned to encourage an attack by the British and then pretend that he had been overcome by surprise.

The ill-starred André was brought to the American headquarters on the morning of September 26, his pitiable circumstances being heightened by a rain through which he had been forced to ride for long hours in the night. He was accompanied by a detachment of American dragoons under the command of Major Tallmadge. Probably anticipating an ardent plea and reluctant to see him anyway, Washington refused to meet André, but he did receive pertinent information regarding the capture from Tallmadge. Brave and artistic young André was sent to West Point and from there taken by barge to Stony Point, then imprisoned at a tavern in Tappan. At Tappan he had time to contemplate his fate, which was not long in being determined.

A board of general officers was convened by the American commander next day and asked to act quickly to "report a precise state of his case, together with your opinion of the light in which he ought to be considered and the punishment that ought to be inflicted." Presiding was temperate and fair-minded Nathanael Greene; on the board were the impetuous Lord Stirling, the emotional and sympathetic Marquis de Lafayette, methodical von Steuben and the young general who five years before had met and spent the night talking to André, had found much in common with him and had liked him very much, Henry Knox. Other members were Generals Arthur St. Clair, Robert Howe, James Clinton, John Glover, Edward Hand, John Stark, Samuel H. Parsons and Jedediah Huntington.

André was interrogated by the board, and he proved disarmingly frank and honest. He did not for a moment deny who he was or his mission. Letters from Arnold, Beverly Robinson and Sir Henry Clinton were read. All insisted that André had come ashore under a flag and had acted under the orders of Arnold while inside the American lines and therefore could not be considered a spy. André said he could not pretend that he was under a flag.

Perhaps if he had lied artfully, André might have been given the benefit of the doubt by his sympathetic group of officers. But he did not choose even to try. By the end of one day of hearing, "he confessed everything," so that the board had no choice but to conclude that he had come ashore in a private and secret manner, and his subsequent movements within the American lines under a feigned name "and in a disguised habit" thus resulted in his being judged a spy. The answer was simple, the sentence was automatic: he was to be executed.

After receiving the report of the board of officers, Washington issued a general order that quoted the board's report and directed "the execution of the above sentence in the usual way this afternoon at 5 o'clock precisely." The usual procedure was death by hanging. So plans were made, but on the afternoon scheduled for this event, October 1, Washington received from Sir Henry Clinton a request for a delay. Washington was glad to have such a request; he hoped that Clinton would offer Arnold in exchange for André, "who came within our lines in the night on an interview with Major General Arnold in an assumed character." But the British appeal contained no such offer.

In the meantime, André showed a calm fortitude that impressed those who had contact with him. He asked Washington if instead of the ignominious method of hanging, he could instead be shot. Under the rules of the day, Washington could not properly grant this request, so it was ignored. It is believed with some basis that members of his staff, particularly Alexander Hamilton and Henry Knox, tried to intervene with Clinton to obtain the exchange of Arnold for André, but their pleas were to no avail. On October 2 Major John André, clad in full regimentals, died bravely on the scaffold at Tappan, being mourned by his foes as well as his friends.

There are those who have criticized Washington for what appeared to them a too-harsh attitude on his part. But interestingly, a British historian, R. E. Graves, has commented: "Washington has been unreasonably censured for not having granted André a more honorable death. To have done so would have implied a doubt as to the justice of his conviction. Washington and André deserve equal honor;

André for having accepted a terrible risk for his country and borne the consequences of failure with unshrinking courage; and Washington for having performed his duty to his own country at a great sacrifice of feelings."

And so it was with sad heart that Washington approached the winter of 1780–1781, not only because of the André incident but because prospects in general appeared to be bleak. His army was encamped through the highlands of the Hudson to Connecticut and also at Morristown, New Jersey. Even with all the efforts its leader and his staff had made, the condition of the American military force was distressingly dismal again. There was a serious lack of food, a dearth of satisfactory shelter and proper clothing and, as was expected by this time, the army was way behind in its payments to the men.

Some accepted the conditions stoically. To read their letters and journals one wonders how they were able to muster as much resolution as they did. But others were extremely dissatisfied. The enlistment agreement of the soldiers of the Pennsylvania Line stated that they were bound "for three years or during the war." This vague wording did not satisfy either the soldiers or their officers. The men interpreted it to mean that their service was limited to whichever came first, the expiration of three years or the ending of the war. Now three years had passed. They felt free to go and asked that they be discharged. But the military authorities held that they must continue to serve until the end of the war even if it lasted beyond three years. Discontent was centered in Anthony Wayne's brigade, which was now in camp near Morristown.

The boiling point was reached on New Year's Day, 1781, when the men were celebrating—to the extent that they could under the austere circumstances. Evening had come, and the Pennsylvanians should have been inside their huts;

instead, they were out on the parade ground in a carousing mood, milling about, running and shouting. Now and then, one would fire his musket. Officers intervened and finally got the revelers back inside their shelters, but at midnight they came out again as noisy as before. As a result of the shooting, one officer was killed and two others wounded. Then the rioters took possession of the artillery park, killing one guard there, to the consternation of Knox.

The report came to Washington that Wayne—a Pennsylvanian himself and highly regarded by his men even though he was a strict disciplinarian—and Colonels Walter Stewart and Richard Butler had tried to handle the situation, but Sergeant William Bouzar, leader of the uprising, refused to obey and demanded on behalf of the men the back pay they were due as well as discharges for all who had served for three years. He added that the men were bent on presenting their complaints to the Continental Congress in Philadelphia. "Mad Anthony" Wayne, a brave man who certainly did not fear his own troops, now was aroused to real anger and faced them calmly. But even his efforts were in vain; six regiments formed in good order and marched off down the road to Trenton. Wayne and his staff followed, and at Princeton they all stopped and waited for a reply to the message the men had already sent to Congress.

This dignified if sometimes erratic body learned of the mutiny with much concern. Not only were they disturbed that part of the army had revolted—especially the part from Pennsylvania, the very state in which the Congress met—but some individual members feared for their own lives and considered fleeing. Cooler heads advised against this, and the president of the state Executive Council, Joseph Reed, went with a committee to Princeton and negotiated with the soldiers. Reed won quite a victory. Promises were made to pay the men their arrears with interest soon, needed clothing was to be furnished and each soldier who had enlisted for "three years or during the war" and had already served for three years was to be discharged. Many were, but most reenlisted.

Washington was appalled at the mutiny and its results. He felt that such compliance with the soldiers' demands was a bad example of lack of discipline, and he was soon proved right. Three regiments of New Jersey troops stationed at Pompton marched off toward Trenton on January 20. This time Washington took direct charge and sent Major General Robert Howe of North Carolina, in command of a detachment of Continental troops from New England, with instructions "to compel the mutineers to unconditional submission and to execute a few of the most active and incendiary leaders." Howe caught up with the mutineers, surrounded them and ordered them to assemble without arms. They complied, and he selected one man from each of the three regiments who was reported to be the most aggressive in the uprising. Tried by court-martial, two were hanged, one reprieved. The mutiny was over.

XI ON LAND, SEA AND IN THE OFFING

GEORGE WASHINGTON DESPISED the Indian method of warfare, having had bitter experiences with it in earlier campaigns. Nevertheless, he would gladly have made peace with the redmen or had them on his side in dire moments of need. As it was, a large proportion of the Indians sided with the Tories and British, and Washington felt that something should be done about this.

By now the Revolution in the northern states had become a defensive war, with the British fleet controlling offshore waters. The British army was mainly confined to New York and Newport. A new opportunity to mount a large-scale offensive presented itself to Washington. In his estimation, he had three choices. One was to expel the British army from its eastern strongholds; another, to keep them boxed in at New York and Newport and attempt to capture Niagara; or third, to send an expedition against the Iroquois Indians.

The first was most appealing to Washington, for he felt it would be decisive. But it would require an estimated twenty-six thousand troops and be very expensive. The second alternative would require almost as many troops and as much expense. So the third operation, that against the Indians, was accepted as most practical because of the shortage of troops and funds.

The frontier settlements of New York and Pennsylvania particularly were being ravaged by the Indians, mainly Iroquois, and by whites who had remained loyal to the Crown. At first Washington offered command of an expedition against them to Horatio Gates, but Gates was more inclined to paper work and felt the assignment would be too strenuous for one his age. Washington then offered the position to the garrulous John Sullivan, who was popular but not generally successful. Washington frankly told Sullivan he was the second choice but then characteristically encouraged him. After some hesitation, Sullivan accepted.

The leaders of the raids against the frontier settlements were Colonel John Butler, his son Walter, Sir John Johnson and the able Indian chief Joseph Brant, under whom Tories and Indians had terrorized western New York since 1778. In the Wyoming Valley massacre carried out by these irregular forces, hundreds of settlers died. Violence was practiced on both sides. Then Butler and Brant struck the Cherry Valley settlement in November, 1778. More than fifty men, women and children were slain, their leaders not being able to restrain the Indians once they started fighting.

A cry was raised to Congress and to Washington, but it was not until the next summer that he was able to do much about it. He resolved to send the Sullivan expedition to destroy the Indian towns and crops and to capture Fort Niagara, which was a base for their raids. "I beg leave to suggest," he wrote Sullivan in those terms of politeness which characterized eighteenth-century gentlemen, even superior officers, "as general rules that ought to govern your operations, to make rather than receive attacks, attended with as much impetuosity, shouting and noise as possible, and to make the troops act in as loose and dispersed a way as is consistent with a proper degree of concert and mutual support. It should be previously impressed upon the minds of the men whenever they have an opportunity, to rush on with the war whoop and fixed bayonets. Nothing will disconcert and terrify the Indians more than this."

Advancing in two columns that totaled almost five thousand men, with Sullivan commanding the right wing and General James Clinton the left, the Americans moved close to their objectives. Sullivan laid waste the town of Chemung, and Clinton destroyed fourteen villages as they progressed. At Newton, near the present Elmira, the Butlers and Brant, with fifteen hundred Tories and Indians, undertook to stop the American advance but were soundly defeated. Sullivan's forces devastated the standing crops of corn, squash and beans and cut down the fruit trees of the Indian tribes as well as their houses and barns, until he could report that only one Iroquois town remained. As a result, during the next winter many Indian families froze and starved to death.

Even so, Sullivan did not reach Fort Niagara. Finding his food supplies low and cold weather coming on, he returned to the east, his expedition incomplete. For this he was criticized, and being a complainer himself, he fired back verbal sallies at his critics. The Board of War recommended that his resignation, which he had sent in in a huff, be accepted by Congress. To Sullivan's surprise, it was, and he found himself out of the army.

Washington tried to persuade him to stay, but it was too late. Sullivan did not have enough supporters in Congress, partly because he had irritated and disappointed so many people. However, he did feel that his Indian expedition was a success, and he was grateful to Washington for his solicitude. "My public and constant declarations have been and I now repeat," he wrote Washington, "that in my opinion, you are the savior of this country, and that to your bravery, fortitude and steady performance, do we owe the independence and freedom we enjoy."

Farther to the west, George Rogers Clark had added to the American laurels by defeating the British and Indians and taking over much of what is now the Midwest for the Patriot cause. Although Washington had little direct connection with this notable expedition, which originated in Virginia under the sponsorship of Patrick Henry, he was gratified that much of the immediate menace of the Indians in the frontier lands had been removed. He had always been interested in western lands, and had it not been for the war would doubtless have spent more of his time and resources in acquiring acres to add to his already extensive holdings in Virginia. As it was, he never ceased to long for Mount Vernon and expressed this in much of his correspondence home when he had the time.

Washington was concerned with not only the vast expanse of land west of the main theater of the war but the broad reaches of the ocean to the east as well. Even though naval historians admit that the American Revolution was primarily a war of armies, they like to point out the significance of sea power and quote Washington's statement that "whatever efforts are made by the land armies, the navy must have the casting vote in the present contest." Of course this judgment was partly hindsight—being written after the victory at Yorktown—but it should be remembered that Washington had insisted that as a condition of his participation at Yorktown he must have available for cooperation "a decisive naval superiority to be considered as a fundamental principle upon which every hope of success must ultimately depend."

Probably the most valuable contributions rendered the war by the navy were general transport and the early supply of munitions from captured British ships, privateers from America preying upon English commerce and the direct coordination of the navy with the army. At the beginning of the war, the colonies had no navy at all, but there was a sizeable maritime population that employed many merchant vessels in both foreign and domestic trade. Here was the natural source of a new navy, and Washington was one of the first to realize this. The British had control of the seas and enjoyed freedom of movement of men and supplies.

The answer was what became known as "Washington's navy"—at first simply a fleet of colonial privateers, mainly armed schooners. Although the records are incomplete, they indicate that over two thousand private armed vessels, carrying some eighteen thousand guns and seventy thousand men (several times larger than the Continental armies at any time), were so utilized during the course of the war. The most spectacular capture in the early part of naval operations was that of the ordnance brig *Nancy*, taken in November of 1775 by Washington's armed schooner *Lee*, commanded by Captain John Manley.

After Washington had organized his little navy, Congress, in 1775, had voted funds for the first fleet, consisting of eight vessels; these embarked the following year under the command of Commodore Esek Hopkins. In the meantime, the British navy was not idle. It sent strong reinforcements to increase the blockade of American ports. Already the Royal Navy was well represented in colonial waters, and hostile squadrons near the coast operated in support of such large military expeditions as those against Charleston and the arrival of General Howe's army at New York City. But the huge task imposed upon the British of supplying their armies in America by sea furnished excellent and profitable opportunities of raiding and capturing their supply ships in order to use their cargoes for the American army. When the French alliance was concluded in 1778, Wash-

ington saw at last the prospect of having proper naval support for his operations. The attack on New York did not
come about—the French were wise enough in siege warfare
to realize how well the city could be defended and that
defenders usually have a two-to-one advantage. But Washington, and Knox especially, never ceased to dream of surrounding New York by land and sea and blasting it open
with heavy cannon. Washington more or less marked time
from this point on until he could have a French fleet to
support his army in a combined operation. Just such an
opportunity was to come later at Yorktown.

Nor was Washington patient during the interim. At first
he felt encouraged by the attitude of the French commanders. Then, as time passed and he did not receive the help
he had hoped for, he wrote, near the end of 1780, "Disappointed, especially in the expected naval superiority, which
was the pivot upon which everything turned, we have been
compelled to spend an inactive campaign, after flattering
prospects at the opening of it." In time, the long-desired
help did arrive. The outcome even inspired a naval historian, Commodore Dudley W. Knox, to comment, "Washington's genius in refusing to employ the French and
American armies in a major attack until a naval superiority
was available for cooperation, and in his conduct of the subsequent joint operations with the fleet of Admiral de
Grasse decided the war. . . . The Continental Navy carried on its heavy burden well throughout the war, but especially so in the early years when the acute need of munitions
for the army had to be met despite an overpowering British
Navy that was gallantly faced alone."

A chapter was now added to the history of the American
navy that has been celebrated both in song and story and in
our sometimes romanticized history. Captain John Paul
Jones, a Scottish-born sea dog, was sent to France in 1779
in an American naval vessel to inform the French of the

surrender of General Burgoyne. Taking advantage of the French bases, he made a cruise around the British Isles and took several prize ships. Finally coming upon the frigate *Serapis,* Jones attacked with his aging and rotten wooden-hulled ship, the *Bon Homme Richard,* named for Benjamin Franklin's "Poor Richard." A three-hour pitched battle by moonlight followed, in which Jones and his crew fought with exceptional courage against great odds. The result was the most colorful victory in our early naval history, making Jones a hero. Most of the vaunted British navy, however, was in distant places at the time and a large French and Spanish fleet was then in the English Channel.

Had Washington been able to determine when and where the war would be fought, there might well have been different results. As it was, the British had decided in 1778 to transfer major military operations to the South. There they expected to find large numbers of active Tories who would flock to the Union Jack once it was plainly unfurled. That such cooperation did not occur there or anywhere else to any appreciable extent during the war is now a matter of record.

Acting on Washington's advice, Congress appointed Major General Benjamin Lincoln as commander of the Southern Department. He was a corpulent but loyal officer from Massachusetts, a Federalist and a close friend of Henry Knox's, who recommended him to Washington. But aside from a few minor victories he had achieved over the British and their Tories in the South, Lincoln was best known for his defeat at Charleston by General Clinton in early 1780 with a loss of over five thousand men, probably the most clear-cut victory won by the British during the war.

Just to the north, the state of Virginia was in a condition of apathy. Its governor, Thomas Jefferson, for all his talent and forcefulness in writing the Declaration of Independence, had not enlisted in the armed forces nor even aroused his fellow Virginians to the danger from the British. Washington had written Jefferson several times that the state probably would be invaded, but apparently the governor had paid little heed to the warnings. Finally, when an enemy fleet was sighted off the Chesapeake capes, Jefferson sent General Thomas Nelson, Jr., of the state militia down to the coastal region to call up the troops there but added that he would wait "further intelligence before we would call for militia from the middle or upper country." Jefferson was obviously not a military man.

None other than Benedict Arnold, now a brigadier in the British army, was approaching Virginia with sixteen hundred men, having been ordered by Clinton to destroy military stores and rally the American Tories. Clinton was trying to prevent reinforcements from being sent to General Nathanael Greene, who had succeeded Gates after his disastrous defeat at the Battle of Camden. No one trusts a turncoat, and Clinton did not trust Arnold. He had directed Arnold to consult with Colonels John Simcoe and Thomas Dundas on anything of importance. Arnold arrived at Hampton Roads on December 30, 1780, shifted his men to small boats and pushed up the James River to Westover, former home of William Byrd. From there he went to Richmond, which he took without opposition.

Arnold wrote a letter to Governor Jefferson, in which he offered to spare the Virginia capital if the British were permitted to sail up the river and take the tobacco from the warehouses. For some reason, Jefferson refused. So Arnold simply burned public and private buildings, as well as state papers. Weapons and military stores were also seized without firing a shot. Thereupon, Arnold and his British and Tory troops marched back to Portsmouth, where they encamped for the winter.

Henry (Light Horse Harry) Lee—often of a suspicious

nature—was no friend of Jefferson's. He pointed out that although Virginia had been partly devastated by British raids and had strained herself to help Greene's army in the Carolinas, the state possessed more than enough resources to have crushed any predatory adventure such as that of Arnold. Lee charged that Jefferson had failed to heed Washington's warning to prepare to meet an invasion and that he left "the archives of the state, its reputation and all the military stores deposited in the magazines of the metropolis at the mercy of a small corps conducted by a traitor."

Hearing of Arnold's incursions, Washington, who had long sought an opportunity to recapture and punish him, now felt that such a chance might be at hand. Arnold's capture, he stated, would be "an event particularly agreeable to this country." He asked Count Rochambeau if there was any way in which the French army and navy could help in the undertaking. Being blockaded by a British fleet at Newport, the French general and Admiral Destouches, though willing, could for the moment provide no aid to Washington.

Then a turn of good fortune came their way. A brisk storm hit the British ships blockading Newport on January 22, 1781, and damaged some of them so heavily that for a time the French had some superiority over their adversary. Destouches at once sent a sixty-four-gun vessel and two frigates to Chesapeake Bay to destroy Arnold's small naval supporting force. But that foxy individual had already withdrawn his ships up the Elizabeth River to Portsmouth. To Washington's disappointment, the French vessels then returned to Newport.

Meanwhile, Washington had dispatched Lafayette with three regiments of light infantry, about twelve hundred men, to Virginia to attack Arnold and, if possible, take him captive. By now, the French general and admiral

heeded the continued pleas of Washington and sent all
Destouches's ships, eight of the line and three frigates,
carrying twelve hundred men, just the number Lafayette
had with him. Lafayette had by this time arrived at Annapolis. But British Admiral Marriat Arbuthnot had heard
of the departure of the French fleet, so he sailed from
Long Island Sound for the Chesapeake. Having faster
ships, the British overtook the French fleet. They fought
off the Chesapeake capes, each having eight vessels but
one of the British ships having heavier guns. Some ships
were disabled on both sides, but the French returned to
Newport, leaving Lafayette without naval help or reinforcements from the French troops aboard.

Washington was worried. The Marquis de Lafayette, a
favorite of his, was threatened by some twenty-five hundred redcoats under General William Phillips, who had
arrived in Portsmouth on March 26. Phillips was to super-
sede Arnold in command. This must have given Phillips
a feeling of triumph, for he had been second in command
under Burgoyne at Saratoga and had distinguished himself
with his artillery activities there, Arnold being just as
active on the opposing side in that engagement.

Phillips sent Arnold with twenty-five hundred men on
a raiding expedition to the north, following Clinton's
order that no major British operation take place at this
time in Virginia. The purpose of the raid was to prevent
the state militia from becoming too active and to destroy
as many local supplies as possible. Arnold marched northward toward Richmond, destroying military stores as he
went. American General Peter Muhlenberg, with a thousand militia, tried to oppose Arnold at Petersburg, but
the British drove them off. At the village of Osborne's, a
few miles below Richmond, the Americans had gathered
a naval force of four ships, five brigs and ten smaller craft,
all filled with tobacco and other supplies destined for ports

in the West Indies. A former sea captain himself, Arnold found no difficulty in sizing up the situation, forming his own artillery on the banks and, with well-directed fire, knocking out the entire American squadron.

By this time Lord Cornwallis had arrived in the region from his North Carolina campaign, and Phillips and Arnold marched to Petersburg to meet him. But soon after arriving there on May 10, General Phillips, who had been ailing for some time, grew worse and died from a fever believed to have been brought on by the warm climate. For a short time Arnold was again in command of the British forces in Virginia; however, Cornwallis arrived and superseded him. Lafayette was now in Richmond with three thousand men and eager to fight, although he was outnumbered almost two to one. He wrote Washington, "Were I to fight a battle, I should be cut to pieces, the militia dispersed and the arms lost. Were I to decline fighting, the country would think itself given up. I am therefore determined to skirmish, but not to engage too far, and particularly to take care against their immense and excellent body of horse, whom the militia fear as they would so many wild beasts. Were I anyways equal to the enemy, I should be extremely happy in my present command, but I am not strong enough even to get beaten."

Washington had sent Wayne's brigade to Pennsylvania to recruit to full strength and then to proceed to join the action in the South. Cornwallis was wary, not intending to be lured into any trap. In early June, he sent the spirited cavalryman Banastre Tarleton, with two hundred and fifty men, against Charlottesville, Virginia, where the legislature of that new state was in session. En route the dashing Tarleton came upon a wagon train carrying clothing for Greene's army and burned it. The legislature heard of the approach of the dreaded British cavalry leader and adjourned before he arrived, but even so, he captured seven

of them before they could get away. Governor Jefferson
was warned only a few minutes before by the son of a
tavernkeeper; he mounted his horse and fled just as
Tarleton and his men were coming up the hill to get him.
Henry Lee called this flight of Jefferson's "a cowardly act."
A sizeable quantity of powder, tobacco and clothing, plus
a thousand muskets, were taken by the British marauders
without opposition.

Washington had been heartened by the results of a small
but intense engagement that took place at King's Mountain
in October. This high, narrow, wooded hill, near the South
Carolina border not far west of Charlotte, had been occupied by Major Patrick Ferguson, the expert British rifle-
man who had almost shot Washington at one time, and
a Tory force of about a thousand men. Despite caution
from Cornwallis, his superior, about fighting the Americans of that rough region, the fiery Ferguson felt he was
securely ensconced on top of the mountain and boasted
that "all the devils in hell" could not drive him from it.
Perhaps not, but the "devils" from westward across the
mountains, woodsmen who knew the terrain and how to
use their long rifles to advantage, were a different story.
Surrounding the little mountain, they worked their way
up in three divisions, under the command of Colonels
Campbell, Shelby and Sevier. Despite the bravery of Ferguson, who rode his horse to and fro and rallied his men
with a silver whistle, the frontiersmen made their way to
the top, aided by crack marksmanship, and captured the
whole Tory force. Major Ferguson, who had determined
he would not be taken alive, went down with several bullets through his body. He was buried atop King's Mountain.

This sharp and decisive loss disappointed Cornwallis in
the power of the local Tories to resist their neighbors, discouraged many Tories regarding their future and changed

the plans of the British general, who had to diminish his southern activities. But as if this was not enough in the way of reverses, General Daniel Morgan dealt the enemy another serious blow. He had been ordered by Nathanael Greene to move ahead of Cornwallis and try to divert his efforts. This "the Old Waggoner" did, retreating strategically to the west but chafing under the humiliation of it, for it was contrary to his fighting nature. Morgan was from Virginia, was Washington's personal friend, and like others of his state—the Lees, John Marshall and James Monroe—had decided that his place in these times was in military rather than legislative activities. Washington admired Morgan, who typified the best in the frontier fighter; the colorful pioneer-scout uniforms he and his men wore were later characterized by Theodore Roosevelt as the most American of any up to that time.

Daniel Morgan decided to stop running. He found a thinly wooded slope near the Broad River called the Cowpens. There he placed his men, the rawest militia in front, the Continentals in the center and his cavalry (under Colonel William Washington, George's cousin) in the rear behind a little rise. Morgan went among his men on the night of January 16 and encouraged them, telling them that he had never lost a fair fight and did not mean to this time, that if they did what he asked them, they would be heroes on the morrow.

With daylight, Banastre Tarleton, who had been sent in pursuit of Morgan with around a thousand regular British troops and a small number of Tories, attacked. As the veteran but tired British assaulted the American lines, they were met by a weak fire from the front lines, a moderate response as they charged forward, a heavy fusillade when they tried to overrun the Continentals and then were surrounded by Colonel Washington's cavalry as they closed in. Again, it was a classic, double-enveloping movement, such as that of Hannibal at Cannae.

As news of the victory at the Cowpens spread, Morgan was hailed as a hero throughout the colonies. Washington, greatly encouraged, was among those who thanked Morgan for the momentous achievement; Congress voted Morgan a medal. As a result of this most sensational victory, Morgan has been rated as the best field general of the Revolution.

Realizing that Cornwallis would soon be upon him with his main army, Morgan cannily retreated northward and soon found that the bad weather and physical ailments forced him to take a rest. But he did get his troops to Greene near what is now Greensboro, North Carolina, at a place called Guilford Courthouse. There Cornwallis attacked him, and a bitter battle ensued. Greene tried to emulate the Cowpens tactics of Morgan but placed his men too far apart and relied too much on the local militia. The conflict seesawed back and forth, but the British came out ahead. Greene was finally forced to withdraw after Cornwallis had ordered his artillery to fire across a clearing —the grapeshot killed not only Americans but his own men and horses, but it was effective. Greene did not win here, nor could it even be called a drawn battle, but he inflicted great losses on the British. Cornwallis's was a Pyrrhic victory, from which he never recovered. The Battle of Guilford Courthouse as well as that of the Cowpens eventually led to his reckoning at Yorktown.

XII THE RECKONING AT YORKTOWN

EVEN DURING the spring of 1781, Washington still longed for a gloriously successful assault on New York. He had never gotten over being driven out of the city; he felt that it represented the new nation in microcosm and sincerely believed that if he could retake it, the American national star would again be in bright ascendancy.

Washington reasoned—and not without advice from his generals—that New York actually could be taken if the French would help him as he desired. Washington had written to Lafayette in Virginia that he felt an attempt to take New York would be preferable to a southern operation, but this letter was intercepted by the British on June 3, 1781. Sir Henry Clinton was delighted at this supposed coup, but when he learned that Washington made light of the disclosure, he wondered if the letter was simply a ruse. Hamilton allowed a known spy to look at a fake map and then was told that the plans were for a move to Virginia. It has usually been accepted that Washington hesitated between the two courses as late as July, but years later he told Noah Webster that he had decided much earlier but had pretended to fix upon New York as an objective in order "to spur the eastern and middle states to greater exertions in furnishing specific supplies, and to render the enemy less prepared elsewhere."

In late May, when the New England flowers added their color to the green leaves and grass, he held another conference with the Count de Rochambeau at Wethersfield, Connecticut. Here he heard good news. Rochambeau informed him that the Count de Grasse was even at that time in all probability operating against the British in the West Indies and might later move his fleet up the eastern coast and unite with French forces at Newport for American action.

Rochambeau felt that with this added naval help, he himself would be more free to aid Washington in the matters at hand. Despite Washington's desire to attack New York, the veteran Frenchman indicated that Virginia would be preferable as an object. Washington pointed out the disadvantage of the humid heat in his native state at this time of year. He persuaded Rochambeau to aid him in making a demonstration just above New York City. On July 22 and 23, the Americans and French sent a reconnaissance force of five thousand men above King's Bridge, led by about one hundred and fifty Continentals. The American and French commanders thoroughly examined British positions along the nearby Harlem River. What they saw—the British solidly ensconced with fourteen thousand seasoned soldiers plus war vessels—convinced both Washington and Rochambeau that they had better not attack.

Washington, meanwhile, was growing anxious. He sensed that the American people were becoming tired of the war, now six years old. Many were already apathetic to its outcome. It was becoming more and more difficult to recruit soldiers, farmers wishing to be at home for planting and harvesting, urban dwellers even more unconcerned with the outcome of the conflict. There was no strong national government that could order a draft, and, as usual, military problems were compounded by a dire financial condition. Washington had over three thousand troops around West Point, the soldiers of New York and New Jersey for the most part guarding their own frontiers, with the Pennsylvania troops mainly in Virginia with Lafayette, and Wayne and Greene having most of regulars from the South. Washington's outlook was dark. Ammunition and food were scarce, and the people were getting tired of having it taken away from them. He summed up the situation on May 1, 1781, when he wrote in his journal, "Instead of having the prospect of a glorious offensive campaign before us, we have a bewildered and gloomy defensive one, unless we receive a powerful aid of ships, land troops and money from our generous allies."

Observing Washington, a French officer stated, "I have never seen anyone more naturally and spontaneously polite. He asks questions, listens attentively and answers in low tones and with few words." The American commander also surprised his foreign friends by playing ball with his aides for hours in camp, throwing the ball as vigorously as much younger men. The Prince de Broglie said of Washington that "he preserves that polite and attentive good breeding which satisfies everybody, and that dignified reserve which offends no one. He is a foe to ostentation and to vainglory. He does not seem to estimate himself at his true worth." But though the Frenchmen were impressed with Washington as a fine man, one of courage with "an uncommon capacity for grasping the whole of a subject," Swedish Count Axel Fersen described him as having "a tinge of melancholy which affects his whole being and which is not unbecoming; it renders him more interesting."

The late John C. Fitzpatrick described Washington's

strenuous work schedule: "Let anyone try to write from eight to twelve letters in longhand on vitally important matters, of from one to four folio pages in length, to Congress, to Governors of states or state legislatures, to commanding and subordinate officers of an army, issue general orders for managing a force of from ten to fifteen thousand men, keep in the saddle for hours, enter up a daily expense account, sign warrants for the disbursement of hundreds of dollars of public funds, plan and continually revise plans for a military campaign, while striving always to keep an army supplied with food, clothing and arms, and on top of all this, make perhaps a forced march and fight a battle, and it can easily be seen that George Washington could have obtained hardly more than three consecutive hours of sleep in any twenty-four, during the eight years of the Revolutionary War. Had he not been a physical giant . . . he could never have stood such a strain."

Washington now saw that it was time to turn his thoughts elsewhere. A swift French frigate was sent to the West Indies to urge the Count de Grasse to move northward.

In the middle of August, de Grasse's reply arrived: his fleet would leave the West Indies for Chesapeake Bay at once, bringing thirty-five hundred men from Haiti. De Grasse would be on hand to take part in a combined action against the British; however, the admiral would have to leave by October 15 because of other commitments and the coming of the hurricane season. Though still disappointed at not being able to attack New York, Washington was wise enough to see that the new opportunity must be seized at once. He rushed orders to Lafayette, telling him to dispose his troops so as to prevent the escape of Cornwallis and sent Colonel Louis le Bèque de Presle Duportail, the able French engineer officer, to Chesapeake Bay with a message for Admiral de Grasse saying that Washington, Rochambeau and a large part of the American army along with French troops would soon meet him there. Washington felt it necessary to leave about three thousand troops under General William Heath north of New York City to protect the region. With a quick slyness that seemed to characterize him when he was in important action, Washington ordered work on the roads leading to Staten Island in order to make the British think he might make an attack on New York. He sent a small French detachment near that island, where they ostensibly began construction of bake ovens as if a siege were being prepared.

On or about August 21—accounts differ as to the exact date—the allied armies broke camp and started south across the Hudson River. The object was to keep Sir Henry Clinton in the dark about their intentions. To further this secrecy, the Americans and French moved across King's Ferry to Stony Point and then marched down behind the New Jersey Palisades through Newark and New Brunswick. Only a few of the highest ranking officers knew the real plans; even Henry Knox, writing to his wife, admitted that he did not know the destination.

James Thacher, the army surgeon, wrote in his journal that "The real object of the allied armies in the present campaign has become a subject of much speculation. Ostensibly an investment of the city of New York is in contemplation. We are left to conclude that a part of our besieging force is to occupy that ground [New Jersey]. But General Washington possesses a capacious mind, full of resource, and he resolves and matures his great plans and designs under an impenetrable secrecy, and while we repose the fullest confidence in our chief, our own opinions must be founded only on doubtful conjectures." Washington's attitude, after having such a traumatic experience in trusting Benedict Arnold, can surely be understood.

The urgent need for secrecy lay in the danger of an attack while the armies were moving out and toward the

South. Washington noted in his journal: "Matters having now come to a crisis and a decisive plan to be determined on, I was obliged from the shortness of Count de Grasse's promised stay on this coast, the apparent disinclination in their naval officers to force the harbor of New York and the feeble compliance of the states to my requisitions for men . . . to remove the French troops and a detachment from the American army to Virginia." As a modern historian has commented, "After three years of dreary inactivity, he was ready and able to seize his opportunity and act with the boldness of high courage and the skill of a great captain."

Washington realized that the immediate danger was the greatest. If Clinton knew of the army's movements early enough, he could either swing his strong force into New Jersey against them or, after they had left the Hudson highlands, give General Heath an overwhelming blow. So the crucial period was within the first few days. Washington took a calculated risk, rightly believing that the timid and vacillating Clinton would in all probability make no decisive move. "Much trouble was taken," Washington recorded, "and finesse used, to misguide and bewilder Sir Henry Clinton, in regard to the real object, by fictitious communications as well as by making a deceptive provision of ovens, forage and boats in his neighborhood. Nor were less pains taken to deceive our own army; for I had always conceived, when the deception does not completely take place at home, it would never sufficiently succeed abroad."

So the combined allied armies threaded their way down through New Jersey during the hot days of late August, the French via Morristown and Somerset, the artillery by way of Bound Brook and the American infantry through New Brunswick. At times they were even in sight of the enemy troops but managed to hide their destination, so that it was not until early September that Clinton knew for certain that Generals Washington and Rochambeau were on their way to Virginia.

Count Dumas observed that along the way men, women and children crowded around Washington whenever they had the chance. Some just wanted to see him, others to touch his feet or his horse. The Abbé Robin was moved by what he saw. "The Americans, that cool and sedate people," he wrote, "are roused, animated and inflamed at the very mention of his name, and the first songs that sentiment or gratitude has dictated, have been to celebrate General Washington."

The soldiers, however, many of them from the North, were disgruntled not only because they were marching south but because they did not know where they were going. Washington sensed that some pay would help matters. He called on Robert Morris "to procure one month's pay in specie for the detachment," pointing out that some of the men had not been paid for a long time and had reminded him of such arrears. Morris had no money, but he resourcefully turned to the war chest of the Count de Rochambeau and borrowed twenty thousand dollars. The cash had a remarkably mollifying effect.

Then a new problem appeared. While riding past Chester, Pennsylvania, on September 5, Washington received word that twenty-eight French warships with thirty-five hundred men had already arrived at the entrance to Chesapeake Bay. Some of his men remarked that they had never seen him so happy, but his joy was short-lived. Another report came that eighteen large British ships of war had appeared off Sandy Hook. Now he was afraid that these additional ships and those already in New York Harbor would enable the enemy to challenge de Grasse successfully. A later report, wisely requested by Washington to confirm his earlier information, revealed that a lesser number of British ships had arrived than was first thought.

The army was welcomed as it passed through Philadelphia, although the streets appeared to be extremely dirty and the weather so hot and dry that the marching soldiers raised a dust like a snow storm. The residents, who had seen numerous parades of both British and American armies, were now intrigued by the colorful French uniforms of white faced with green. But Washington did not allow his forces to delay in Philadelphia or anywhere else along the route. He knew that time was of the essence.

Meanwhile, Admiral de Grasse had arrived at Yorktown, Virginia, and set up a naval blockade of the British garrison. He then landed troops to join those of Lafayette for the purpose of hemming in Cornwallis's army. The British fleet under Admiral Thomas Graves appeared off the Chesapeake on September 5 and de Grasse moved out to meet it. There was some sharp fighting followed by three days during which the opposing ships tried to maneuver into more favorable positions. Then on the ninth, Count Barras and his French vessels arrived from Newport to strengthen de Grasse, and Admiral Graves left the scene of action to return to New York for repairs.

Hearing of this withdrawal, Washington, more relaxed, felt that his trap had closed. It was high time. In Philadelphia he tried to maintain composure in front of the people, though his heart was anxious about the arrival of the French fleet. Here in this Pennsylvania metropolis Washington had six years before accepted the position of commander-in-chief when it was offered by the Continental Congress. On that day he had told Patrick Henry that because of this he fully expected "the ruin of my reputation." He now went to the Congress and paid his respects briefly. As the tall commander walked through the lighted city at dusk, a crowd of people of all ages followed, cheering him.

Having received word from Lafayette that Cornwallis had occupied Yorktown, Washington replied, thanking him for the news. "But my dear marquis," he added, "I am distressed beyond expression . . . for fear that the English fleet by occupying the Chesapeake may frustrate all our flattering prospects. . . . You see how critically important the present moment is. If you get anything new from any quarter, send it, I pray you, on the spur of speed for I am almost all impatience and anxiety." And Lafayette complied. On his way south soon afterward, Washington saw a horse gallop toward him in the dust ahead. The rider dismounted and gave him a message: the French had blockaded the Chesapeake. Washington was elated, and the Count Dumas remarked that he had "never seen a man moved by a greater or more sincere joy."

Washington wheeled his horse and trotted back to Chester to tell Rochambeau the news. As some of those accompanying him noted, it was one of the rare times they had seen him smile broadly and repeatedly. To their even greater surprise, as he came in sight of Rochambeau, Washington waved his hat and a white handkerchief.

Soon he again turned south and came to the Head of Elk, as it was called, a tributary of the upper Chesapeake. Washington issued an order bearing the information to his men, stating his highest pleasure at being able to bring them such good tidings, felicitating them upon the auspicious occasion and calling upon "the gentlemen officers, the brave and faithful soldiers, to exert their utmost abilities in the cause of their country and to share with him the difficulties, dangers, and glory of the enterprise." He and his forces had had little to cheer about during their two-hundred-mile march in just fifteen days, and now the news was joyful.

After getting off a number of letters to Maryland officials asking their aid in helping to transport troops and supplies, Washington rode rapidly to Baltimore, with Rochambeau following him more slowly. As Washington reached the approaches to that city in the late afternoon, he was met by a company of local militia, which had come out to welcome him. Artillery salutes were fired, and he was given a tumultuous welcome, riding through crowds in the streets. Finally he reached the Fountain Inn, where he spent the night. There Maryland officials formally welcomed him. The city was especially illuminated for the occasion, and it was a late hour before the celebration, probably premature, ceased. Then Washington went to bed, rising before daylight to make a coveted side trip.

Mount Vernon was his destination. He was only sixty-six miles away, and although this was not a short distance on horseback, Mount Vernon was not far out of the way of Yorktown. He had not seen his home in six years and four months, and the temptation now was too great. Accompanied only by his aide David Humphreys and his servant Billie Lee, Washington traveled hard and crossed the Potomac on late Sunday, September 9, 1781, and that evening rode up the winding lane to Mount Vernon. From here on May 4, 1775, he had departed for Philadelphia to become commander. He was warmly greeted by Martha and some new grandchildren.

It had taken Washington two days to reach Mount Vernon, and he spent only forty-eight hours there. Even so, he took time from his personal visit to send a letter to a local militia officer asking him to work on the rutty roads so that the American army could pass over them. When Washington's servants came to the big house and greeted their master, they were sorrowed to see his face "so changed by the storms of campaigns and the mighty cares which had burdened his mind during more than six years of absence." He found opportunity to confer with his manager about the plantation and the crops and invited in the neighbors for a festive time the next day when Rochambeau and his staff, including the noted writer-soldier, the Marquis de Chastellux, were to arrive.

Washington managed to keep abreast of the military situation during all the pleasant time he spent at home. He obtained a carriage to carry Rochambeau and Chastellux from there to Yorktown. "Every day we now lose," he wrote to General Benjamin Lincoln, "is comparatively an age." Just before dawn on September 12, he sent a dozen servants from Mount Vernon to Fredericksburg to see that forage for his horses would be ready when he and his party passed that way to the south. He and the French leaders left soon afterward with his stepson Jacky Custis, who had begged Washington to let him see a little of the war, something he had not yet experienced.

Between September 14 and 24, the allied troops arrived in Williamsburg by both land and sea. En route Washington and his staff stopped at a farmhouse for breakfast one morning. When the meal was over, Henry Knox noticed an elderly man, a resident of the neighborhood, come into the room and slowly approach General Washington. The old man stood for several moments and stared into the impressive face of the commander-in-chief without saying a word. Those in the room grew silent as they watched. Finally the patriarch turned his dim eyes away from Washington and, solemnly looking upward, said in a hushed prayer: "Lord, now lettest thou thy servant depart in peace, for mine eyes have seen thy salvation."

On September 18, Washington, Knox and some other American officers paid their first visit to Admiral de Grasse aboard his flagship the *Ville de Paris*. Containing one hundred and twenty guns, it was at the time the largest and finest warship in the world. The meeting was important because Washington not only wanted to be sure of de Grasse's plans but wished to coordinate French and American efforts. The two officers had not yet met. As Washington—six feet two inches tall and weighing two hundred and ten pounds—reached the quarterdeck, he was greeted by the taller French admiral, who rushed to greet him, threw his arms around him and, in typical French style, kissed him on both cheeks.

"My dear little general!" exclaimed de Grasse, and the aides tittered. Fat Henry Knox could not restrain his mirth and laughed so loudly that his sides shook.

Washington could see thirty-one other French ships of the line lying at anchor around him and the sight fulfilled his ardent hopes of more than six years. He found de Grasse as cordial and cooperative as Rochambeau. The admiral informed Washington that he had now decided to stay until the end of October if necessary and would furnish a detachment of sailors and marines for land operations if it could be done briefly.

Back at his headquarters in Williamsburg, Washington learned that another English naval force had arrived in New York to reinforce Graves. Admiral de Grasse had heard the news at about the same time and sent a message telling Washington and Rochambeau that rather than wait for the British to come down to Virginia to attack him, he intended to sail there and fight at once, leaving only a few vessels for the Yorktown blockade. Both generals were alarmed and sent urgent replies to de Grasse, pointing out the necessity of keeping Chesapeake Bay strongly blocked off. Washington thought the message so important he sent Lafayette to carry it. De Grasse sent back word that he would remain at the mouth of the bay.

Now Washington could turn his full attention to preparations for action against Yorktown. Though almost a century old, it was still little more than a drowsy village, with five churches, a courthouse and numerous houses built along a northern cliff. A few fine dwellings fronted the York River, which flowed into the bay. Williamsburg was some twelve miles to the west on the peninsula. Across the river and opposite Yorktown, a point of land projected on which the village of Gloucester was located; at this point the York narrowed to about one-half a mile in width. In these waters, Cornwallis had placed his small fleet consisting of two frigates, three large transports and some smaller craft.

In selecting Yorktown, Cornwallis had chosen his terrain well. To its west and southwest was Yorktown Creek, which flowed through a ravine resembling a moat. On the south, Wormeley Creek flowed eastward into the York River two miles below the town. Between the two creeks was a flat plain, only half a mile wide, known as the Pigeon Quarter and forming the only good approach by land to Yorktown. Since early September, Cornwallis and his army of 7,800 men had been busy preparing defenses. For once, the Americans and their allies had more troops. Washington had 9,500 men and Rochambeau 7,500 which, along with some marines de Grasse furnished, made a total force of over 18,000 men.

The British had erected fortifications that curved around Yorktown and comprised seven redoubts with batteries. There was also a line of batteries on the river side, one of which had eleven heavy guns that commanded the waterway between the town and Gloucester Point. These fortifications were supported by outworks. Cornwallis had also fortified Gloucester Point in order to control both sides of the York River. Commanding Gloucester was the dreaded cavalry leader, Banastre Tarleton. But the disparity of forces placed most of the fear on the side of the British, who, as soon as they knew of the strength of the combined armies and sea power facing them, had little hope for a victorious outcome.

In his last days at Williamsburg before the attack, Washington could not help but be conscious of familiar things. There was the old capitol building where he had served as a member of the Virginia House of Burgesses a score of years before. He passed Bruton Church, where, as a young legislator, he had often attended services. At the home of his old friend George Wythe, Washington made his headquarters. Wythe, who had accompanied him to the Congress and signed the Declaration of Independence, was at one time Thomas Jefferson's law teacher. There Washington got off a note to General Heath in New York, saying that "Lord Cornwallis is incessantly at work on his fortifications, and is probably preparing to defend himself to the last extremity; a little time will probably decide his fate; with the blessing of heaven, I feel it will be favorable to the interests of America."

Washington and his men marched out of Williamsburg early on the morning of September 28, along the sandy road to Yorktown, twelve miles distant. Just a little over a month before, they had left New York. Across the wide river almost one hundred seventy-five years ago, Captain John Smith had struggled to found a new country.

At noon, the army halted for two hours. Fires for cooking sprang up along the hot roadsides. Then an order from Washington was read to the troops. It stated that if the British were to come out to meet them they were to use bayonets in hand-to-hand fighting. About the middle of the afternoon, a few enemy pickets were sighted by the advance scouts, but the former only fell back silently.

By this time, Washington himself was anxious for some action or at least an encounter that would give him more knowledge of his foe. He rode to the front on a new horse, a light sorrel, large and with a white face and legs. With a telescope, he peered ahead. Soon he saw Cornwallis's fortifications, with his flanks anchored on the river above and below the "town of York." In the center of the British position, he could see the land rising above the creeks on either side. He judged that the best way to reach the town's defenses was across the Pigeon Quarter. Now he could make out British sentries on Gloucester Point and opposite them, enemy ships riding at anchor.

The first night before Yorktown was spent out in the open. Since no tents had as yet arrived, Washington slept under a mulberry tree. The night was quiet except for the sound of men building bridges across the marshy waters.

Up the next morning, the men found a scarcity of drinking water; what little was available was muddy and "full of frogs." But the woods around abounded with hogs; soon some of the fatter ones fell prey to the hungry soldiers, and the aroma of roast pork filled the air. An atmosphere of optimism was plainly present as Dr. Thacher recorded in his diary, "an unbounded confidence in our commanders." It was doubtless much easier to have confidence with such impressive help from the French and an obvious preponderance of troop strength. The worn headquarters tents Washington had used since taking command of the army in Boston were again pitched. He worked in these and slept on a simple cot in the smaller tent. Another shelter was large enough for fifty officers to be entertained at dinner. These tents were outside of range of the enemy artillery and were constantly guarded by members of Washington's Light Guard, who checked all visitors very carefully.

Ordinarily Cornwallis would have sensed defeat from the start of this siege movement, but he kept receiving encouragement from Clinton, who told him that a British fleet would soon come to his relief. As a consequence, Cornwallis wrote Clinton that "I have ventured these last two days to look General Washington's whole force in the face in the position on the outside of my works. . . . There was but one wish throughout the whole army, which was that the enemy would advance."

The British commander would get his wish—but not in the manner and circumstance he desired.

The Americans, in keeping with the tradition of the day, moved into camp on the right of the line and the French on the left, forming a semicircle extending from Wormeley Creek to the York River above Gloucester Point. The Duke de Lauzun was meanwhile placed to contain Banastre Tarleton in the defenses of Gloucester. On the morning of September 20, the allied forces experienced a pleasant surprise: during the night, Lord Cornwallis had withdrawn from his outlying redoubts southwest of the town. This was hard to believe. Here was already a small victory without a fight.

Cornwallis, as usual, had a reason for his action. He had received a message from Clinton just the day before, saying that five thousand men would be sent to Yorktown on British ships to aid both the army and navy in just a few days. Expecting this help, Cornwallis had felt it best to constrict his forces and await reinforcements. But hardly had the redcoats abandoned the trenches, when the Americans and French filled them. Now Washington wrote to John McKean, president of the Continental Congress: "We are in possession of very advantageous grounds, which command their line of works."

Washington wanted to be sure not to leave anything to chance, so he and several of his generals rode out to reconnoiter the terrain. The first redoubt he reached was under some tall trees and thus was an inviting target. Soon a cannon ball looped across above the heads of the party and gave them a start, but they did not change their position.

When a second shot pounded into the dirt not many feet away, all the officers galloped to the rear—all, that is, except Washington, who sat on his big horse, his telescope fixed on the British lines. Though he remained there for several minutes in characteristic indifference, for some reason the enemy did not fire again.

There were many details to see to. Deserters had to be apprehended, particularly those with smallpox so that they would not spread the disease. Washington also had to urge his men, despite the scarcity of uniforms, to dress with at least some similarity, otherwise they might be shot. A soldier on duty wearing red clothing made a prime target, too. And he gave orders for more than a thousand men to labor at strengthening the earthworks in front of the British.

Sometimes, Washington found, one's friends can be more of a problem than one's enemies. A favorite, the Marquis de Lafayette, to whom Washington was plainly devoted, had the effrontery to ask him to be put in command of all the American forces at Yorktown in place of General Benjamin Lincoln, a seasoned senior officer. After all, argued the impulsive young Frenchman, Lincoln had already made his reputation, and now Lafayette felt it was time to allow him to make his own. With fatherly firmness tempered by gentleness, Washington turned down the request and left Lincoln in charge as second in command of the siege operations.

In order to be sure that the men realized the urgency of the situation, Washington issued the following orders: "The general expects and requires the officers and soldiers to pursue the duties of their respective departments with the most unabating ardor. The present moment will decide American independence . . . the liberties of America and the honor of the Allied Arms." As a practical follow-up, the general sent a sizeable fraction of his forces into the nearby woodlands to cut saplings and branches to be tied into bundles for use as fascines, to fill trenches and earthworks. Gabions were formed by driving saplings into the ground in circles and then filling the enclosures with dirt. Washington planned to use these near the enemy and to open parallels as close as possible. Then the heavy artillery brought from the North by Knox and by his French compatriots was placed in position; it would prove to be a decisive element in the battle.

Of course all this activity could not escape the eyes of the British. Gunners fired constantly at the allied positions in an effort to prevent the placing of the artillery pieces. At first, the intrepid but reckless Americans exposed themselves needlessly to British fire. As a result, a drummer was hit by a cannon ball; a militiaman who had climbed on top of a parapet and showed off for hours, daring the enemy to hit him, drew their aim and his battered body ended up in a trench. A chaplain's hat was covered with sand from an artillery projectile, and Washington joshed the owner by suggesting he carry it home to show his family.

As is usually the case, there were deserters on both sides. Washington issued a stern warning: "Every deserter from the American troops, after this public notice is given, who shall be found within the enemy's lines at York, if the place falls into our hands, will be instantly hanged."

During the first week in October, the allied forces were preparing to advance their siege and tighten the noose around Cornwallis. By dawn of October 5, Washington was almost ready to open a parallel, or new trench, in advance of his line, nearer to the enemy. The idea was to complete the trench in one night so that the British would not observe the work. Washington had given instructions that no gun would be fired until all artillery was properly in place. He wanted the first sudden, massive salvo to have an overwhelming effect on the already jittery enemy. The weather turned cold and windy. Rain swept in from the bay. Men hunched close beside their campfires, while others tried to sleep.

By the evening of October 6, they were ready to dig the trench across the Pigeon Quarter between Wormeley Creek and Yorktown. The rain had stopped, and darkness had settled upon the fields. Washington could hear no sound from the British side except for the yelping, every now and then, of the watchdogs in the biggest British redoubt. The night hours passed slowly, the beat of picks and shovels keeping up a muffled staccato. A light rain fell. As morning approached, a chill crept over the area and stiffened the diggers.

A story is told that while the men were working in the darkness, a tall man wearing a cape appeared beside them, so wrapped up that they could not tell who he was. He asked questions, talked and then left. Sergeant Joseph Plumb Martin of the Americans recorded in his diary that the man said as he left, "If you're captured out here, be sure the enemy doesn't find out that you're sappers and miners." He and his detachment already realized this, Martin noted, knowing that if they were captured, they would, according to the rules of war of that day, be summarily executed. They dug on. Hearing the engineers call the stranger "Your Excellency," Martin concluded that the man was Washington and added, "Had we dared, we might have cautioned him for exposing himself so carelessly to danger at such a time, and doubtless he would have taken it in good part if we had."

Fifteen hundred men were hard at work preparing the parallel trenches. Columns of panting men brought forward gabions and fascines, while others struggled to mount the heavy guns. Soon after dark, the troops moved out behind the engineers. They did not stop until they were less than a thousand yards from the British lines. The miners and sappers were at the same place where they had met the shadowy figure of Washington the previous night. Here he was again, and according to Sergeant Martin's account, Washington took up one of the pickaxes and struck a few blows with it, "so that it might be said," Martin recorded—perhaps with tongue in cheek—"that General Washington with his own hands first broke ground at the siege of Yorktown."

This brief ceremony over, the men immediately went to work placing the gabions, the sandy soil being thrown into them, in proper rows, so that the new trench was now behind a kind of dirt breastwork. Fortunately the enemy remained quiet for several hours while the troops were completing the two-thousand-yard trench, extending from the head of Yorktown Creek across the Hampton Road and then in the shape of a crescent to the bluff above the York River. At around 9 P.M. some firing broke out unexpectedly. Washington was told that a French deserter had slipped out and reported their positions to the English. But the work went on. Rain continued to fall, but it hindered the firing of the British more than it did the work of the allies.

For three days they labored. Though the men made typical soldierly complaints, their efforts were beginning to pay off. The big siege guns were dragged forward and emplaced, under the direction of Henry Knox, who seemed to be everywhere at once. The huge, dumpy mortars were mounted on special carriages invented by Knox in order to elevate the barrels of the large guns so that their shells would lob high into the air and then fall into Yorktown. On orders from their commanders, the troops still held their fire.

Then at three o'clock in the afternoon of October 9, the French let loose with a resounding boom a battery of four-pound cannon, along with six mortars and howitzers. The battle had begun. Soon afterward, Washington was walking with Knox for a last-minute inspection of the American batteries. Seeing the cannon all set neatly in their places, primed and loaded and ready for the torch to be put to the fuse, Washington apparently felt a great desire to start the firing himself. Knox, who doubtless also wished to do this, picked up a torch, lighted it and handed it to his chief. Washington strode over and touched it to the fuse of a fat, smooth-bore twelve-pounder cannon, and the first American artillery shot of the siege of Yorktown rammed into the British lines.

The first shot was said to have crashed into the house where British staff officers were gathered for mess, killing Commissary General Perkins and wounding three of his companions. Colonel Philip van Cortlandt reported that "I could hear the ball strike from house to house, and I was afterwards informed that it went through the one where many of the officers were at dinner, and over the tables, discomposing the dishes and either killed or wounded the one at the head of the table." A later shot from the same American battery decapitated a Major Cochrane as he stood beside Lord Cornwallis, who came so close to being hit himself that he ducked under a cliff for protection. One of his enlisted men, Johann Conrad Doehla, wrote, "One could not avoid the horribly many cannon balls, either inside or outside the city. Many men were badly injured or mortally wounded by the fragments of the bombs which exploded partly in the air and partly on the ground, their arms and legs severed or themselves struck dead. One saw men lying nearly everywhere who were mortally wounded. I saw bombs fall into the water and lie there for 5, 6, 8 and more minutes and then still explode. Fragments and pieces of these bombs flew back again and fell on the houses and buildings of the city and in our camp, where they still did much damage and robbed many a brave soldier of his life or struck off his arm and leg."

Washington was naturally encouraged by the results of his artillery fire. But he and Knox generously admitted that the French fired even more accurately although Lafayette just as gallantly denied it. Trouble was caused by faulty American ammunition that sometimes failed to explode. Even so, Doehla reported, "They threw bombs in here from 100, 150 pound and also some of 200 pounds. . . . Most of the inhabitants who were still found here at Yorktown fled with their best possessions eastward to the bank of the York River and dug in among the sand cliffs. But many were badly injured and mortally wounded by the fragments of bombs which exploded partly in the air and partly on the ground."

Washington must have managed a smile at the sight of a huge bulldog belonging to the British that, every time they fired from a certain sector, would follow their shots across the trenches. Some of the allied officers restrained their men from firing at the animal, suggesting instead that they capture him, attach a message for Cornwallis to his tail and then send him back across the lines.

Early next morning Washington rode out to observe the skill of the French gunners, who had acquitted themselves well by smashing targets in the town with fine accuracy. These ebullient gunners made the boast that they could fire six consecutive shots into the same narrow opening.

As Washington watched, a white flag appeared on the enemy's works. An old man, afflicted with gout, limped toward him on the arms of two soldiers, followed by a servant carrying a bundle of family silver. This was the uncle of Governor Thomas Nelson of Virginia, who was with the American and French forces at the time. After his elegant house had been battered by American artillery, Cornwallis had sent the elderly man out. The house had been used as headquarters, and the British had had to move. Washington heard from his unexpected guest that Cornwallis had moved to an underground headquarters, that a thousand horses had been killed and that many Negroes had fallen victim to the bombardment. Governor Nelson next asked that his own fine house in Yorktown be fired upon, and it was.

In the next day, red-hot shot from French guns set fire to the British frigate *Charon*. The flames, Dr. Thacher said, "spread with vivid brightness among the combustible rigging, and running with amazing rapidity to the tops of the several masts, while all around, the thunder and lightning from our numerous cannon and mortars made one of the most sublime and magnificent spectacles which can be imagined." Two British transports were also set ablaze and burned to the water's edge during the night.

By now, some fifty allied siege guns were pounding the defenses of the enemy and steadily diminishing their response. With such great destruction by the artillery at distances of only eight hundred to one thousand yards, Washington decided to open a second allied siege line or parallel, so as to bring his guns even closer to their objective. Work on this began on the night of October 11 and lasted almost three days. Every conceivable kind of digging tool was used to move the dirt for the new artillery position. The work was plainly seen by the British and drew a heavy fire of musketry, canister, grapeshot and bombs, but to little avail. The second parallel was completed.

Washington, Lincoln, Knox and their aides were standing in an exposed position, shells from the enemy falling nearby. Becoming alarmed, Colonel David Cobb, an aide to the commander, looked nervously at him and finally cried out, "Sir, you are too much exposed here. Had you not better step back a little?"

Calmly returning his gaze, Washington replied, "Colonel

Cobb, if you are afraid, you have the liberty to step back."

The works needed to be extended to the river, but as two large British redoubts intervened, this could not be done until they were taken. Washington ordered all the guns within range to begin firing upon these redoubts in order to soften them up so that they could be assaulted. This was vigorously done, and it was then decided that two columns, one French, the other American, would attack the objectives. Lafayette wanted his aide to lead the American attack, but Alexander Hamilton, now a lieutenant colonel and itching for a fight, as he had been for a long time, insisted that he have the opportunity. The dispute went to Washington. He was in a quandary, because he had promised Lafayette considerable leeway in the operations, of which the French were such a vital part. But he also remembered how much Hamilton wished to get into combat before the war was over. Hamilton then reminded his commander that he was officer of the day at this time, October 14. That gave Washington a technical out. He designated Hamilton.

The two redoubts were taken in spirited and effectual assaults, and by 10 P.M. the workers were busy extending the parallel northeastward to the York River. But the wily Cornwallis was not yet finished. Just before dawn on October 16, he sent a picked force of redcoats against the new second parallel at a place where the French sector joined that of the Americans. For a while the brave attackers succeeded, spiking seven of the allied guns. They inflicted seventeen casualties while losing twelve of their own men. But the British were hit by a sharp counterattack from the French and driven back. Washington inspected the position soon after daylight and was told by his cannoneers that they had already "unspiked" their guns and showed him that they were again ready for action.

Viewing the activity, Dr. Thacher—who seems to have had a penchant for close observation and vivid description—

wrote "the bomb shells from the besiegers and the besieged are incessantly crossing each other's path in the air. They are clearly visible in the form of a black ball in the day, but in the night they appear like fiery meteors with blazing tails, most beautifully brilliant, ascending majestically from the mortar to a certain altitude, and gradually descending to the spot where they are destined to execute their work of destruction. . . . the whole peninsula trembles under the incessant thunder of our infernal machines."

Lord Cornwallis, the best British field general in America, later to distinguish himself in India, was to make yet another try at escape. He felt there was a bare possibility to save his army by a retreat such as that which Washington had made after the Battle of Long Island. His idea was to ferry his men across the York to Gloucester, join the rest of his army there and overcome the French force that was holding the British above that point. With captured French horses, he and his men might dash off northward and up through Maryland. (Lafayette, incidentally, had correctly predicted Cornwallis's escape route across the York.)

Under the cover of night on October 16, Cornwallis put into effect his desperate plan. He had a number of boats loaded with troops, and these sailed across the river to Gloucester. But fate and weather were against the British. A furious storm arose that, with its wind and rain, soon grew into a gale. Some men were landed on the opposite shore, but most of the boats were driven down the river into Chesapeake Bay. The last effort to escape had to be abandoned.

The next day, October 17, was a bad day in British history. It was, ironically, the fourth anniversary of the surrender of Burgoyne at Saratoga. At least a hundred cannon opened up on the Yorktown garrison, and the shells dropped upon it "more horribly than ever before." The British defenses "were tumbling into ruin; not a gun could be fired from them." This was partly because ammunition was exhausted. Lord Cornwallis entered his hornwork and took a final look at the situation. Then even he decided he had had enough.

Shortly after 9 A.M., a drummer boy climbed to the top of the British parapet and began to beat a signal for a parley. So loud was the roar of the bombardment that his little drum could not be heard. But sentries watching from the allied trenches spotted him and called to their commanders. "He might have beat away until Doomsday," recorded Ebenezer Denny of the Pennsylvania Line, "if he had not been sighted by men in the front lines. The constant firing was too much for the sound of the single drum; but when the firing ceased, I thought I had never heard a drum equal to it—the most delightful music to us all."

Soon a brightly clad British officer joined the valiant drummer boy and stood beside him waving a white handkerchief. The drum continued its beat. Then an American officer sprang out of his trench and ran to meet the enemy officer. After tying his own handkerchief over the eyes of the redcoat, he led him back into the allied lines and then to Washington's headquarters. There Washington read a note carried by the officer from Lord Cornwallis: "Sir, I propose a cessation of hostilities for twenty-four hours, and that two officers may be appointed by each side, to meet at Mr. Moore's house, to settle terms for the surrender of the posts at York and Gloucester."

Washington replied immediately: "My Lord: I have had the honor of receiving your Lordship's letter of this date.

"An ardent desire to spare the further effusion of blood, will readily incline me to listen to such terms for the surrender of your posts and garrisons of York and Gloucester, as are admissible.

"I wish previously to the meeting of Commissioners, that your Lordship's proposals in writing may be sent to the

American lines; for which purpose, a suspension of hostilities during two hours from the delivery of this letter will be granted."

Trying to bargain until the last, Cornwallis replied within the time limit given him but asked that his troops be returned to England. They would not serve against America or France during the war or until they might be exchanged. The response from Washington was naturally no, with the grim comment that "the same honors will be granted to the surrendering army as were granted to the garrison of Charleston."

This meant that the British and German soldiers would be received as prisoners of war. Washington agreed that the British might retain their personal property but he refused to grant immunity to any Tories and deserters within the British lines. Details of the negotiations were worked out by commissioners at the Moore house, behind the allied lines. Lieutenant Colonel Thomas Dundas and Major Alexander Ross represented Cornwallis. Washington named Lieutenant Colonel John Laurens, and Rochambeau selected Lafayette's brother-in-law, Viscount de Noailles, as allied commissioners. The four argued long over the details. Military and naval personnel were to be surrendered as prisoners of war, those of the navy becoming prisoners of France while the soldiers would go to the United States. The officers would be allowed to go on parole to New York, Europe or any American post in the possession of the British.

It was almost midnight when the allied commissioners returned to their headquarters. Though exhausted, they did bring a rough draft of the surrender terms. Washington read over the document carefully and approved ten of the fourteen articles. But as expected, he declined to approve immunity for Tories and deserters who had lined up with the

British. He also stated that merchants who were with the British army should be considered war prisoners. The enemy, he insisted, should provide for its own sick and wounded men.

Early the next day—it was an auspicious occasion and none of the victors minded getting up at dawn—Washington directed that the articles of surrender be copied in final form. They were then sent to Cornwallis with orders that they be signed by 11 A.M. and the garrison march out and give up its arms at 2 P.M. This was a new role for George Washington, supervising the capitulation of a British army, and he thoroughly enjoyed it.

Shortly before the designated hour of eleven, Washington and Rochambeau rode out to a captured redoubt, where they were joined by a representative of Count de Grasse, who had come down with an attack of asthma. A few minutes later, the papers were returned to them by Cornwallis, duly signed by him and his chief naval officer, Captain Thomas Symonds. At the bottom Washington had added the line, "Done in the trenches before Yorktown in Virginia, October 19, 1781." Then he signed his name as "G. Washington."

The news of the forthcoming ceremonies had reached the ears of the civilian populace, and from all around the countryside the people gathered, traveling in wagons, on horseback and in carriages. The equipages and servants of the local planters impressed the foreign visitors very much. Now the French formed along the main road that led from Yorktown past the Pigeon Quarter and to the trenches of the allied forces. They looked magnificent in their white linen uniforms faced by pastel colors. Quite a contrast they were to the shabbily clad Americans in "small jackets of white cloth, dirty and ragged and a number of them almost barefoot. But what does it matter?" asked the Baron von

Closen. "These people are much more praiseworthy to fight as they do, when they are so poorly supplied with everything."

Finally, to the cadence of a roll of drums, the British made their belated appearance. Their color guard carried their flags furled. Allied troops strained their eyes to catch a sight of the renowned British commander, but Cornwallis was not there. Being so ashamed at his misfortune, he had pleaded illness and did not appear for the surrender ceremonies. Instead, leading the brilliantly dressed troops was Brigadier General Charles O'Hara, second in command. According to a French account, O'Hara at first approached the Count de Rochambeau to offer his sword to him, seemingly preferring to surrender to the French rather than the upstart Americans. But the French commander waved him aside and motioned for him to go to Washington instead.

O'Hara again proffered his sword, but again he was waved on. Being a secondary officer, he was not considered eligible by protocol to present himself directly to the commander-in-chief. So Washington designated Major General Benjamin Lincoln, his deputy commander, to receive the surrender from his corresponding officer in the British army. Whether Washington had had it in mind is not known; however, it does seem appropriate that the general who had surrendered to the enemy at Charleston should be the one to receive the surrender near Yorktown.

Many accounts of the ceremonies state that the British band played sadly and slowly the tune, "The World Turned Upside Down." But Richard S. Hill, head of the Reference Section, Music Division, of the Library of Congress takes a different view, based upon extensive research. "Anyone with the slightest familiarity with military music in the eighteenth century would be immediately suspicious of the tale," he comments. Instead, he contends, several marches were played by the various British and German band units.

Lincoln indicated to O'Hara where the British troops were to lay down their arms. It was in a nearby field of the Pigeon Quarter, just beyond where Washington and his staff were stationed. There, a large circle of French hussars sat astride their horses, and inside of the circle, each regiment was to march, stack its arms and then march back out. Although they were in bright, new uniforms, the enemy soldiers, Dr. Thacher thought, "were disorderly and unsoldierly, their step was irregular and their ranks frequently broken." There probably was a reason for this, as one American officer observed that the "prisoners appeared to be much in liquor." Some of the British officers were said to have bitten their lips; some pouted, while others wept unashamedly. Many of the soldiers seemed sullen when ordered to ground their arms and threw them violently into a pile until General Lincoln noticed it. He then ordered them to stack their weapons in an orderly way, which they did.

With the details of the surrender well underway, Washington issued an invitation to General O'Hara and the other senior British officers to dine with him that evening, and returned to his headquarters. He had reason for satisfaction. The British had surrendered 7,257 troops and 840 seamen, had lost 156 dead and 326 wounded, with 70 missing. The Americans lost 23 dead and 65 wounded, with 30 missing. The French suffered 60 dead and 193 wounded.

On the same day that Cornwallis surrendered, Clinton sailed from New York for Virginia with seven thousand troops and thirty-five ships. Hearing of the surrender, he returned to New York, but had Cornwallis waited just ten days more to capitulate—which he might have done—Yorktown might have been a different story.

The dinner at Washington's headquarters was a pleasant occasion, especially for the victors. Even the British seemed relaxed and relieved. They chatted with the French and

American officers as if they had never been adversaries, which was characteristic of the professional soldier. Washington was concerned over the health of his stepson Jacky Custis, who had insisted on seeing the ceremonies, against the advice of doctors.

But Henry Knox was overjoyed with the outcome of the operation against the British. He wrote his friend John Adams that it had been necessary for Washington to bring the main army down and settle the situation or give the South up as lost. "The consequences will be extremely beneficial," he said with understatement. "Our beloved General Washington, whose distinguished patriotism and worth rises every day, demands the pen of some animated republican to do him justice."

Not forgetting the men who had made the victory possible, Washington issued an order of congratulations to the army. He was so occupied with details of the surrender that it was nighttime before he got around to sending a message to Congress: "Sir: I have the honor to inform Congress, that a reduction of the British Army under the command of Lord Cornwallis, is most happily effected. The unremitting ardor which actuated every officer and soldier in the combined Army in this occasion, has principally led to this important event more than my most sanguine hopes had induced me to expect." The proud commander-in-chief went on to praise other officers who had distinguished themselves in the campaign.

Washington then selected Lieutenant Colonel Tench Tilghman, an engaging Marylander and one of his most loyal aides, who had shared many command secrets, to carry the message to Philadelphia. Although extremely anxious to hurry, Tilghman, just recovering from a fever, sailed down the York and up the bay, but his small sailboat then ran aground on an island. After spending an impatient night, he made only twenty miles the next day because of a mild wind. Then thirty miles below Annapolis, the wind died down completely, and Tilghman became ill again. But he managed to get ashore, obtained a horse and dashed off for the capital. He arrived chilled and shaken at midnight, after changing horses several times. He aroused President Thomas McKean of the Congress, who was so overjoyed at news of the vital victory that he had the Independence Hall bell tolled until dawn broke over the city.

Meanwhile, those who learned the news turned the city into a fiesta of celebration. Windows flew open and candles were lighted, the streets soon filled with cheering throngs, some of whom stoned the homes of Quakers, who had opposed the war. Salutes were fired, and many toasts were drunk at joyous banquets. Congress offered prayers of thanks, but some of the members shouted angrily that Cornwallis should be hanged because of his atrocities in the South and demanded that Washington be ordered to execute him. Then it was pointed out that the earl had surrendered in good faith, and such an order would upset Washington and reflect upon his integrity. The proposal was defeated, but by only a small majority.

The enemy prisoners were sent out of Yorktown to various destinations, some of them fading into the countryside, there to remain for the rest of their lives. Washington then had the Gloucester garrison disarmed and went out to visit the French fleet and to thank Admiral de Grasse for his help, which now seemed more important than ever. In a move that appeared impetuous, Washington had the stockades opened and all the prisoners, no matter what their offense, freed. He showed mercy to the Tories, but to the deserters who had once served under him and then changed sides, he meted out sentences of hanging. The French thought this fair.

In line with eighteenth-century officer camaraderie, Washington and his staff entertained Cornwallis and his aides at several banquets. But when it came the turn of Baron von Steuben, that improvident individual was embarrassed, because he was "completely broke." He even sold his horse so he could have the money to entertain, but still had to borrow five half-joes (Portuguese coins worth about eight dollars each) from Henry Knox. Said the baron, "I will give one grand dinner to our allies, should I eat soup with a wooden spoon forever after." So he spent all he had obtained, and finally, before he left Yorktown, von Steuben suppressed his pride enough to borrow twenty guineas from Washington himself. The army at that time owed the baron an estimated eighty-five hundred dollars, most of which he never received, though he was given some worthless treasury certificates.

On November 3, 1781, Washington and his staff rode west, and Cornwallis and O'Hara sailed for New York. That evening, after stopping at Williamsburg to see patients in the hospital, Washington reached Eltham at the head of the York River, where Burwell Bassett, his brother-in-law, lived. There he was grieved to find Jacky Custis gravely ill; in fact, he died during the night, leaving four young children.

A week later, the young widow Custis reached Mount Vernon with Washington. Though it was a sad homecoming, he could be thankful for his signal victory. Now he could look ahead to the end of hostilities and to his return to his home and hearthside.

XIII AFTERMATH

ALTHOUGH YORKTOWN did not mark the official ending of the Revolution, the war was practically over. The British prime minister, Lord North, predicted that his cause was lost, although it was six months before he left office. The English people were tired of the war, and their resources had undergone a great strain. In March of 1782, Parliament passed a resolution recommending that the conflict be terminated. King George III was finally convinced, and by early April conversations began between British and American commissioners in Paris.

At Mount Vernon, George Washington relaxed briefly with his family and friends and discussed the condition of his estate with his cousin, Lund Washington, also its manager. After only a week at home, the general and his wife set out for Philadelphia. Stopping en route at Annapolis, Maryland, they received a hearty welcome and a sumptuous dinner, along with "good wine and bad poetry."

Washington arrived in Philadelphia on November 26 and found that Congress was glad to see him but wanted the war continued in the South. He agreed. However, he wrote to Nathanael Greene that he was afraid "Congress, viewing this stroke at Yorktown in too favorable a light, may think our work too nearly closed, and will fall into a state of languor and relaxation. To prevent this error, I shall employ every means in my power, and if unhappily we sink into that fatal mistake, no part of the blame shall be mine."

Most of the members of Congress seemed to share Washington's view that his victory had created a lull, so plans were made for the future. For fifteen weeks, Washington and his wife remained in Philadelphia, and although he had the usual small problems of his command reported to him, on the whole it was a pleasant period. He and Martha enjoyed a round of social festivities, and many of his friends were invited to his quarters at the house of Benjamin Chew on South Third Street. Wherever he went, crowds followed him, whether he was hunting in the suburbs or worshiping each Sunday at Saint Peter's Church. By the end of March, with the end of the winter weather, he let it be known that he would like to return to his soldiers. He was accordingly given permission by Congress, which assured him of their esteem and confidence and commended him to the "protection of Divine Providence." In his reply, Washington expressed his gratitude and said that nothing in his power would prevent him from promoting the views of Congress "to insure a successful campaign." Then he departed.

Arriving in the Hudson highlands, Washington found Generals William Health and Alexander McDougall feuding over jurisdictional matters. He turned the dispute over to a court-martial, as was his custom in such things. He also learned that Captain Richard Lippincott of the Associated Loyalists in New York—of which William Franklin, illegitimate son of Benjamin, was president—had received permission to take three Patriot prisoners from jail in New Jersey, where they were to be exchanged. Before reaching Henry Knox and Gouverneur Morris, commissioners who had been appointed by Washington to negotiate, Lippincott had decided to execute one of the prisoners, Joshua Huddy, because a Loyalist named White had been put to death previously by the Americans. Huddy was thereupon taken to Morristown and hanged, with a sign placed on him by Lippincott that read, "Up Goes Huddy for Phillip White."

People of the neighborhood discovered the body and notified Knox, who informed Washington. Washington was so incensed that he wrote General Clinton that unless the murderer was given over to the Americans, he would hang a British captain in retaliation. So lots were drawn, and a British prisoner, Captain Charles Asgill, nineteen, became the intended victim. Protests reached Washington from Europe as well as America. Even Alexander Hamilton wrote Knox that "a sacrifice of this kind is entirely repugnant to the genius of the age we live in and is without example in modern history. . . . It is a deliberate sacrifice of the innocent for the guilty and must be condemned. . . . I address myself to you on this occasion, because I know your liberality and your influence with the General."

Knox replied to Hamilton that he had talked to Washington, who felt that it was impossible for him to "recede from his full determination." Washington had assured Knox, however, that only after everything possible had been done to resolve the issue would he go through with the punishment. An out was found; the British decided to try Captain Lippincott by court-martial, so Washington set young Asgill free. The incident did serve to break up the organization of Associated Loyalists.

In the spring of 1782, Washington received a letter from Colonel Lewis Nicola, head of the Invalid Regiment, stationed at West Point, containing the surprising suggestion that the new nation become a monarchy with Washington as its king. Washington, roused to unusual anger, treated the idea with contempt. He answered, "Be assured, sir, no occurrence in the course of the war has given me more sensations. . . . I must view it with abhorrence and reprehend it with severity."

Military action was largely superseded by administrative activities. A celebration of the birth of the French dauphin was observed at West Point on May 31. Washington climaxed it with a dinner for over five hundred guests in a temporary bower, 214 by 70 feet in size. Such a setting would have seemed too elaborate to the public at this time of austerity had not Washington taken pains to explain that all of it had been prepared by his soldiers with material they had cut in the woods. One toast given during the gay occasion especially appealed to him. "A new edge to our swords, until they shall have opened the way to independence, freedom and glory; and then may be converted to the instruments of peace."

The Purple Heart Badge of Military Merit was established by Washington in a general order of August 7, 1782. The order, which set up a permanent award for men of all ranks, reads in part as follows:

"The general, ever desirous to cherish a virtuous ambition in his soldiers, as well as to foster and encourage every species of military merit, directs that whenever any singularly meritorious action is performed, the author of it shall be permitted to wear on his facings over the left breast, the figure of a heart in purple cloth or silk, edged with narrow lace or binding. Not only instances of unusual gallantry but also of extraordinary fidelity and essential service in any way shall meet with a due reward. . . . The road to glory in a patriot army and a free country is thus open to all."

As the summer wore on, Washington learned sadly of the death of young John Laurens, a favorite aide at one time, in South Carolina, while resisting a British raid. General Charles Lee also passed away soon afterward. That resentful and erratic individual had paid his final respects to Washington by writing to his sister that Washington's understanding was of "so slow a sort as not to be of any use in that situation to which the infatuation of the people has raised him; but he has an ample share of cunning which enables him, by direct or indirect means (but the latter is his favorite mode) to work the ruin of every man who has excited his jealousy or offended his pride." The dawning of 1783 brought also the news of the death of Lord Stirling, which touched Washington deeply.

Soon there came word that both officers and men were complaining bitterly to Congress that they had not been paid. They feared that when they were discharged the government would forget what it had promised them and leave them impoverished after they had spent some of their most active years in the service.

Washington wrote to a friend: "Peace has given rest to speculative opinions respecting the time and terms of it. The first has come as soon as we could well have expected it under the disadvantages which we labored; and the latter is abundantly satisfactory. It is now the bounden duty of every one to make the blessings thereof as diffusive as possible."

Then prophetically Washington added these words: "We now have a National Character to establish, and it is of the utmost importance to stamp favorable impressions upon it; let justice then be one of its characteristics and gratitude another. . . . This Army is of near eight years' standing, six of which they have spent in the field without any other shelter from the inclemency of the seasons than tents or such houses as they could build for themselves without expense to the public. They have encountered hunger, cold and nakedness. They have fought many battles and bled freely. They have lived without pay. . . . Many of them to do better and to dress as officers have contracted heavy debts or spent their patrimonies. Is there no discrimination then, no extra exertion to be made in favor of these men in these peculiar circumstances, in the event of their military dissolution? . . . Are they to be turned adrift soured and discontented, complaining of the ingratitude of their country? . . . For permit me to add, tho every man in the army feels his distress—it is not every one that will reason to the cause of it."

On February 20, 1783, Alexander Hamilton had confided to some of his friends that "the army had secretly determined not to lay down their arms until due provision should be afforded on the subject of their pay." He also stated that Washington had become unpopular with many of the men because of his "known dislike to every unlawful proceeding." Hamilton added that he knew "General Washington intimately and perfectly, that his extreme reserve, mixed sometimes with asperity of temper, both of which have increased of late, had contributed to the decline of his popularity, but his virtue, patriotism and firmness would never yield to any dishonorable or disloyal plans into which he might be called. He would sooner suffer himself to be cut to pieces."

In the army, as the weeks passed, the cry for pay grew louder. The soldiers stated with reason that they had done their part and more for their country, now it was time it did its part for them. Henry Knox told his friend Benjamin Lincoln that "the expectations of the army, from the drummer to the highest officer, are so keen for *some* pay, that I shudder at the idea of their not receiving it. The utmost period of suffering upon that head has arrived. To attempt to lengthen it will undoubtedly occasion commotions."

General Knox was correct. There was much commotion. Some high-ranking officers went to Philadelphia, asked for payment and were turned down—partly because Congress had so many other financial obligations and could not depend on voluntary help from the states. These men then returned to their main encampment at Newburgh, New York, and bitterly attacked their government. Their sentiments were contained in an anonymous letter signed "Brutus" and probably written by Major John Armstrong, aide to General Horatio Gates. It stated that the army should not disband until its members were duly paid; that the recipient of the letter should be silent about receiving it, but be vigilant; and that conditions were such that the army "should not lose a moment." This was followed by a second letter urging the men to meet on March 11 and draw up a final remonstrance, which if not heeded by Congress, would justify them in defying that body and moving to the west. It meant a virtual mutiny.

Washington was aware of these letters and of course was depressed and alarmed. He issued a general order forbidding the meeting of March 11. Realizing that something must be done, he called for a regular meeting of his officers on March 15. A weak man would have held back. A rash one would have tried to suppress the meeting. Washington did neither but quietly took charge of the whole movement. He realized that now he must exert his utmost efforts to curb the uprising before it could really get underway. Hamilton and others had urged that he make the cause of the dissident officers his own.

Instead of waiting for more reports to come to him, he planned to appear before the meeting himself. His correspondence at this time reveals that such a step was distasteful for him, but experience had taught him that often one must do what he dreads most. Keeping in mind what Congress had already promised and trying to gain a prior sense of the feelings of his officers, he prepared a paper he would take with him to the meeting.

On March 15 he went to a large wooden building beside

the Hudson River that the soldiers had completed only a few weeks before. It was called The Temple and was used both as a chapel and a dancing academy. A hush fell on the audience when his tall figure strode to the simple lectern at the front of the room. Every eye was upon him, and there was surprise that he would appear here in this hostile atmosphere.

As he began speaking, rather haltingly at first, he pointed out that when he had issued the order for the meeting, he had not intended to participate in the proceedings. But the anonymous Newburgh Addresses had made such an impact that his presence was necessary. He explained that he had put his thoughts into writing, and that with their permission, he would read the result. He admitted that the Addresses were well written and designed to impress their readers with the idea that there was "premeditated injustice in the sovereign power of the United States." He reminded his listeners of his own long army service and deplored the hint of mutiny in the anonymous papers, which could only leave the country defenseless or even in danger of attack by its own warriors. He denounced any such sentiments and promised that "in the attainment of complete justice for all your toils and dangers . . . you may freely command my services to the utmost of my abilities."

By this time, the veteran officers were tensely attentive, leaning forward to catch every word spoken by this voice so familiar to them on the field. "Let me entreat you, gentlemen," he went on, his voice becoming more resonant and earnest, "on your part, not to take any measures which, viewed in the calm light of reason, will lessen the dignity and sully the glory you have hitherto maintained . . . You will, by the dignity of your conduct, afford occasion for posterity to say, when speaking of the glorious example you have exhibited to mankind, 'had this day been wanting, the world had never seen the last stage of perfection to which human nature is capable of attaining.' "

Washington paused. According to some of those present, there was an almost electric silence in the room. Then he slowly pulled a letter from his pocket and explained that it was from Joseph Jones, a discerning member of Congress from Virginia. The letter explained some of the tremendous financial problems Congress had to face, including that of the army's demands. Apparently the letter was written in a small, hard-to-read hand, for Washington now paused and reached into his pocket, took out his new spectacles and put them on. "Gentlemen," he said emotionally, "you must pardon me. I have grown gray in your service and now find myself growing blind."

There were lumps in many throats and tears in some eyes. Washington quietly withdrew. Then a committee headed by Henry Knox moved to give Washington a vote of thanks. This was passed, and so was a resolution expressing the confidence of the officers in the justice of Congress. The assemblage repudiated the proposals of the anonymous addresses and asked Washington to act in their behalf. Only Colonel Timothy Pickering seemed dissatisfied. Major Samuel Shaw, Knox's aide, later wrote about Washington: "He spoke—every doubt was dispelled, and the tide of patriotism rolled again in its wonted course. Illustrious man! What he says of the army may with equal justice be applied to his own character."

The tide of patriotism had been heightened by the arrival on March 12 of Captain Joshua Barney—on a ship appropriately named the *Washington*—bringing Congress the official text of the treaty of peace between the United States and Great Britain. It had been signed in Paris on November 30, 1782, but was not final. When he first learned of it, Washington was skeptical and said it was so incon-

clusive that his country should be "prepared for either
alternative, war or peace." But his initial fears were quieted
as confirmation of the significance of the treaty continued
to come from Europe. "The news," said Washington in
understatement, "has filled my mind with inexpressible
satisfaction."

And so, fittingly, on April 19, exactly eight years after
the fighting on Lexington Green, from the steps of The
Temple, near Newburgh, the "cessation of hostilities between the United States and the King of Great Britain"
was joyfully announced.

The military historians, Colonels R. E. and T. N. Dupuy,
have attributed the victory to "the unselfish genius of
George Washington, who could transform stubborn freemen, who refused to submit to unjust law, into professional
soldiers capable of meeting on equal terms the best that
Europe could produce. His was the inspiration which
guided these men to discard the primal instinct of self-
preservation for that of the patriotic will to win. His was
the iron will and military acumen which substituted victory for defeat, no matter how hopeless the situation."

But for Washington, the task was not finished. He longed
to place his ideas about the future in the hearts and minds
of those to whom it would mean the most. Accordingly, he
wrote another of his "Circulars to the States" which he had
sent so frequently during the war (and often with disappointing results), urgently asking for supplies such as
powder, recruits, arms, clothing and food. In this his last
such communication, he reminded the states that "this is
the moment when the eyes of the world are turned upon
them, this is the moment to establish or ruin their national
character forever . . ." Then again with a perspicacity that
is clear to us today, he added, "For, according to the system
of policy the states shall adopt at this moment, they will
stand or fall, and by their confirmation or lapse, it is yet

to be decided, whether the Revolution must ultimately be considered as a blessing or a curse: a blessing or a curse, not to the present age alone, for with our fate will the destiny of unborn millions be involved."

Although he produced a document highly significant for the future of his new nation, Washington was becoming bored with the inactivity at Newburgh. He made a trip through the surrounding countryside and returned to find Martha ill, though not seriously. He must have been in good health himself, for in August a record was made of the weight of his immediate officers and himself:

General Washington	209 pounds
General Lincoln	224
General Knox	280
General Huntington	132
General Greaton	166
Colonel Swift	219
Colonel M. Jackson	252
Colonel Henry Jackson	230
Lt. Col. Huntington	232
Lt. Col. Cobb	186
Lt. Col. Humphreys	221

Eight of the eleven officers weighed over two hundred pounds, making it difficult to believe that they had suffered extreme hardship in the service.

Meanwhile, Henry Knox had come forward with an idea for a fraternal organization of the Continental officers in order to perpetuate their wartime association and help their families and descendants. It was called the Society of the Cincinnati, named for the illustrious farmer-general Lucius Quinctius Cincinnatus, who in 458 B.C. left his plow to lead his Roman countrymen to victory over the Aequians, returning by his own choice not to stately honors but to the peacefulness of his farm. The constitution of the society was adopted by a meeting of officers at Fishkill, New York, on May 13, 1783.

Although Washington did not attend any of the organizing meetings, he was elected president of the Society of the Cincinnati and served until his death. Knox served as the group's secretary. It soon had about two thousand members and, incidentally, has about the same number today. At first Washington evidently knew little about his new organization, for he wrote to Knox saying he would appreciate knowing "in precise terms what is expected from the President of the Cincinnati." He might, he said, "for want of information of the part I am to act, neglect some essential duty which might not only be injurious to the Society but mortifying to myself, as it would discover a want of knowledge or want of attention in the president."

Some historians have intimated that Washington was not much in sympathy with the aims of the Society of the Cincinnati. This is not borne out by his subsequent letter to Knox, informing him "that it has always been my intention to present the Society with $500." The elegant insigne of the organization is a colorful badge on which is engraved a bald eagle in gold, with decorations added. This brought humorous scorn from Benjamin Franklin, who wrote his daughter, "I wish the bald eagle had not been chosen as the representative of our country; he is a bird of bad moral character . . . besides he is a coward and is therefore by no means a proper emblem for the brave and honest Cincinnati of America, who have driven the kingbirds from our country."

Other prominent men of the time took up the cudgel of adverse criticism of the society. Samuel Adams thought it was a "disgustful" organization having "the mere pageantry of nobility"; John Jay was worried lest the society might eventually divide the country into "two mighty factions"; Elbridge Gerry expressed fears that the members might control elections; James Madison was apprehensive that the members might "elect the Chief Magistrate in every instance"; Thomas Jefferson wrote a diatribe against the society. Later, at the Constitutional Convention, its members, according to recent historians, were men of wealth enough to be able to hold onto the worthless Continental currency and thus influence the proceedings. (It will be noted, however, that virtually all those opposed to the Society of the Cincinnati in its early years had *not* had military service, a significant factor in itself.) Washington apparently thought enough of the organization to wear its badge over his left breast when he sat for a portrait by Edward Savage.

The evacuation of New York by the British armed forces was now imminent. Washington corresponded with the new British commander, and it was decided that the evacuation would be on November 25. Five days earlier, Washington issued his last official paper at West Point, an order discharging some dragoons, and quietly rode down to the Harlem River. There he met Governor George Clinton of New York and they crossed the river over which Washington had fled with his troops seven years before.

On the morning of the British departure, the weather was brisk and clear, and a smart wind blew down from the northwest. Washington and Clinton rode south toward what had once been the British lines, but no redcoats were present now. They had left this city—named for one of their kings when he was duke—and were in the harbor preparing to return to their venerable homeland. Washington was mounted on a fine gray horse, Clinton on a bay gelding, their escort being a detachment of Westchester militia.

For the next few days Washington was praised by citizens in elaborate church and civic ceremonies. He listened with patience and appreciation as one official after another read eulogies and was thankful that his efficient and literary aide, David Humphreys, could draft fitting replies so that each seemed different enough to fit the occasion. Tired as he was, Washington could not help but be grateful for these eloquent expressions of thankfulness from simple and well-placed citizens.

He was anxious, however, to leave New York as soon as his work was done. Knox would succeed him as commander of the army. In New York were a number of other veteran officers, and Washington knew he must see them once more before he took his leave. This touching event took place at noon on December 4, 1783, the very day General Carleton and the British were leaving. The place selected for the parting ceremonies was picturesque Fraunces Tavern, an inn at the corner of Broad and Pearl streets, which had been converted from a warehouse to an eating place and was owned by Samuel Fraunces, a West Indian mulatto. The tavern, incidentally, under the stewardship of the Sons of the Revolution, still enjoys a large clientele.

Outwardly showing his customary unemotional calm, Washington found this a harder occasion to face than many of his battles. Here he was to see, for the last time, old friends and comrades with whom he had served in the most trying periods of their lives. Thinking of the event, he prepared no formal remarks nor did his deep sincerity need any. His entry into the agreeable, oblong room of Fraunces Tavern just past the hour of noon on this winter's day was as inconspicuous as he could make it. Nevertheless, he found the place packed with his officers. They stood as soon as they realized he was present. One observed, "On finding himself surrounded by his old companions in arms, who had shared with him so many scenes of hardship, difficulty and danger, his agitated feelings overcame his usual self-command."

For the moment, Washington could think of nothing

better to do than go to the refreshment table and nervously try some tidbits of food. Even this was not very successful in hiding his feelings. Then he picked up a glass of wine. The others joined him and filled their own. Holding up his glass, Washington said in a choking voice to the silent and attentive group, "With a heart full of love and gratitude, I now take my leave of you. I most devoutly wish that your latter days may be as prosperous and happy as your former ones have been glorious and honorable."

From the group arose a low, responsive murmur. All emptied their glasses. By now, Washington was so filled with emotion that tears were in his eyes. "I cannot come to each of you," he managed to say, "but I shall feel obliged if each of you will come and take me by the hand."

Henry Knox was the first to come. He was his youngest major general and the one who in eight years of faithful association had never given Washington worry, but only eminent service and warm devotion. Knox, his own eyes full of tears, took Washington's hand, looked into his eyes and both were so overcome that Washington threw his arms around him and kissed him on the cheek. Both wept but neither said a word.

The others then came, their eyes wet, and received the embrace of their beloved commander. They passed by in eloquent silence. "Such a scene of sorrow and weeping," one recorded, "I had never witnessed before and hope I may never be called upon to witness again." Major Benjamin Tallmadge wrote, "The simple thought that we were then about to part from the man who had conducted us through a long and bloody war, and under whose conduct the glory and independence of our country had been achieved, and that we should see his face no more in this world seemed to me utterly insupportable."

And finally, when Washington had bade them all good-bye, he made his way to the door, raised his arm in a silent farewell and left the taven. He walked through the open ranks of a guard of honor, past men, women and children, and entered the barge at Whitehall Ferry that was to take him on the first leg of his journey home. Once on the barge, Washington turned and looked back. Then he raised his hat and waved it at the silent throng along the shore. "I do not think," one of them later said, "that there ever were so many broken hearts in New York as there were that day."

Pausing in Philadelphia, Washington received the loud acclaim of thousands who flocked to see him, as indeed, they did later at Wilmington and Baltimore. But it was at Annapolis, Maryland, that he was received most dramatically. Here he found the Continental Congress assembled —or at least seven of the states were represented. This group had been shifted around during the war to whatever spot seemed safe. Washington had received his commission as commander-in-chief from the Congress; now he was to return it. He wrote the president of the group—who happened to be Thomas Mifflin of Pennsylvania—that he wished to resign and asked in what manner they would like to have him do so. His letter was read in Congress, and the date for the ceremony was set for December 23. Washington decided to leave immediately afterward in order to keep his promise to have Christmas dinner with Martha at home.

A recent governor of Maryland has written that "Washington at that time was surrounded by a popularity that was close to worship. Only a few men in history have been so rapturously taken to a nation's heart. Had he declared himself dictator, the American people by all indications would have been happy to have him. His response was to withdraw from public life entirely." But for three days, he was so feted and entertained that he was doubtless glad when the final moments arrived. At a colorful dance, he took part in every set, to the delight of the admiring ladies.

Washington arrived at the Congress at noon, as requested, accompanied by two aides. He occupied the seat assigned to him and waited for the president of the Congress to ask him to speak. Then he rose and bowed; the members took off their hats momentarily but did not return the bow. This was part of their plan to demonstrate that the civilian government was still and was to remain, above the military—and that was the order Washington, as President, was to favor. He took his address out of his pocket and held it with a trembling hand.

"Mr. President," he began, "the great events on which my resignation depended having at length taken place; I have now the honor of offering my sincere congratulations to Congress and of presenting myself before them to surrender into their hands the trust committed to me, and to claim the indulgence of retiring from the service of my country. Happy in the confirmation of our independence and sovereignty and pleased with the opportunity afforded the United States of becoming a respectable nation, I resign with satisfaction the appointment I accepted with diffidence. . . . The successful termination of the war has verified the most sanguine expectations, and my gratitude for the interposition of Providence and the assurance I have received from my countrymen, increases with every review of the momentous Contest. . . ." Now both his hands shook, and Washington had difficulty controlling himself. After commending the future of the new nation to God, he concluded with the words, "Having now finished the work assigned me, I retire from the great theater of action; and bidding an affectionate farewell to this august body under whose orders I have so long acted, I here offer my commission and take my leave of all the employments of public life."

From Maryland he went rapidly to his beloved Mount Vernon, there to be greeted by family and friends with affection and admiration such as few men have received. He wrote from Mount Vernon in reply to a warm letter from Knox: "I feel as I conceive a wearied traveller must do, after treading many a painful step with a heavy burden on his shoulders, and is eased of the latter, having reached the haven to which the former was directed; and from his own housetop is looking back and tracing with an eager eye the meanders by which he escaped the quicksands and the mines which lay in his way; and into which none but the all-powerful Guide and Dispenser of human events could have prevented his falling."

XIV APPRAISAL

THE GENERAL THUS BECAME George Washington, Esquire, a civilian gentleman-planter, the role he had formerly had and always loved. He was not to don his uniform again for field service, although there would come a time when war with France threatened and he felt he might have to assume military leadership anew.

Now he turned his attention to the broad acres of Mount Vernon. True, he was not to be permitted to linger long in this pastoral setting before he would be called to an even bigger role in the new nation. Meanwhile he turned his thoughts and dreams back to the welcome and refreshing tasks of agrarian activity and was thankful that fortune smiled upon him in the reaches of sunlit Virginia. Here, in his home from the beginning, with his family and friends, his servants and neighbors, he worked on his fine plantation; and it in turn gave him renewed strength and peace.

Washington himself expressed it best when he wrote to Lafayette: "I have not only retired from all public employments, but I am retiring within myself. Envious of none, I am determined to be pleased with all; and this, my dear friend, being the order for my march, I will move gently down the stream of life, until I sleep with my fathers."

So for a time the planter spent his days enlarging the

house at Mount Vernon, experimenting with mahogany, palmetto and other foreign trees as well as with grasses and grain. He also tried to recoup his financial losses incurred during the Revolution, but this was impeded by an endless number of visitors. So many came to see him that he and his own family seldom sat down alone to dine.

Some commissioners from Virginia and Maryland met at Mount Vernon in the spring of 1785 to negotiate regarding the navigation of the Potomac, and from this grew the convention to create the national constitution. Washington took note of the chaotic policy of the several states and warned them that they must decide "whether the Revolution must ultimately be considered a blessing or a curse."

After the end of hostilities, but before the formal signing of the Treaty of Paris in 1783, a committee of Congress under the chairmanship of Alexander Hamilton asked Washington for his ideas on a system of defense of the states. Washington conferred with Knox, Pickering, Heath, Putnam and von Steuben and then formulated what has come to be known as his *Sentiments on a Peace Establishment.*

The main points of these ideas were:

First. A regular and standing force, including a navy, to protect trade, prevent foreign encroachments and guard the nation from surprise attacks.

Second. A well-organized militia similar in character, in all the states.

Third. Arsenals containing all kinds of military stores.

Fourth. Academies, including one for the instruction of the military art.

Fifth. Factories to manufacture military equipment.

For the time being, Congress did nothing with Washington's recommendations.

The necessity for improvement of the Articles of Confederation was emphasized by the Shays Rebellion. In west-

ern Massachusetts the farmers were in a turmoil because
their taxes were so high that their farms were being fore-
closed. Daniel Shays, a former captain in the army, led a
group of rebels against the system, and courts were closed
by force and intimidation. Henry Knox, now Secretary at
War under the Confederation government, was alarmed
and feared that civil war against propertied interests was
in the offing. David Cobb, former aide to Washington, was
a judge in the affected part of Massachusetts. He commented, "I shall die as a general or sit as a judge." The
matter did not come to this extreme, however; General
Benjamin Lincoln, then in Massachusetts, with local troops
aided by some national soldiers ostensibly recruited to fight
the Indians, routed Shays and his dissidents, and the rebellion subsided. But it worried Washington, Hamilton
and Knox, and it confirmed their belief that a strong national government was necessary.

In May of 1787 there was a call for a convention "to
render the Constitution of the Federal Government adequate to the exigencies of the Union." The story of how
Washington was selected as chairman of the Constitutional
Convention and presided over it in silence, with only one
interruption, is well known. But that he did influence the
proceedings as "the perfect chairman" is also generally accepted. (While in Philadelphia, he also attended a meeting
of the Society of the Cincinnati.) His purpose, in his own
words: "To establish good order and government and to
render the nation happy at home and respected abroad."
He told the delegates that he was "sure the mass of citizens
in those United States *mean well,* and I firmly believe they
will always *act well* whenever they can obtain a right understanding of matters."

Washington became the first American President, but
protested that at the age of fifty-six he had "no wish beyond
that of living and dying an honest man on my own farm."

He said his ascent to the Presidency was "accompanied by feelings not unlike those of a culprit, who is going to the place of his execution." The drain on his cash reserves had been so heavy, he had to borrow money to make the trip from Mount Vernon to New York, the first capital. On April 30, 1789, he took the oath of office from Chancellor Robert R. Livingston of New York, on the balcony of the Federal Building at Broad and Wall streets. He was clad in a brown velvet suit; Knox had obtained the suit for him, being careful to follow Washington's instructions to make sure it was made in America.

One of the notable achievements of his first administration was to make peace, with Knox's help, with the southern Indians. A delegation of thirty chiefs headed by Alexander McGillivray came to New York and was wined and dined by the new government. After they had all sat down with the President and his Secretary of War and smoked the pipe of peace—which Washington found very distasteful—and had all drunk thirteen toasts to the thirteen states, the Indians seemed to be ready to sign, with their marks, most any treaty. The settlement was helped by the astute move of making McGillivray a brigadier general in the American army. The peace lasted well into the nineteenth century.

In 1794 Washington had to resort to military force to keep peace in the young nation. He and Knox had assigned General Josiah Harmar to subdue the Western Indians. This attempt had failed, as had a succeeding one by General Arthur St. Clair, both of them because of bad planning and excessive drinking on the part of their leaders. Then Anthony Wayne was given the job, and by careful supervision of the campaign plus boldness on his own part, he succeeded in defeating the Indians at the Battle of Fallen Timbers. Thus he opened up the West, convincing the British it was time for them to evacuate their posts in the region.

During the same period the excise taxes put through by Alexander Hamilton aroused the resentment of the farmers of western Pennsylvania. They felt the taxes were discriminatory, because whiskey was their most important economic commodity. The farmers rebelled, Washington sent in troops—first under himself and Henry Lee and then Daniel Morgan—and the uprising was quelled. In characistic moderation regarding civilians, Washington pardoned the leaders of the rebellion.

After trying in vain to retire at the end of his first term as President, Washington succeeded at the end of his second and again went home to Mount Vernon. There he busied himself for a year. Then the threat of war with France brought about his appointment by President John Adams as commander of the army. Somewhat petulantly he insisted that Hamilton be his second in command, to the discomfiture of Adams and of Henry Knox—who was a major general when Hamilton was only a lieutenant colonel and was asked to serve under Hamilton. But the war did not materialize, and the master of Mount Vernon was able to remain at home.

The rift between Washington and Knox was healed. Washington wrote Knox a warm letter of friendly expression, to which the former Secretary of War, now residing on a huge estate in Maine, replied in kind: "I may not wish you the greatest blessing by wishing you a long life, because I believe that while you continue here, you are detained from a much better condition. But I pray fervently that your days on earth may be days of felicity, without clouds, sickness and sorrow."

Knox's letter was dated December 22, 1799. Because of the slow communications of the day, its writer did not know that eight days before, on December 14, George Washington had died. In his soldierly tradition, his almost final words were, "I am not afraid to go." He had lived through most of the golden years of the eighteenth century, lasting until within a few days of the advent of the next one; as Chateaubriand aptly remarked, "he blended his existence with that of his country."

The memorable words of Henry Lee—relished and quoted by his son Robert—are universally known: "First in war, first in peace and first in the hearts of his country-men." They probably best describe George Washington. He was first of all a soldier, though not by choice. In the elegant drawing room of the Duke of Wellington was a portrait of Washington, hung in a prominent place. Wellington, eminent warrior that he was, considered Washington "perhaps the purest and noblest character of modern times and among the great captains of the eighteenth century."

Pages of eulogy could be quoted, but the comment of Abigail Adams seems appropriate: "History will not produce to us a parallel." Samuel Livermore, president pro tempore of the Senate, said, "Let his countrymen teach their children never to forget that the fruit of his labors and his example, are their inheritance." A kind of crowning tribute came not many years ago when the eminent historian, Samuel F. Bemis, then president of the American Historical Association, stated in reply to adverse criticism, "His detractors may try to tear him down, but Washington still stands like Pike's Peak, towering above the lower mountains."

Douglas Freeman did not live to express his full evaluation of Washington, but he did give his appraisal of him as a general. His vital principle, Freeman wrote, was discipline; Washington believed it was the "soul of an army." A commander should set an example of discipline; justice called for both reward and punishment; justice should be meted out conscientiously and so that it would not be questioned by any ranks; rewards should not be bestowed so freely that they lose their value; an officer should always be a gentleman; every man was entitled to a courteous hearing of his suggestions and complaints; inspiration can be more important than admonition; an officer should be given an opportunity, whenever possible, to apply his special abilities; and in leadership as well as discipline, the prime essential is patience. What he was, he made himself by will, by effort, by discipline, by ambition and by perseverance. For the long and dangerous journeys of his incredible life, he had the needful strength and direction because he walked that "straight line."

To some Europeans, Washington's tactics were bolder than those of the British generals; his use of guerrilla riflemen mystified as well as drew admiration. His refusal to recognize that any season, such as winter, precluded a battle, astounded military leaders.

As Washington wrote to Joseph Reed, "In modern wars, the longest purse must chiefly determine the event." This lends substantiation to the theory that Washington did not really win the war but Britain lost it, mainly to circumstances rather than the American enemy. The obligation to win the war lay with the British commanders in the field, and this they failed to do, even though at times, especially in New York and New Jersey, they could have. Washington himself admitted that he could have been overcome at Valley Forge. The British defeat, therefore, was owing to political bungling in London and military failure in America.

"There was," wrote Sir George Trevelyan, "one American who did not over-rate George Washington; and that was George Washington himself. He put in no claim to the possession of a heaven-born genius for war. . . . In the course of the prolonged and dreary struggle for American independence, he scored very few of those master-strokes of victory which elicit a thunder of applause from the crowded benches of the world's amphitheater. His warlike successes, like his personal qualities, were unostentatious and unsensational, but of great and durable value."

Any appraisal of Washington as a soldier and man taxes the ability of the historian. For he falls into no standard category. To compare him with other national heroes is to risk losing sight of the fact that Washington had no precedent to follow, as most of them did. He was our leader at the head of our armed forces on land and sea when independence was won for the new nation, then headed it for its first eight vitally formative years.

In a time when he could have made the military supreme in our land, he wisely insisted upon civilian rule of the government and its people and turned down a dictatorship which he could have had for the asking. Instead, his far-reaching voice cried out to posterity to avoid self-destructive conflict and enjoy domestic peace.

BIBLIOGRAPHICAL NOTE

THE INTRODUCTION to this book sets forth the principal primary sources from which the account is taken. In addition to those mentioned, there are of course numerous other collections of informative documents about George Washington as soldier and man. Many of these are in printed form or on microfilm. Essential to any detailed study of the subject are *The Writings of George Washington* in fourteen volumes, edited by W. C. Ford and published 1889–93, and another great work of the same title edited by J. C. Fitzpatrick and published 1931–44 in thirty-nine volumes. *Journals of the Continental Congress, 1774–89*, edited by W. C. Ford and others and published in thirty-four volumes, 1904–37, are also indispensable.

Selected from among other manuscript sources as being pertinent to this volume and worthy of examination are the Sir Henry Clinton Papers at the Clements Library, University of Michigan; the Emmet Collection, New York Public Library; Horatio Gates Papers, New York Historical Society, which also has the Alexander McDougall Papers; the William Smith Diaries, New York Public Library; and the Anthony Wayne Papers in the Historical Society of Pennsylvania.

Recommended for further reading are the following:

Adams, John, *Papers*, L. H. Butterfield, ed., Vols. I–IV (1961)

Alden, J. R., *A History of the American Revolution* (1969); *Gen. Charles Lee* (1951)

Allen, G. W., *Naval History of the American Revolution*, two vols. (1913)

Anderson, T. S., *The Command of the Howe Brothers During the American Revolution* (1936)

André, John, *The Case of Major John André* (1780)

Bakeless, John, *Turncoats, Traitors and Heroes* (1959)

Baurmeister, C. L., *Confidential Letters and Journal* (1957)

Bemis, S. F., *The Diplomacy of the American Revolution* (1965)

Bill, A. H., *The Campaign of Princeton* (1948); *Valley Forge: The Making of an Army* (1952)

Billias, G. A., ed., *George Washington's Generals* (1964)

Boatner, Mark M., *Encyclopedia of the American Revolution* (1966)

Bliven, Bruce, *The Battle for Manhattan* (1956)

Braeman, John, *The Road to Independence* (1963)

Burnett, E. C., *The Continental Congress* (1941)

————, ed., *Letters of Members of the Continental Congress*, eight vols. (1921–26)

Callahan, North, *Henry Knox: General Washington's General* (1958)

————, *Daniel Morgan: Ranger of the Revolution* (1962)

————, *Royal Raiders: The Tories of the American Revolution*, Vol. I (1963)

————, *Flight from the Republic: The Tories of the American Revolution*, Vol. II (1967)

Chastellux, Marquis de, *Travels in North America* (1963)

Clark, W. B., *George Washington's Navy* (1960); *Naval Docs. of the Revolution*, four vols. (1964)

Clinton, Sir Henry, *The American Rebellion*, W. B. Willcox, ed. (1954)

Closen, Baron Ludwig von, *Revolutionary Journal* (1958)

Cresswell, Nicholas, *Journal* (1924)

Cunliffe, Marcus, *George Washington, Man and Monument* (1958)

Curwen, Samuel, *Journals and Letters, 1775–84*, G. A. Ward, ed. (1842)

Custis, G. W. P., *Recollections of Washington* (1860)

Davis, Burke, *The Campaign that Won America . . . Yorktown* (1970)

Dorson, R. M., ed., *America Rebels* (1953)

Dupuy, R. E. and T. N., *The Compact History of the Revolution* (1860)

Field, T. W., *The Battle of Long Island* (1869)

Fitzpatrick, J. C., *George Washington Himself* (1933)

Fleming, Thomas J., *Beat the Last Drum* (1963)

————, *The Man Who Dared the Lightning* (1970)

Flexner, J. T., *George Washington, the Forge of Experience* (1965)

————, *George Washington in the American Revolution* (1967)

Force, Peter, compiler, *American Archives*, nine vols. (1837–53)

Ford, P. L., *The True George Washington* (1898)

Freeman, Douglas S., *George Washington*, seven vols. (1948–57) finished by J. A. Carroll and M. W. Ashworth

French, Allen, *The Day of Concord and Lexington* (1925); *First Year of the American Revolution* (1934)

Gottschalk, L. R., *Lafayette Joins the American Army* (1937)

Graydon, Alexander, *Memoirs of His Own Time* (1846)

Greene, Jack P., ed., *Colonies to Nation* (1967)

Greene, G. W., *The Life of Nathanael Greene*, three vols. (1867–71)

Hamilton, Alexander, *Papers*, Vols. I–III, H. C. Syrett, ed. (1961–62)

Heath, William, *Memoirs of the American War* (1904)

Heitman, F. B., *Historical Register of the Officers of the Continental Army*

Howe, William, *Narrative* (1780)

Hughes, Rupert, *George Washington,* three vols. (1926–30)

Jefferson, Thomas, *Papers,* Julian Boyd, ed., Vols. I–VI (1950–52)

Jensen, Merrill, *The New Nation* (1950)

Johnston, H. P., *The Campaign of 1776 Around New York and Brooklyn* (1878)

Jones, Thomas, *History of New York During the Revolutionary War,* two vols. (1879)

Knollenberg, Bernhard, *Washington and the Revolution* (1940)

Lafayette, Marquis de, *The Letters of Lafayette to Washington,* Louis Gottschalk, ed. (1944)

Lee, Charles, *The Lee Papers,* four vols. (1872–75)

Lee, Henry, *Memoirs of the War in the Southern Department of the U.S.* (1827)

Little, Shelby, *George Washington* (1929)

Lossing, B. J., *The Pictorial Field Book of the Revolution,* two vols. (1852)

Lundin, C. H., *Cockpit of the Revolution* (1940)

Mackesy, Piers, *The War for America, 1775–83* (1964)

Mahan, A. T., *Major Operations of the Navies in the War for Independence* (1913)

Malone, Dumas, *Jefferson the Virginian* (1948)

Marshall, John, *George Washington,* five vols. (1926)

Miller, J. C., *Alexander Hamilton* (1959)

Millis, Walter, *Arms and the Man* (1956)

Mitchell, Broadus, *Alexander Hamilton, the Revolutionary Years* (1970)

Montross, Lynn, *Rag, Tag and Bobtail* (1952)

Montresor, John, *Journals* (1882)

Moore, Frank, *Diary of the American Revolution,* two vols. (1865)

Morris, R. B. and Commager, H. S., *The Spirit of Seventy-Six,* two vols. (1958)

Nettels, Curtis, *George Washington and American Independence* (1951)

Patterson, S. P., *Horatio Gates* (1941)

Peckham, Howard, *The War for Independence* (1958)

Rankin, Hugh, *The American Revolution* (1964)

———, with George Scheer, eds., *Rebels and Redcoats* (1957); *Private Yankee Doodle* (1962)

Robson, Eric, *The American Revolution in its Political and Military Aspects* (1955)

Rochambeau, Marshal Count de, *Memoirs* (1838)

Rush, Benjamin, *Letters,* L. H. Butterfield, ed., two vols. (1951)

Serle, Ambrose, *American Journal* (1940)

Shaw, Samuel, *Journals* (1847)

Shy, John, *Toward Lexington: The Role of the British Army* (1965)

Smith, Page, *John Adams,* two vols. (1962)

Sparks, Jared, ed., *Correspondence of the American Revolution,* four vols. (1853)

Stevens, B. F., *Facsimiles of Manuscripts* (1895)

Stryker, W. S., *The Battles of Trenton and Princeton* (1898); *The Battle of Monmouth* (1917)

Sullivan, John, *Letters and Papers,* O. G. Hamilton, ed., three vols. (1930–39)

Tallmadge, Benjamin, *Memoir* (1904)

Thacher, James, *Military Journal of the American Revolution* (1827)

Thayer, Theodore, *Nathanael Greene* (1960)

Trevelyan, Sir George Otto, *The American Revolution,* four vols. (1899–1907)

Valentine, Alan, *Lord Stirling* (1969)

von Riedesel, Baroness, and the American Revolution, M. L. Brown, ed. (1965)

Wallace, W. M., *Appeal to Arms* (1951)

Ward, Christopher, *The War of the Revolution,* two vols. (1952)

Whittemore, C. P., *A General of the Revolution: John Sullivan* (1961)

Whitridge, Arnold, *Rochambeau* (1965)

Wickwire, Franklin and Mary, *Cornwallis* (1970)

Willcox, W. B., *Portrait of a General: Sir Henry Clinton* (1964)

INDEX

Adams, Abigail, 19, 90, 278
Adams, John, 4, 15–19, 22, 36, 39, 60–61, 84, 90, 277
Adams, Samuel, 22, 118, 266
Addison, Joseph, 4
Aequians, 265
Agrarian activities of Washington, 273
Albany, N.Y., 89
Alleghany Mts., 67
Allentown, Pa., 148
Allied Arms, 238
Alexander, Gen. William (Lord Stirling), 44
American Commissioners, 255
American Historical Association, 278
Ammunition, shortage of, 27
André, John, 36, 144, 197–204
Annapolis, Md., 253–54, 270
Arbuthnot, Adm. Marriat, 217
Armstrong, Gen. John, 105, 261
Arnold, Benedict, 30–33, 115, 147–48, 195–204, 215, 217
Arnold, Mrs. Benedict, 144, 148, 197, 200–2
Articles of Confederation, 274
Articles of War, 61, 188
Artillery horses, 127
Asgill, Capt. Charles, 257

Associated Loyalists, 256–57
Associators of Philadelphia, 81
Assunpink Creek, 70, 75

Baltimore, Md., 231, 270
Barbados, 5
Barney, Capt. Joshua, 263
Barras, Count de Jacques-Melchior, 229
Bassett, Burwell, 254
Bear Mt., 176
Bemis Heights, 115
Bemis, Samuel F., 278
Bennington, Vt., 115
Berkshire Mts., 38
Bethlehem, Pa., 106
Birmingham crossroads, 72
Birmingham Meetinghouse, 97
Black Watch, 60
Bland, Col. Theodorick, 96
Board of War, 210
Bon Homme Richard, ship, 214
Bordentown, N.J., 76
Boston Gazette, 13
Boston, Mass., 39–41, 166, 167
Boston Massacre, 35
Boston Tea Party, 14
Boudinot, Col. Elias, 86
Bound Brook, N.J., 88, 227
Bounties, offer of, 77

Braddock, Gen. Edward, 11–13, 22
Brandywine Creek, Battle of, 1, 93–
  100
Brant, Joseph, 209, 210
Bridges Creek, Va., 2–3
British Crown, its offer of pardon,
  69
British troops, appearance of, 63
Broad River, 220
Bronx, N.Y., 58
Brooklyn, N.Y., 43
Brooklyn Heights, N.Y., 50, 51
Bronx River, N.Y., 62
Brown, Maj. John, 195
Brown, Joseph, 99
Bruton Church, 235
"Brutus," 261
Burgoyne, Gen. John, 38, 89, 114–17
Burlington, N.J., 79
Burr, Aaron, 32, 58
Bushnell, David, 130
Butler, Col. Richard, 177, 206
Butler, Sir John, 172, 209, 210
Butler, Walter, 209, 210
Byrd, William II, 215

Cadwalader, Lt. Col. John, 70
Caldwell, Mrs. James, 191
Campbell, Col. William, 219
Cambridge, Mass., 19, 20, 27, 33–35,
  40
Camden, Battle of, 215
Canada, 29, 33, 34, 117, 164
Cannae, Battle of, 105, 106, 221
Carleton, Gen. Sir Guy, 30, 33, 268
Carlisle Peace Commission, 146, 172
"Cavalier" ancestry of Washington,
  3
Cavalry, lack of, 55
Chadd's Ford, Pa., 93–95, 97, 98
Channing, Edward, 1
Charleston, S.C., 52
Charlotte, N.C., 219
Charlottesville, Va., 218
Charon, frigate, 244

Chateaubriand, François, 278
Chatterton Hill, 63
Chaudière River, 30
Cherry Valley Massacre, 209
Chesapeake Bay, 91, 225, 228, 230
Chester, Pa., 112, 228
Chew, Benjamin, 256
Chew House, 109–11
Cheyney, Thomas, 97
Christmas, 1776, 71
Cincinnatus, Lucius, 265
"Circulars to the States," 264
Clark, George Rogers, 172, 211
Clark, Maj. Jonathan, 180
Clinton, George, 114, 267
Clinton, Sir Henry, 47, 49, 52, 67,
  115, 131, 143, 145–61, 162, 167–68,
  172–74, 183, 197, 204, 222, 226–28,
  236–37, 251
Clinton, Gen. James, 203, 210
Cobb, Col. David, 244–45, 275
Cochran, John and Mrs., 171
Coldstream Guards, 158
Comb's Hill, 157
Commissioners for surrender, 247
Connecticut Farms, N.J., 191
Constitution, U. S., 275
Constitutional Convention, 275
Continental Congress, 15, 17, 22, 27,
  29, 34, 55, 56, 60, 66, 68, 77, 78, 86,
  87, 104, 117, 118, 120, 123, 130, 139,
  146, 161, 182, 210, 212, 214, 221,
  253, 270–71
Continental Journal and *Weekly
  Advertiser*, 116
Continental Navy, 212–14
Conway Cabal, 142
Conway, Gen. Thomas, 117–20
Cornwallis, Lord, 47, 49, 67, 68, 78–
  79, 80–84, 104, 157, 158, 160, 183,
  218–21, 230–53
Corporal punishment, 188
Cowpens, Battle of, 24, 220–21
Cranbury, N.J., 148, 150
Crisis, The, 70
Cumberland, Md., 7

Custis, Jacky, 232, 252, 254
Custis, Mrs. Jacky, 254

Danbury, Conn., 168, 170
Dauphin, French, 258
Dearborn, Lt. Col. Henry, 123
Death of Washington, 277
de Broglie, Prince, 224
de Chastellux, Marquis, 232
Declaration of Independence, 46, 47
de Fermoy, Gen. Roche, 79
de Fleury, Lt. Col. François, 178
de Grasse, Admiral, 193, 223, 225, 227–29, 232, 253
de Kalb, Baron, 185
de la Rouerie, Marquis, 128
de Lauzun, Duke, 237
Delaware, frigate, 112
Delaware River, 67, 104, 112, 144, 147, 148
Denny, Ebenezer, 247
de Noailles, Viscount, 248
d'Estaing, Count, 163–67, 183
Destouches, Adm. Charles, 216, 217
Dickenson, Gen. Philemon, 146, 149, 152
Dinwiddie, Gov. Robert, 7, 8, 11
Discipline, military, 25, 42–43
Discouragement of Washington, 60, 119
Divine Providence, 256
Dobbs Ferry, N.Y., 199
Doehla, Johann, 242
Dog of General Howe, 144
Donderberg, 176
Dorchester Heights, 39, 40
Duchess of Gordon, ship, 45
Duke of Wellington, 278
Dumas, Count, 230
Dundas, Col. Thomas, 215
du Plessis, Chevalier de Mauduit, 109
Duponceau, Pierre-Etienne, 129, 134
Duportail, Col. Louis, 225
Dupuy, Cols. R. E. & T. N., 264
Durham Boats, 70

Eddis, William, 78
Edinburgh, Scotland, 2
Egg Harbor, N.J., 169
Elizabeth, N.J., 170
Elkton, Md., 91
Elmira, N.Y., 210
Empress Catherine, 84
English Channel, 214
Englishtown, N.J., 150, 162
Enlistments, expiration of, 77
Enos, Lt. Col. Roger, 33
Erskine, Gen. Sir William, 79
Ewing, Gen. James, 70

Fairfax, Lord, 4, 5,
Fallen Timbers, Battle of, 101, 276
Farewell, in New York, 269
Fascines, 239, 240
Federal Building, N.Y. City, 276
Ferguson, Lt. Col., Patrick, 1, 2, 95, 169
Ferguson rifle, 1
Fersen, Count Axel, 224
Feu de joie, 140
Fishkill, N.Y., 170, 202
Fitzpatrick, J. C., 224, 281
Flag used Jan. 1, 1776, 37
Flexner, James T., xii
Food, scarcity of, 185–86
Forbes, Gilbert, 45
Forbes, Gen., John, 14
Ford, W. C., 281
Fort Duquesne, 9, 11, 12
Fort George, 36
Fort Lee, 45, 62–64
Fort Mercer, 112
Fort Mifflin, 112
Fort Necessity, 9, 10
Fort Pitt, 14
Fort Washington, 45, 62–64
France, 166, 167, 183
Fraunces, Samuel, 268
Fraunces Tavern, 268
Franklin, Benjamin, 34, 130, 132, 191–92, 266

Franklin, William, 256
Frederick the Great, 132
Fredericksburg, Va., 2, 3, 232
Freehold Meeting House, N.J., 154, 155
Freehold, N.J., 149
Freeman, Douglas S., xi, xii, 278
Freeman's Farm, 115
Freeman's Journal, 114
Freemen's Tavern, 85
French gunners, 243
Fry, Col. Joshua, 9

Gabions, 239
Gage, Gen. Thomas, 27
Gardiner, Me., 31
Gates, Gen. Horatio, 115–17, 209, 215
George II, 83
George III, 48, 138, 255
Germain, Lord George, 172
Germantown, Pa., Battle of, 89, 100–12
Gerry, Elbridge, 22, 266
Gibbons, Lt. James, 178
Gist, Christopher, 8
Gloucester, Village of, 234, 246
Glover, Gen. John, 53, 62, 70, 165
Grant, Gen. James, 51, 73, 95
Grant's Tomb, 59
Graves, R. E., 204
Graves, Adm. Thomas, 192, 229
Grayson, Col. William, 65, 151
Great Meadows, 9
Great Valley Road, 96
Greaton, Gen., John, 265
Grey, Gen. Charles, 102–5, 168
Greene, Col. Christopher, 113
Greene, Gen. Nathanael, 22, 40, 42, 50, 56, 58, 71–83, 87, 119, 126–27, 133, 156–57, 165, 202, 203, 215, 220, 221, 224, 255
Greene, Mrs. Nathanael, 128
Greene, William, 45
Guide and Dispenser of human events, 272
Guilford Courthouse, Battle of, 221

Hackensack, N.J., 64
Haiti, 225
Half-joes, Portuguese money, 254
Hamilton, Col. Henry, 172
Hale, Nathan, 62
Halifax, N.S., 41
Hamilton, Lt. Col. Alexander, 19, 83, 104, 119, 133, 135, 158, 170, 200, 204, 222, 245, 257, 260, 261, 275, 277
Hampton Road, 241
Hancock, John, 100
Hand, Col. Edward, 49, 79
Harmar, Gen. Josiah, 101, 276
Harlem Heights, N.Y. City, 56, 58–60
Harlem River, 223
Harrison, Benjamin, 34
Hartford, Conn., 193, 200
Harvard University, xii, 43
Haslet, Col. John, 55
Haverstraw, N.Y., 199
Headley, J. T., 110
Heath, Gen. William, 42, 164, 226, 227, 256
Hell's Gate, N.Y. City, 61
Henry, Patrick, 172, 211, 229
Hessians, 51, 57, 64, 72–75
Hickey, Thomas, 45
Hill, Richard S., 250
Historical Society of Pennsylvania, 281
Hitchcock, Col. Daniel, 83
Honeyman, John, 69
Honorary degree for Washington, 43
Hopkins, Commodore Esek, 212
Hopkinson, Francis, 130
Hornwork, Cornwallis', 247
Howe, Admiral Lord Richard, 47, 48, 162, 166
Howe, Gen. Robert, 203, 207
Howe, Gen. Sir William, 37–41, 47, 48, 52, 53, 56–61, 65, 67, 68, 88, 89, 102–12, 130, 131, 143–44, 173
Huddy, Joshua, 257

Hudson River, 29, 205, 226
Humphreys, David, 231, 268
Huntington, Jedediah, 203
Huntington, Gen. Samuel, 265

Independence Hall, 253
Independent Chronicle, 110
Indians, southern, 276
Indian warfare, 208
Internecine warfare, 171–72
Invalid Regiment, 257
Iroquois Indians, 208–10
Irving, Washington, 155

Jackson, Col. Henry, 265
Jackson, Col. Michael, 265
James River, 7, 215
Jameson, Lt. Col. John, 199
Jay, John, 266
Jefferson, Thomas, 4, 214–16, 219, 235, 267
Johnson, Lt. Col. Henry, 177
Johnson, Sir John, 209
Jones, Capt. John Paul, 213–14
Jones, Joseph, 263
Journal of James Thacher, 19
Journal of Major George Washington, The, 9
Julius Caesar, 138
Jumonville, Count de, 9, 10

Kaskia, Ill., 172
Kennebec River, 30
Kennett Meetinghouse, 94
Kentucky rifle, 24
King's Mt., Battle of, 2, 24, 219
Kip's Bay, N.Y. City, 57
Kingship, "offer of" to Washington, 257
Knights of the Blended Rose, 144
Knights of the Burning Mountain, 144
Knox, Commodore Dudley, 213
Knox, Henry, xi, 22, 35, 36–41, 44, 60, 68–83, 91, 109, 119, 122, 127, 130, 133, 155, 157, 161, 165, 187, 189, 200, 203, 204, 206, 213, 233, 241–44, 252, 254, 256, 257, 260, 263, 265, 268, 269, 272, 275–77
Knox, Mrs. Henry, 35, 128, 161
Knox, Henry, Papers, xi
Knowlton, Lt. Col. Thomas, 58
Knyphausen, Gen. Wilhelm von, 64, 98, 152, 190

Lafayette, Marquis de, 91, 119, 128, 144, 145–47, 150, 200, 203, 216–18, 222, 224, 229, 230, 238, 243, 245, 246, 248, 273
Lake Champlain, 19
Lake George, 18, 38
Lake Mahopac, 168
Laurens, John, 109–10, 128, 133, 135, 141, 160, 248, 258
Lee, Billie, 231
Lee, Gen. Charles, 22, 44, 55–56, 62, 65, 143, 147, 150–55, 169, 258
Lee, Col. Henry, 179–83, 186, 215–16, 219, 278
Lee, Richard Henry, 118
Lee, schooner, 212
L'Enfant, Major Pierre, 129
Library of Congress, xii
Lincoln, Gen. Benjamin, 87, 214, 232, 250, 251, 260, 275
Lippincott, Capt. Richard, 256–57
Livermore, Samuel, 278
Livingston, Col. James, 199
Livingston, Robert R., 276
Livingston, Gov. William, 156
Lockwood, Maj. Ebenezer, 169
London, England, 11, 84
Loring, Mrs. Joshua, 67, 143
Lossberg, Gen. von, 69
Louis XVI, 129
Lynch, Thomas, 34

McDougall, Gen. Alexander, 77, 256
McGillivray, Alexander, 276
McKean, John, 237
McKonkey's Ferry, 70, 76

McLane, Capt. Allen, 107, 126, 145, 175, 179–80
Mackenzie, Capt. Robert, 22
Maclean, Col. Allen, 31
Madison, James, 267
Madrid, 84
Magaw, Col. Robert, 64
Manhattan, N.Y. City, 52–61
Manley, Capt. John, 212
Marblehead Mariners, 53, 71
Marshall, John, 220
Martin, Sgt. Joseph, 240
Martinique, 167
Massachusetts Historical Society, xii
Matthews, David, 45
Mawhood, Lt. Col. Charles, 81, 83
Maxwell, Gen. William, 92, 94, 95
Mercenary troops, British, 73–75
Mercer, Gen. Hugh, 71, 81
Middlebrook, N.J., 170
Mifflin, Gen. Thomas, 54, 118, 270
Miles, Col. Samuel, 50
Mischianza, 144, 197
Mohawk Valley, 115
Monckton, Lt. Col. Henry, 158
Money, shortage of, 28
Monmouth, N.J., Battle of, 149–61
Monroe, James, 220
Montgomery, Gen. Richard, 31–32
Morale, low in army, 65
Morgan, Gen. Daniel, xi, 21, 23, 92, 106, 115, 132, 149, 175, 195, 220, 221, 277
Morgan, Daniel, Papers, xi
Morris, Gouverneur, 45, 256
Morris, Robert, 138, 228
Morristown, N.J., 85, 170, 184, 190, 205, 227
Mt. Vernon, 4, 5, 6, 11, 14, 211, 231, 255, 271, 272, 273, 274, 276, 277
Muhlenberg, Gen. Peter, 217
Musgrave, Lt. Col. Thomas, 107

Nancy, brig, 212
Nash, Gen. Francis, 105
Nassau Hall, 80

National Character, 259
Negroes in service, 27
Nelson, Gen. Thomas, Jr., 215, 243, 244
Newark, N.J., 226
New Bridge, N.J., 182
New Brunswick, N.J., 149, 162, 226, 227
Newburgh, N.Y., 261
Newburgh Addresses, 262, 263
New Hampshire Gazette, 186
Newport, R.I., 193, 208, 216
New York City, 42–45, 117, 160, 166–68, 173, 208, 222, 223, 270
New York Historical Society, 281
New York Public Library, xiii
Niagara, 208
Nicola, Col. Lewis, 257
North, Lord, 3, 48, 146, 172, 255
Norwich, Conn., 195

Odell, Rev. Jonathan, 197
O'Hara, Gen. Charles, 250, 251
Oriskany, Battle of, 24

Paine, Thomas, 70
Paoli Massacre, 100–3
Parallel trenches, 241
Paramus, N.J., 162, 181
Paris, France, 255
Paris, Treaty of, 1783, 263, 274
Parson, Gen. Samuel H., 203
Passaic, N.J., 161
Patriarch and Washington, 232
Patterson, James, 48
Paulus Hook, N.J., 179–83
Pay, dissatisfaction regarding military, 260
Peace and its responsibilities, 259
Pennsylvania Line, 205
Penn, William, 90
Pennington Road, 72
Pennsylvania Gazette, 139
Percy, Lord, 47, 64
Perkins, Commissary General, 242

Philadelphia, Pa., 15, 65, 68, 88, 89, 93, 104, 117, 121, 124, 130, 142, 143–47, 197, 229, 255, 256, 260, 270, 271
Phillips, Gen. William, 217, 218
Physical condition of Washington, 137
Pickering, Col. Timothy, 108, 263
Piel, Lt. Jacob, 74
Pigeon Quarter, 234
Pigot, Sir Robert, 163
Pittsburgh, Pa., 9
Plains of Abraham, 31
Poor, Gen. Enoch, 89
Pope, Alexander, 4
Portsmouth, Va., 215
Potomac River, 3, 274
Potsdam, 84
Pottstown, Pa., 103
Pound Ridge, N.J., 169
Prescott, Gen. Richard, 143
Presidena, Washington as, 275
Princeton, N.J., 80–84, 206
Prussian type drill, 134–35
Pulaski, Count Casimir, 112, 169
Punishment, military, 26
Purple Heart Badge of Military Merit, 258
Putnam, Gen. Israel, 22, 39, 42, 50, 58
Putnam, Gen. Rufus, 39

Quaker Meeting House, N.J., 81
Quebec, 24, 30–33, 196

Rainbow, ship, 49
Rall, Col. Johann, 69, 73–75
Ramapo, N.J., 170
Raritan River, 67
Reed, Joseph, 28, 37, 48, 59, 66, 196, 206, 279
Religion of Washington, 187
Rhode Island Historical Society, xiii
Richmond, Va., 217
Rift between Washington and Knox healed, 277

Robespierre, Maximilien, xii
Robin, Abbé, 228
Robinson, Col. Beverly, 197, 203
Rochambeau, Count de, 192, 193, 216, 223, 225, 230–53
Rodney, Caesar, 55
Roosevelt, Theodore, 1, 220
Ross, Maj. Alexander, 248
Ross, Lt. Col. James, 96
Roxbury, Mass., 39
Rush, Dr. Benjamin, 118, 125

St. Clair, Gen. Arthur, 101, 276
St. Lawrence River, 29, 31
St. Leger, Col. Barry, 115
St. Lucia, 170
St. Peter's Church, 256
Sandy Hook, 149, 160, 162
Saratoga, Battle of, 24, 147, 196
Savage, Edward, 267
Savannah, Ga., 183
Schuylkill River, 102, 103, 104, 112, 121, 145
Schuyler, Elizabeth (Hamilton), 170
Schuyler, Gen. Philip, 18, 19, 30, 38
Scotch Plains, N.J., 162
Scott, Gen. Charles, 151, 155
Sentiments on a Peace Establishment, 274
Serapis, frigate, 214
Sevier, Col. John, 219
Shaw, Maj. Samuel, 263
Sharpe, Gov. Horatio, 13
Shays Rebellion, 274–75
Sheldon, Col. Elisha, 169
Shenandoah Valley, 4
Shirley, Col. William, 13
Shuldham, Adm. Molyneux, 40
Simcoe, Col. John, 215
Smallpox, 86–87
Smallwood, Gen. William, 105, 146
Smith, John, 122, 235
Smith, Lt. Col. William, 109
Society of the Cincinnati, 265, 267, 275

Somerset, N.J., 227
Spanish-American War, 171
Spectacles, new ones of Washington, 263
Springfield, Mass., 38
Springfield, N.J., 191
Stansbury, Joseph, 197
Stark, Gen. John, 115
Staten Island, N.Y., 46, 164
Stephen, Gen. Adam, 71, 73, 87, 111
Stewart, Col. Walter, 206
Stony Point, N.Y., 173-79
Stirling, Lady, 128
Stirling, Lord, 44, 50-51, 67, 71, 87, 203, 259
Sullivan, Gen. John, 40, 42, 50, 68, 69-83, 87, 164-67, 209-11
Sutherland, Maj. William, 180
Swift, Col. Herman, 265
Symonds, Capt. Thomas, 249

Tallmadge, Maj. Benjamin, 194, 202, 203, 269
Tappan, N.Y., 203
Tarleton, Lt. Col. Banastre, 68, 169, 218-21, 234
Tarrytown, N.Y., 199
Thacher, Dr. James, 19, 184, 188, 226, 236, 244, 245
The Gentleman's Observer, 93
"The old fox," nickname for Washington, 80
The Temple, 262
Ticonderoga, 30, 32, 36, 38, 115
Tilghman, Lt. Col. Tench, 252
Tories, American, 18, 35, 38, 41, 45, 46, 54, 56, 89, 92, 97, 102, 104, 142-43, 168, 172, 174, 182, 190, 194, 196, 197, 208, 214, 219, 248
Torn Mt., 176
Treatise on Military Discipline, 26
Trenton, N.J., 68-76, 206, 207
Trevelyan, George M., 53, 76, 84, 111, 279
Trumbull, Jonathan, 23
Trumbull, Joseph, 23

Tryon, William, 18, 19, 45
Typhus, 125

Uniforms of the army, 20-21
United States Military Academy, 189
University of Michigan, 281

Valiant, H. M. S., 113
Valley Creek, 125
Valley Forge, Pa., 121-41
van Cortlandt, Col. Philip, 242
Varnum, Gen. James, 89, 165
Verplanck's Point, 173, 174, 198
Vienna, 84
Ville de Paris, ship, 232
Vincennes, Ind., 172
von Heister, Gen. Leopold, 47
von Steuben, Baron, 129, 132-40, 147, 183, 203, 254
Vulture, sloop of war, 178, 199, 200, 202

Wadsworth, Jeremiah, 129
Walker, Capt. Benjamin, 135
Ward, Gen. Artemas, 21, 42
Washington, Augustine, 3
Washington, John, 3
Washington, Lawrence, 3, 5
Washington, Lund, 29, 255
Washington, Martha, 14, 25, 127, 128, 231, 256, 265, 270
Washington, Mary Ball, 6
Washington, Sarah, 5
Washington, Col. William, 75, 220-21
Washington's expense account, 17
Washington's Light Guard, 236
"Washington's Navy," 212
Washington, George, Papers, xii
Washington, ship, 263
Watchung Mts., 88
Waterford, Pa., 7
Wayne, Gen. Anthony, 94, 97, 101-3, 156, 157, 161, 175-79, 205, 206, 224, 276

Wayne, Mrs. Anthony, 128
Webster, Noah, 222
Welch's Tavern, 94, 96
Wellington, Duke of, 278
Westchester militia, 267
Westfield, Mass., 38
Westminster Abbey, 47
West Point, N.Y., 173, 176, 183, 184, 198–205, 224, 257, 258, 267
Wethersfield, Conn., 223
Whigs, English, 48
Whitehall Ferry, 270
White Marsh, 121
White Plains, N.Y., 62–64, 168

Wilkinson, James, 69, 118
Williamsburg, Va., 232–35
Wilmington, Del., 91, 93
Wolfe's Cove, 32
"World Turned Upside Down," tune, 250
Wormeley Creek, 234, 237, 240
Wyoming Valley massacre, 209
Wythe, George, 235

"Yankee Doodle," tune, 90
York River, 234
Yorkshire, 2
Yorktown, Va., 211, 213, 230–53

ABOUT THE AUTHOR

PROFESSOR NORTH CALLAHAN was born in Tennessee in 1908. He graduated with honors from the University of Tennessee, Chattanooga, and received a master's degree in American history from Columbia University and the degree of doctor of philosophy in American civilization from New York University, where, as a professor, he teaches American history. In 1964, he received the honorary degree of Doctor of Humane Letters from his alma mater. Professor Callahan is a member of the American Historical Association, American Studies Association, Conference on British Studies, and an Associate at Columbia University in the Seminar of Early American History. He is Historian of the Southern Society in New York and of The Tennessee Society of New York, a former president of the Civil War Round Table of New York and chairman of the American Revolution Round Table. He has lectured at British universities. Recently he was appointed to the Historical Commission of the New York City Bicentennial Committee. He was a colonel in World War II.

Professor Callahan's previous books include *Smoky Mountain Country; Henry Knox: General Washington's General; Daniel Morgan: Ranger of the Revolution; Royal Raiders: The Tories of the American Revolution, Vol. I; Flight from the Republic: The Tories of the American Revolution, Vol. II; Carl Sandburg: Lincoln of Our Literature. George Washington: Soldier and Man* is North Callahan's tenth book. Many years of research and teaching in the period of early American history preceded the two years Professor Callahan spent writing his work on Washington. The idea for it was suggested to him by a number of librarians who had read *Henry Knox* and *Daniel Morgan* and who felt there was a need for a similar popular one-volume biography based on impeccable scholarship.

921

DATE DUE

OCT 1 9 2004		
OCT 1 9 2004		